ISBN 0-918178-18-5

200 MADISON AVE., NEW YORK, N.Y. 10016
IN CANADA, DOMINION SIMPLICITY PATTERNS LTD., 120 MACK AVE., SCARBOROUGH, ONT., M1L 1N3

EDITORIAL DIRECTOR
Janet Du Bane
PROJECT EDITOR
Diane Friend
ART DIRECTOR
Susan Kretschmer
COPY STAFF
Marion Mylly Bartholomew
Susanna Pfeffer
EDITORIAL ASSISTANT
Elsa Rohlehr
ART TRAFFIC
Ellen Wall
Pearl M. Sullivan
PRODUCTION
Ralph Fierro, Jr.
Linda Gold
CREATIVE DIRECTOR
Richard Ference

Needlepoint and Embroidery

Blossoms and bunnies in beautiful stitches . . . delicate flowers embroidered on a tea cozy and tray cover, a bouquet and a pert cottontail pillow . . . a spray of oleander for a needlepoint pillow.

Tea Cozy, tray cover and floral picture: Coats & Clark/Pillows: Erica Wilson; Photo: Mort Mace

Needlepoint geometrics . . . a jewelry pillow to hold precious pins, a brilliant bargello belt, a large dazzling pillow, a tidy pincushion, and a bracelet pillow for bangles.

Designs: Sara Gutiérrez; Yarn: DMC; Photo: Mort Mace/Photographed at the home of Dr. & Mrs. J. Hyman, Suffern, N.Y.

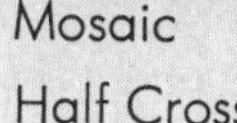

Needlepoint

How to do it!

Terms

Needlepoint is embroidery worked over the counted threads of canvas with the stitches following and entirely covering the grid. The term is interchangeable with Canvas Embroidery which, however, sometimes includes other embroidery stitches as well.

The familiar Tent Stitches are often thought to be the only needlepoint stitches. Needlepoint, however, can claim well over a hundred stitches as well as the whole family of Florentine or Bargello patterns—those straight up and down stitches in stepped rows, no two of which seem to be alike.

Needlepoint is further categorized by gauge. The size or gauge of the canvas refers to the number of threads (or pairs of threads) or "meshes" to the inch (2,5 cm). Petitpoint has sixteen or more meshes to the inch (2,5 cm), grospoint eight to fifteen and quickpoint three to seven. Grospoint is the most commonly done work and quickpoint is usually reserved for rugs.

Materials

Canvas

Needlepoint canvas is usually made of cotton, heavily sized to keep the threads in place. It comes in white, yellow or tan. Choose whichever you find most comfortable for your eyes. Don't buy canvas that has knots or frayed places. Although the stiffness may make the early part of the stitching cumbersome, the canvas will soften up as you proceed.

Mono canvas is woven with single vertical and horizontal threads. Penelope canvas, on the other hand, has pairs of vertical and horizontal threads. These permit you to work sections of the piece in petitpoint. Thus, 10-mesh Penelope canvas can be worked twenty to the inch (2,5 cm), with four stitches of petitpoint occupying the space of a single stitch of grospoint.

MONO CANVAS

GROSPOINT AND PETITPOINT

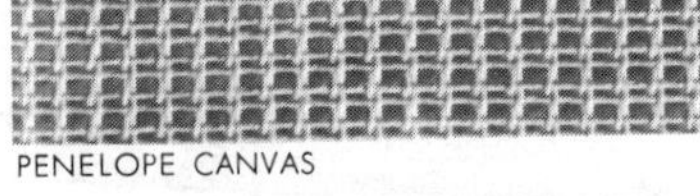

PENELOPE CANVAS

QUICKPOINT ON PENELOPE CANVAS

Yarn

The wool yarn used for needlepoint should be colorfast and permanently mothproofed.

Persian-type Wool is a beautiful versatile yarn made of three loosely twisted strands which can be used separately or together. This yarn, also called crewel yarn, has a slight sheen and a ravishing color range. It may be bought by the skein or by the ounce.
Used separately, Persian-type Wool is thin enough for petitpoint. Or, with several strands in the needle, it will also cover large mesh canvas. Tapestry Yarn cannot be separated and usually fits 10-mesh canvas. It comes in small skeins of about eight yards (7,35 m) and in larger ones of forty (37 m). Rug Wool to fit 3 or 5-mesh canvas is sold by the pound. Knitting wools are not recommended for needlepoint. They fuzz up as they are pulled through the canvas.

Actually, many types of materials, such as silk thread and pearl cotton, are suitable for needlepoint, providing that they cover the canvas adequately.

Needles, etc.

Tapestry needles are used, for they have large eyes, blunt points and a convenient length. A size 18 or 20 is a good size for most grospoint and size 22 is good for petitpoint. Test a threaded needle in your canvas before you begin. It should pass easily through the mesh and the yarn should pass easily through the eye. Also see that the yarn covers the canvas.

Except for cutting canvas, you will need only a small sharp-pointed pair of scissors for cutting yarn. A thimble will help prevent a sore middle finger. Have masking tape or seam binding and, for blocking, aluminum pushpins or thumb tacks.

You may find that stapling your work to a canvas stretcher like the one shown on page 21 of Embroidery is a help. The stretcher or a needlework frame will help keep the work straight.

TRACE DESIGN WITH MARKING PEN

FINISHED DESIGN

Preparation

Design

You can use a transfer pattern designed for embroidery on needlepoint canvas. Just be sure to place and iron it according to the directions with the transfer.

Before you stamp, take care with the placement of the design on the canvas. If there are strong upright lines which should be on the grain, place the transfer so that they fall along a single mesh. If you need to center the design within a larger outline, such as a chair seat, draw center lines on the transfer. Draw the larger outline and center lines on the canvas as well. Place the two sets of center lines over each other before you pin and stamp.

If you have used the transfer and wish to use the design again, you can trace it. To trace a transfer or other design, place the canvas on top. Keep them both in place, on a white table or paper, with tape or weights. Trace on the canvas with a waterproof marking pen.

You may color the marked canvas, but be sure the paint is permanent and colorfast, such as acrylic paint, or it may bleed when you block. Test a patch, if you are in doubt, by painting a small piece of canvas. Let it dry, then wet and rub it. If the color smears, it is not colorfast.

TAPE EDGES

Geometric and repeat designs that demand exact counting of stitches should be drawn on graph paper and referred to as you work. Each block on the graph paper represents one stitch not a hole.

Canvas

Cut the canvas along the mesh, the size of your finished design, plus any extra needed in the finishing, plus about two inches all around to be used for blocking. Tape the edges with masking tape or bind them with seam binding so they won't ravel while you work.

Yarn

When you buy a pattern especially for needlepoint, it will include an estimate of the yarn you'll need. This estimate will be correct only for the specific stitch and canvas gauge called for. If you change either, you will need to make your own estimate: Work a square inch (2,5 cm) of your canvas, measuring and jotting down the length of yarn in your needle before you start. When you finish you will know how many inches of yarn you need for one square inch. Multiply this figure by the number of square inches of the piece and you will have the total amount of yarn required. When you have determined the quantities needed for each color, buy the yarn and don't skimp. Remember that it is sometimes impossible to match your dye lot when you go back to the store later.

Needles

To thread the needle, fold the yarn over the needle. Hold it tightly against the needle between the thumb and the index finger.

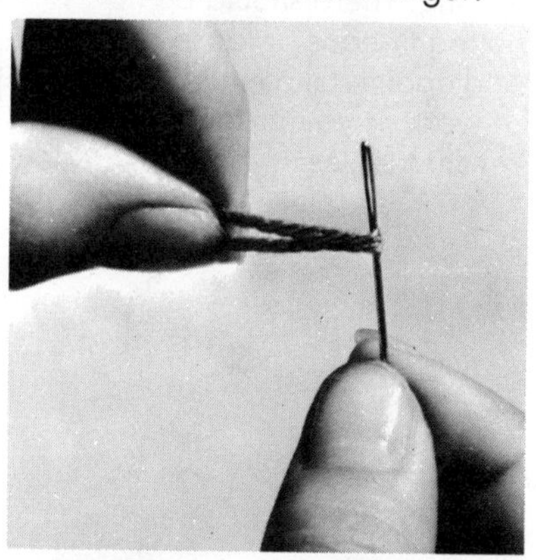

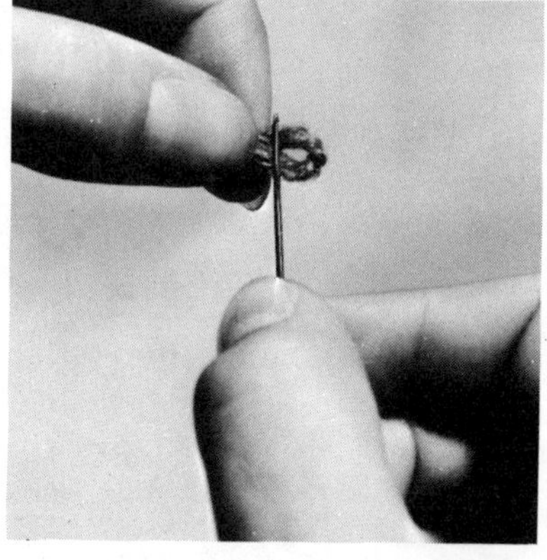

Slide it off the needle, still holding tightly, and push the loop through the eye of the needle.

Use strands about twenty inches long. Keep the tension uniform and loose enough to make plump stitches. Don't let your thread get twisted. If it should start to, let the needle dangle and the thread will unwind.

When inserting the needle into the canvas, bring it through the canvas completely before inserting it in the next hole. Wool wears out quickly from being pulled through more than one hole at once.

Begin a new thread by weaving about an inch (2,5 cm) of it through the back of some previous work. Or hold it against the back of the row you are working on and cover it as you work. Don't run colored strands under pale thread as they may show through, and never carry more than ½ inch (1,2 cm) across the back without weaving it through a few stitches. End a thread, also by weaving it through some under-stitching. There should be no knotted threads or loose ends in needlepoint. Clip ends close to the work as you progress to prevent tangles.

Dictionary of Needlepoint Stitches

FRONT OF ALL TENT STITCHES

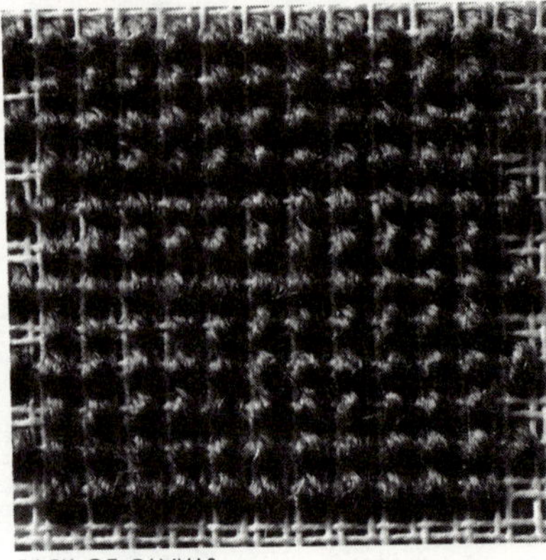

BACK OF CANVAS

From the many, many needlepoint stitches, one type is more commonly associated with needlepoint than the others. This is the Tent stitch including the Half-Cross, Continental and Basket Weave stitches.

Half-Cross and the next two stitches, Continental and Basket Weave, all look alike on the front of the work—like half a cross stitch slanting upward from the left to right. From the back of the canvas, however, you can see they are worked differently.

On the front of the canvas, stitches form neat little "beads", all equal in size and loosely covering the canvas so that no part of the canvas shows to the right side.

This uniform closely-covered look is characteristic of needlepoint and should be your goal in all of the needlepoint stitches.

Half-Cross Stitch

Half-Cross will not work well on mono canvas. While it is very easy and economical with yarn, it is not recommended for pieces that will experience hard wear, for the yarn on the back is very scanty.

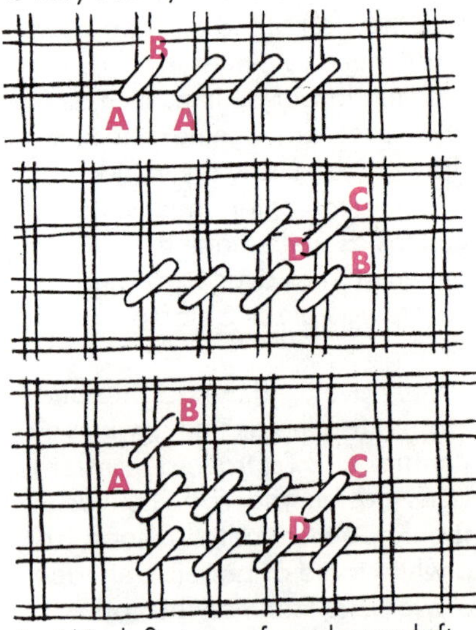

1. Work first row from lower left corner. Bring the needle up (A).
2. Put it down (B) 1 mesh above and to the right of A. Bring it up (A) 1 mesh directly below. Complete row.
3. For second row bring needle up (C) 1 mesh above B. Turn work around.
4. Put it down (D). Work third row same as row 1.

BACK OF CANVAS

Continental Stitch

The stitch you see most often in needlepoint is the Continental. It is very easy, but does have a tendency to pull the canvas out of shape. It wears longer and covers back of the canvas better than the Half-Cross.

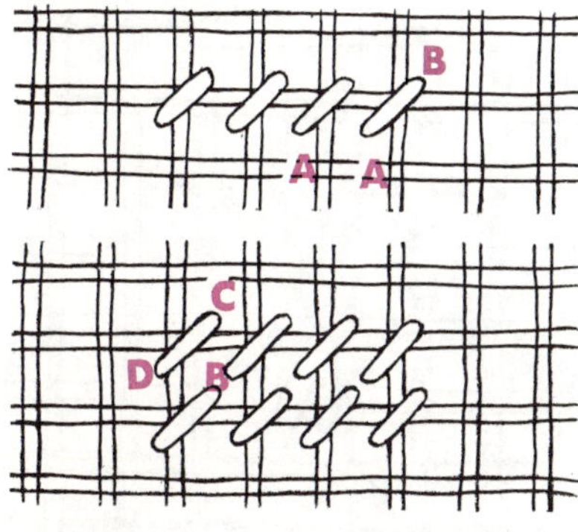

1. Work from right to left. Bring needle up (A).

2. Put it down (B) 1 mesh above and to the right of A. Bring it up (A) 1 mesh below and 2 meshes to the left of B. Complete row.

3. For second row bring needle up (C) 1 mesh above B. Turn work around.

4. Put it down D. For next row, repeat step 2.

BACK OF CANVAS

Basket Weave

The Basket Weave is very well padded on the back. It is worked diagonally across the canvas which helps to keep your work square. It is extremely durable because it reinforces the weave of the canvas.

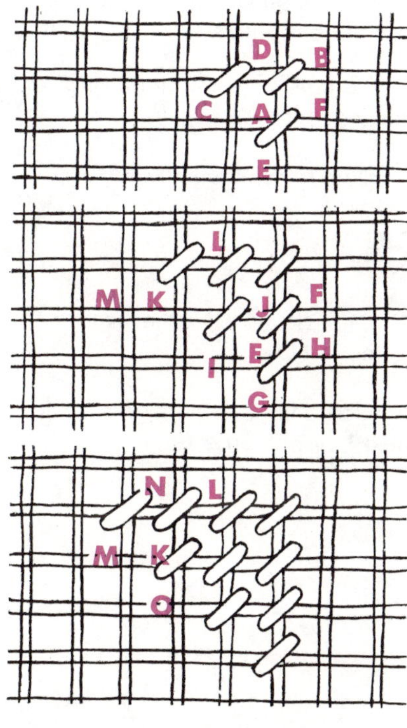

1. Work from upper right corner. Bring needle up (A). Put it down (B) 1 mesh above and to the right of A. Bring it up (C) 1 mesh to the left of A.

2. Put it down (D) 1 mesh above and to the right of C. Bring it up (E) 2 meshes directly below D.

3. Put it down (F) 1 mesh above and to the right of E. Bring it up (G) 1 mesh directly below E.

4. Put it down (H) 1 mesh above and to the right of G. Bring it up (I) 2 meshes directly to the left.

5. Put it down (J) 1 mesh above and to the right of I. Bring it up (K) 2 meshes directly to the left.

6. Put it down (L) 1 mesh above and to the right of K. Bring it up (M) level with and 1 mesh to the left of K.

7. Put it down (N) 1 mesh above and to the right of M. Bring it up (O) 2 meshes directly below.

Stitches are worked diagonally across the canvas.

When you reach top or bottom and have to change direction, put your needle in directly to the left of the beginning of the previous stitch. When you reach one of the sides, put your needle in directly below the beginning of the previous stitch.

Cross-Stitch

The familiar Cross-Stitch is quick and economical. By working some crosses, at regular intervals, in contrast color, you can make a dotted pattern.

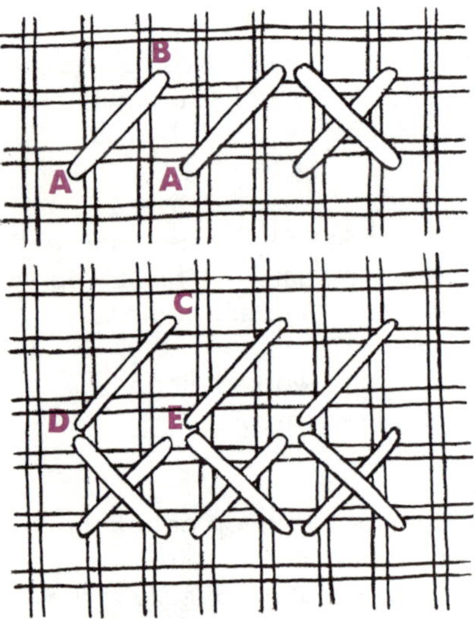

1. Work Cross in squares ot 4 meshes. Bring needle up (A) in lower left corner of square.

2. Put it down (B) 2 meshes to the right of and 2 meshes above A.

3. Bring it up (A) 2 meshes directly below. Complete row.

4. At end of row work stitch in the opposite direction to complete the crosses. For second row bring it up (C) 2 meshes above B.

5. Put it down (D) 2 meshes to the left of and 2 meshes below C.

6. Bring it up (E), which becomes first row's A.

Repeat from Step 2 of first row.

Smyrna Stitch

Smyrna is also known as the Double Cross, which describes it exactly. The top cross can be in contrast color to the cross underneath. Work it in 2 strands of Persian-type wool.

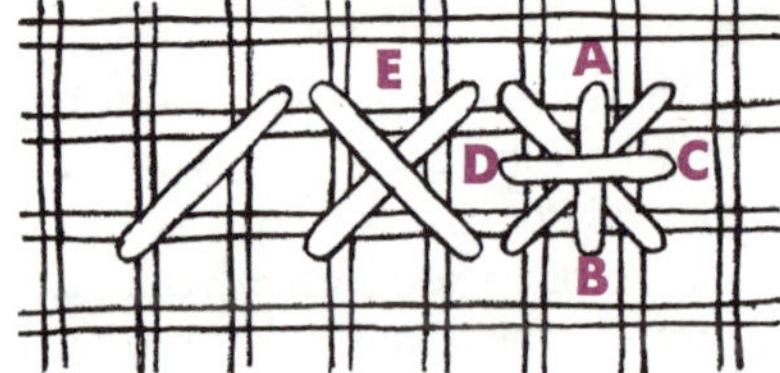

Work first row of Cross-Stitch. Then work an Upright Cross over each Cross-Stitch.

1. Complete cross, then bring needle up at A.

2. Put it down (B) 2 meshes below A.

3 Bring it up (C).

4. Put it down (D) 2 meshes to the left of C.

5. Come up at E to begin next Upright Cross.

Long Legged Cross Stitch

A row of Long Legged Cross looks like a rich braid. Use it for a beautifully ridged surface or for a natural border.

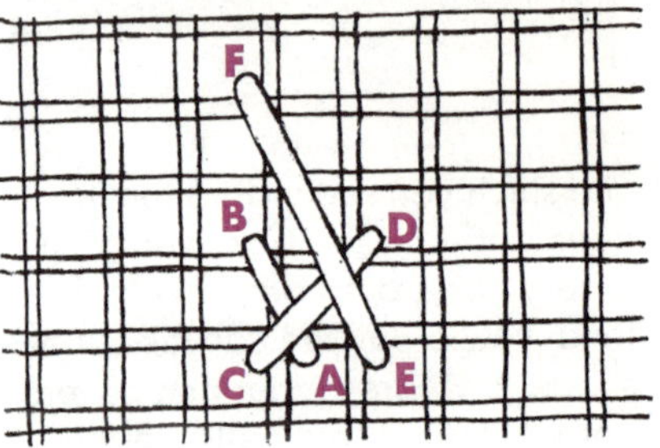

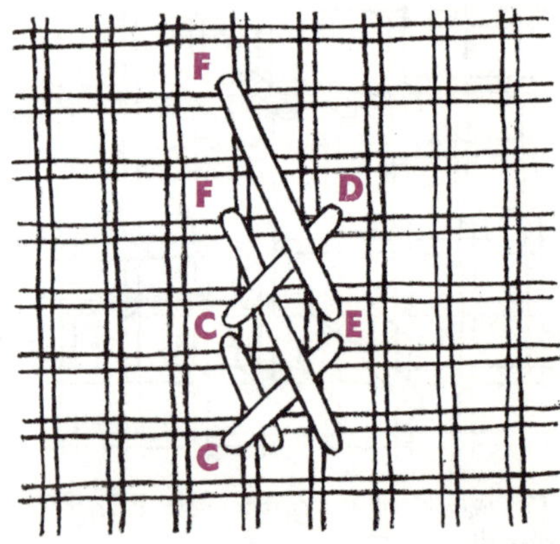

1. Work from bottom to top. Bring needle up (A).

2. Put it down (B) 2 meshes above and 1 mesh to the left of A. Bring it up (C) 2 meshes below B.

3. Put it down (D) 2 meshes to the right of B. Bring it up (E) 2 meshes below D.

4. Put it down (F). Bring it up (C) 2 meshes below F. Repeat from Step 3.

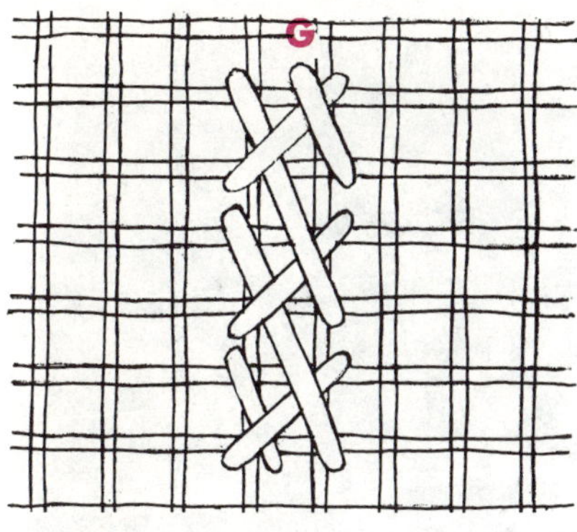

At end of row after Step 3 put needle down at G. Turn the canvas and repeat from Step 1.

Cubed Cross

Cubed Cross is also known as the Leviathan Stitch. The steps below are for working a complete cross over a 4 mesh square.
Work it with 2 strands of wool in the needle. Contrasting colors can be interesting. Be sure that each cross is worked in the same sequence.

Starting at lower left corner.

1. Bring needle up (A).

2. Put it down (B) 4 meshes to the right and 4 meshes above. Bring it up (C) 4 meshes below B.

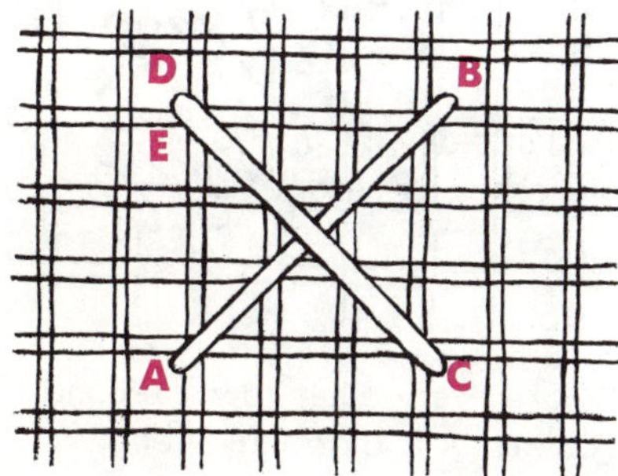

3. Put it down (D) 4 meshes above A. Bring it up (E) 1 mesh below D.

4. Put it down (F) 1 mesh above C. Bring it up (G) 1 mesh to the left of C.

5. Put it down (H) 1 mesh to the right of D. Bring it up (I) 1 mesh to the left of B.

6. Put it down (J) 1 mesh to the right of A. Bring it up (K) 1 mesh above A.

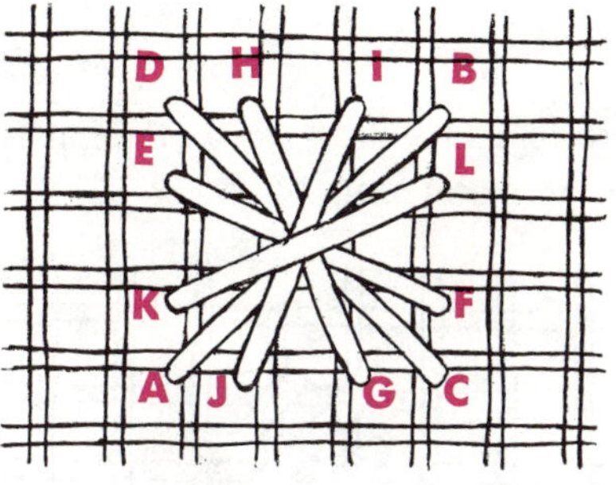

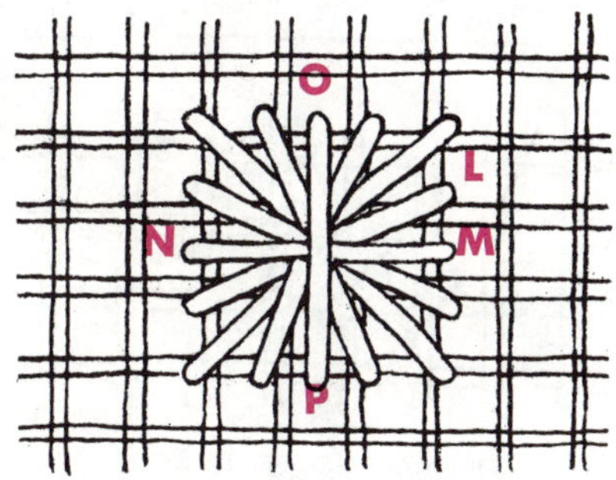

7. Put it down (L) 1 mesh below B. Bring it up (M) 1 mesh below L.

8. Put it down (N) 1 mesh below E. Bring it up (O) 1 mesh to the right of H.

9. Put it down (P) 1 mesh to the right of J.

Cashmere Stitch

The Cashmere resembles the Mosaic, but the units are rectangular rather than square. It, also, is often worked in alternating colors to look checked.

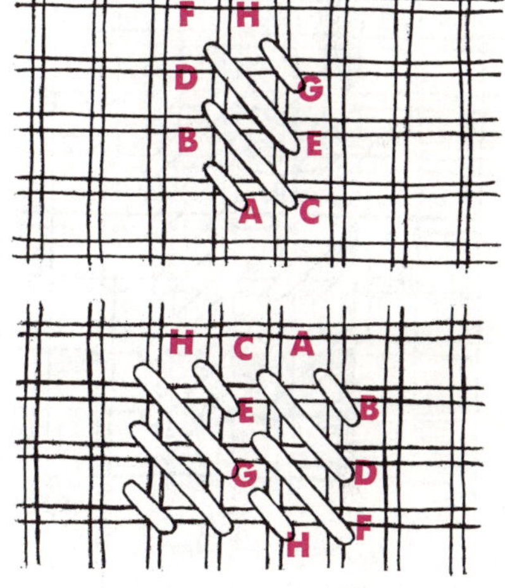

1. Work from lower left corner. Bring needle up (A).

2. Put it down (B) 1 mesh above and to the left of A. Bring it up (C) 1 mesh to the right of A.

3. Put it down (D) 1 mesh above B. Bring it up (E) 1 mesh above C.

4. Put it down (F) 1 mesh above D. Bring it up (G) 1 mesh above E.

5. Put it down (H) 1 mesh to the right of F. Bring it up (A) 2 meshes to the right of H.

Repeat from Step 2 for the second block, reversing direction.

Cashmere Variation

The Cashmere Variation works strong straight lines across the canvas. The rows often alternate colors or directions and it makes either filler or background stitching.

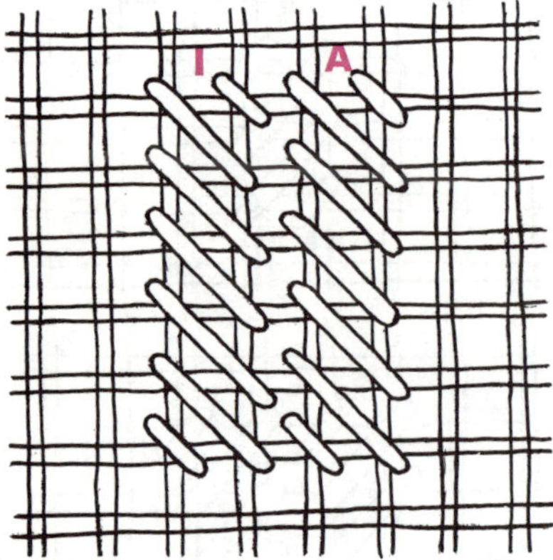

1. Work the first 3 steps of Cashmere.

2. Continue 2 and 3 until row is finished.

3. End row by putting needle down at I.

4. For second row, bring it up (A) two meshes to the right of I.

Repeat from Step 2, reversing direction.

Mosaic Stitch

The tile-like Mosaic is worked in blocks of three stitches.

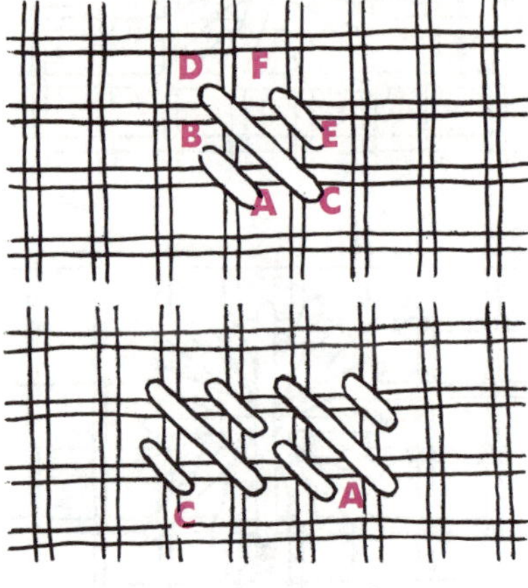

1. Work from lower left corner. Bring needle up (A).

2. Put it down (B) 1 mesh above and to the left of A. Bring it up (C) 1 mesh to the right of A.

3. Put it down (D) 1 mesh above B. Bring it up (E) 1 mesh directly above C.

4. Put it down (F) 1 mesh to the right of D.

Bring it up (A) 1 mesh to the right of C.

Repeat from Step 2. The long stitches of each block touch each other in the same hole.

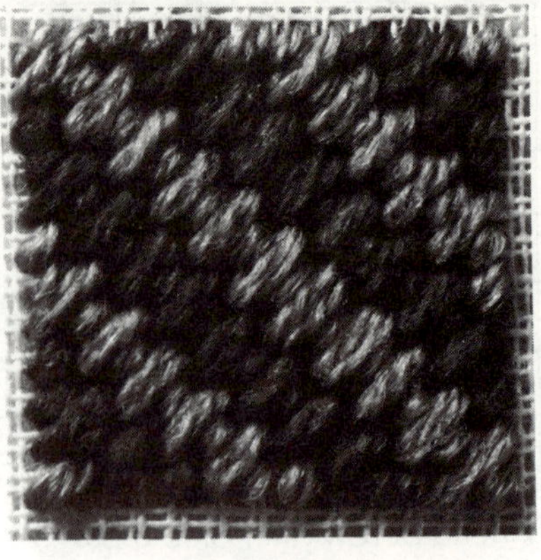

Diagonal Mosaic Stitch

For large areas you will enjoy the rhythm of working Mosaic diagonally. Avoid working with too tight a tension, which will pull your canvas out of shape.

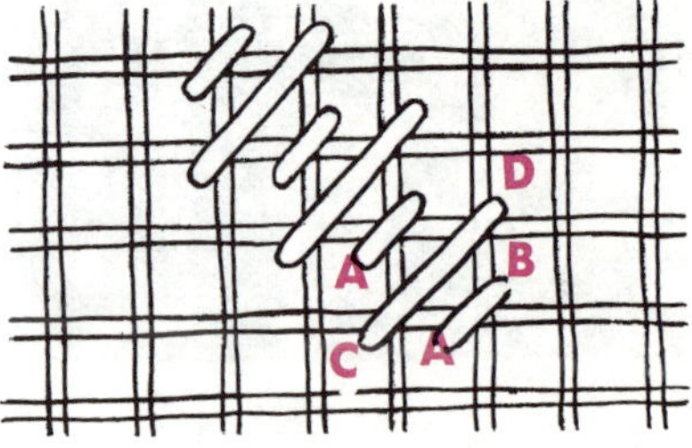

1. Work from lower right corner. Bring needle up (A).

2. Put it down (B) 1 mesh above and to the right of A. Bring it up (C) 1 mesh to the left of A.

3. Put it down (D) 1 mesh above B. Bring it up (A) 1 mesh above C.

Repeat from Step 2. The long stitches of one row touch short stitches of other row.

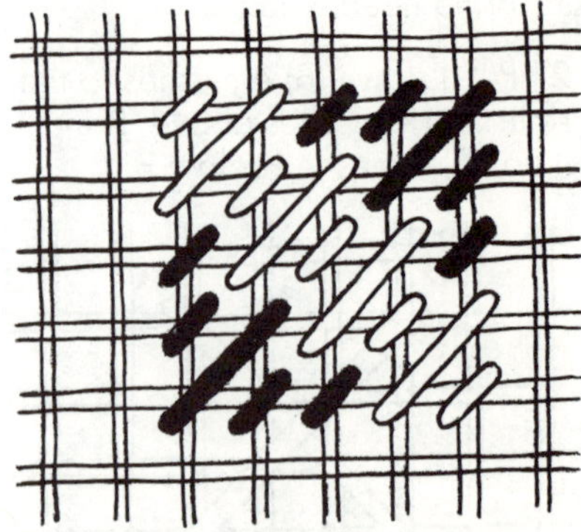

Make every other row a second color, for a diagonal effect.

Scotch Stitch

Resembling the Mosaic, the Scotch Stitch can occupy larger squares. Don't let the stitches get too long, if the piece you are making will be subject to snagging.

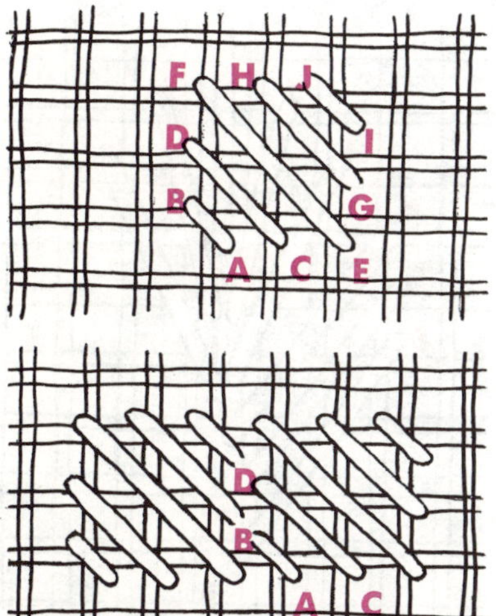

Mark the canvas off in squares of 3, 4, 5 or 6 meshes. These steps are for a square of 3 by 3.

1. Work from lower left corner. Bring needle up (A).

2. Put it down (B) 1 mesh above and to the left of A. Bring it up (C) 1 mesh to the right of A.

3. Put it down (D) 1 mesh above B. Bring it up (E) 1 mesh to the right of C.

4. Put it down (F) 1 mesh above D. Bring it up (G) 1 mesh above E.

5. Put it down (H) 1 mesh to the right of F. Bring it up (I) 1 mesh above G.

6. Put it down (J) one mesh to the right of H. Repeat from Step I.

You may work second square to the right of first, or above.

Scotch Variation

Many patterns can be achieved by working the Scotch Stitch in two colors. Squares in alternate colors produce a checkerboard effect. Changing the stitch direction on alternate squares produces the effect of a square four times as large.

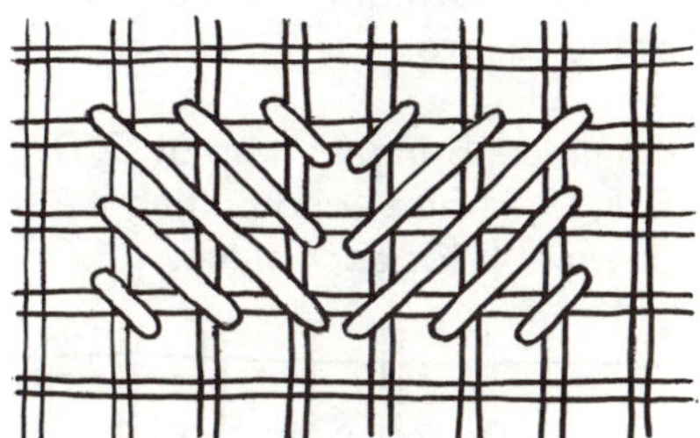

This variation can be further enhanced by using contrast thread in the longest stitch in each square, giving the effect of an overplaid.

Crossed Scotch Stitch

A variation of Scotch and combined or worked by itself will give an interesting texture.

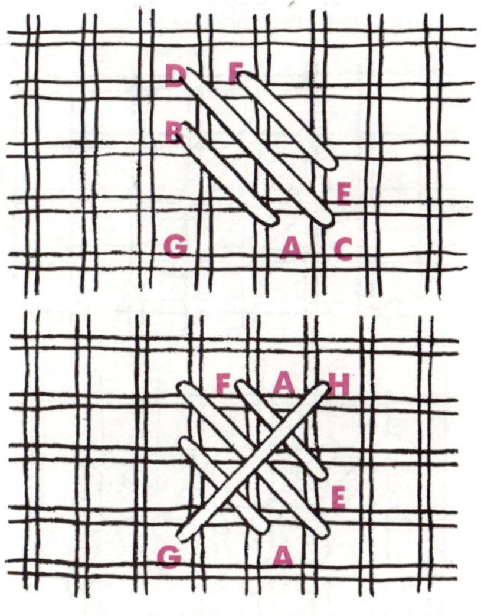

1. Work from lower left corner. Bring needle up (A).

2. Put it down (B) 2 meshes above and 2 meshes to the left of A. Bring it up (C) 1 mesh to the right of A.

3. Put it down (D) 1 mesh above B. Bring it up (E) 1 mesh above C.

4. Put it down (F) 1 mesh to the right of D. Bring it up (G) 2 meshes to the left of A and 2 meshes below B.

5. Put it down (H) 2 meshes to the right of F and 2 meshes above E. Starting at A work next block directly above.

Crossed Scotch Variation

By alternating the directions and colors of each square in crossed scotch, you can achieve an interesting design effect working this one stitch alone.

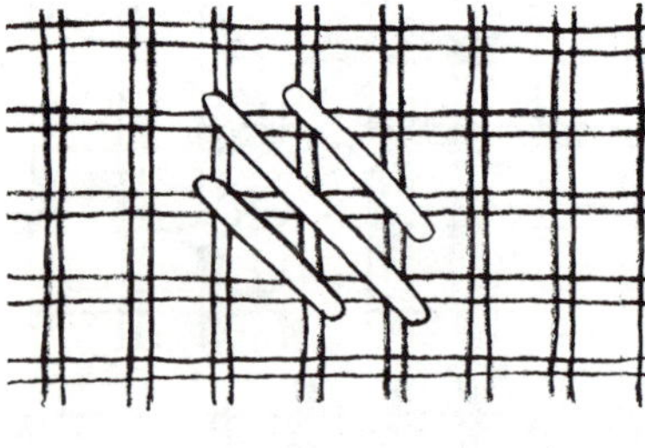

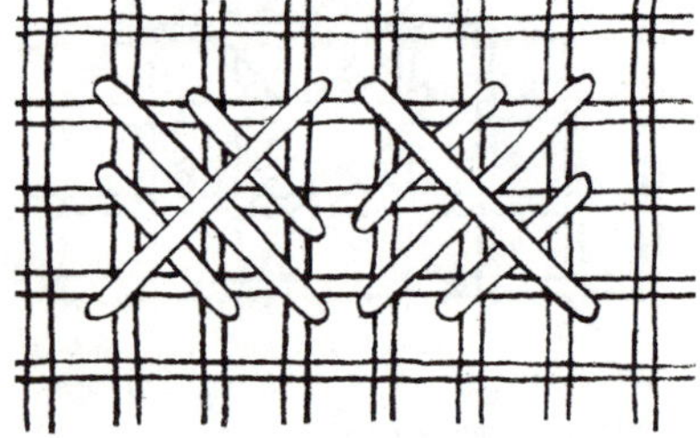

Star Stitch

This decorative stitch is worked clockwise, with the needle always coming up from the outside and going down into the center. New stars begin in the same holes as a corner of the previous star.

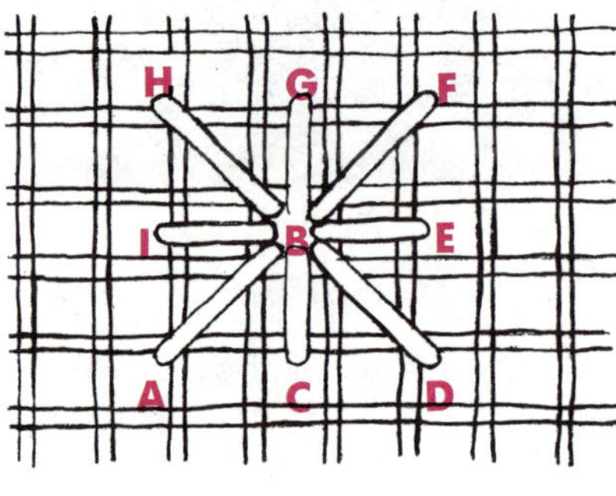

1. Mark canvas off in squares of 4 by 4 meshes. Bring needle up (A) in lower left corner of the square.

2. Put it down (B) in the center of the square.

Continue, bringing it up at C, D, E, F, G, H and I and putting it down at B for each stitch.

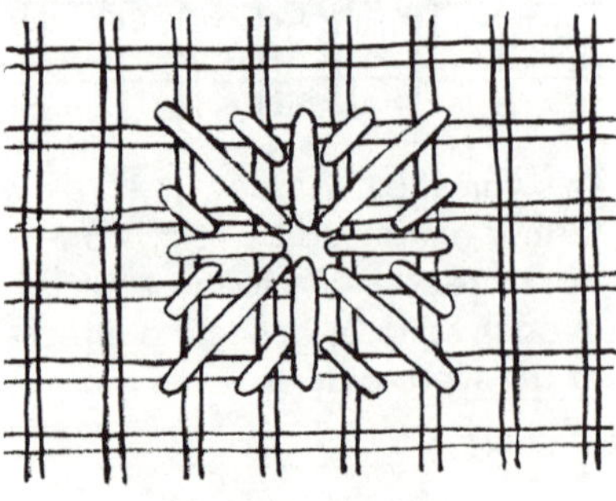

A short filler stitch can be worked between the legs as shown.

Leaf Stitch

A surface of Leaf Stitches is lovely in one or in several colors. The leaves work up quickly but it is necessary to pay attention to the stitch count.

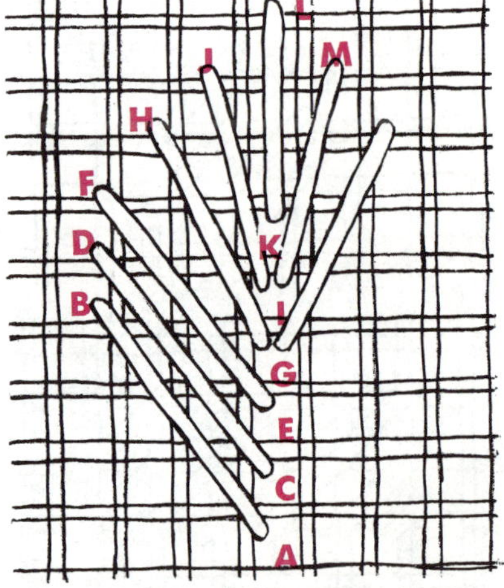

1. Bring needle up (A) 3 meshes in from the left corner of your work.

2. Put it down (B) 4 meshes above and 3 meshes to the left of A. Bring it up (C) 1 mesh above A.

3. Put it down (D) 1 mesh above B. Bring it up (E) 1 mesh above C.

4. Put it down (F) 1 mesh above D. Bring it up (G) 1 mesh above E.

5. Put it down (H) 1 mesh above and to the right of F. Bring it up (I) 1 mesh above G.

6. Put it down (J) 1 mesh above and to the right of H. Bring it up (K) 1 mesh above I.

7. Put it down (L) 4 meshes directly above K.

8. Bring it up (M) one mesh below and to the right of L.

9. Put it down (I) one mesh below K.

Work the right side of the leaf in the same way. Start the next leaf 6 meshes to the right. Start the next row of leaves at F and 1 mesh above L.

Jacquard Stitch

Jacquard makes a bold zigzag diagonally across a canvas. In smaller areas, it is a good filler. It alternates wide and narrow rows. Work it in two or more colors or very elegantly in one color.

1. Start at lower right corner. Bring needle up (A).

2. Put it down (B) 1 mesh above and to the right of A. Bring it up (C) one mesh to the left of A.

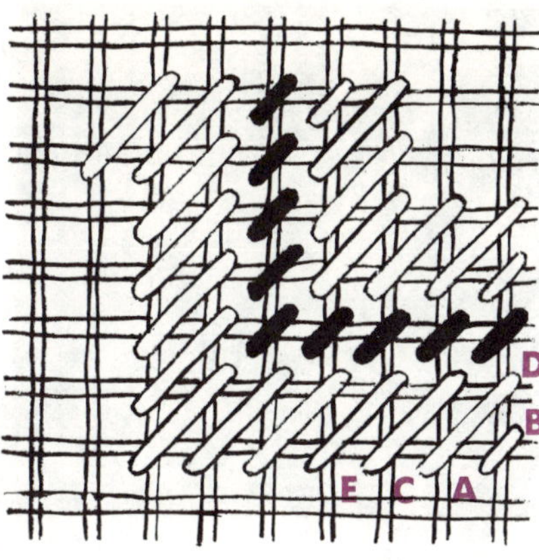

3. Put it down (D) 1 mesh above B. Bring it up (E) 1 mesh to the left of C.

4. Repeat Step 3 for five more stitches but, after the last stitch, bring the needle up 1 mesh directly above the beginning of that stitch.

5. Work five more stitches directly above the last horizontal stitch. But, after the last stitch, bring the needle up 3 meshes to the left and 2 below the end of the last vertical stitch.

Repeat from Step 4.

Frame both sides of the Jacquard row with Continental Stitch in contrast color. Alternate the two patterns and colors.

Milanese Stitch

Milanese makes a triangular pattern that appears to reverse in each row. The pattern has most clarity when worked in two or more colors.

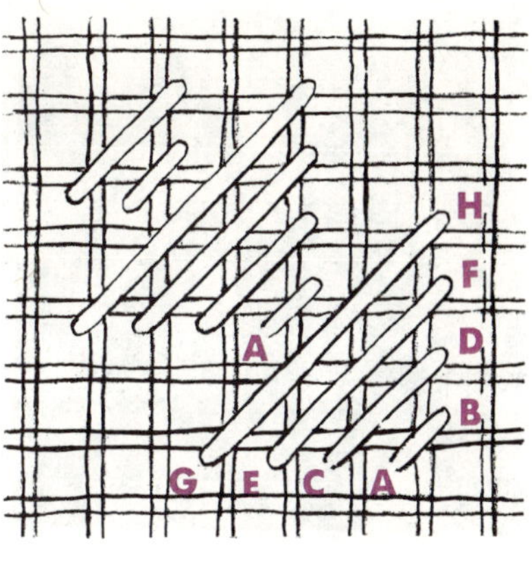

1. Start at lower right corner. Bring needle up (A).

2. Put it down (B) 1 mesh above and to the right of A. Bring it up (C) 1 mesh to the left of A.

3. Put it down (D) 1 mesh above B. Bring it up (E) one mesh to the left of C.

4. Put it down (F) 1 mesh above D. Bring it up (G) one mesh to the left of E.

5. Put it down (H) 1 mesh above F. To repeat stitch, bring it up (A) 1 mesh to the right of and 2 above G.

Repeat from Step 2. Turn the canvas to work second row and start so that the first stitch will share a hole with the longest stitch of the first row.

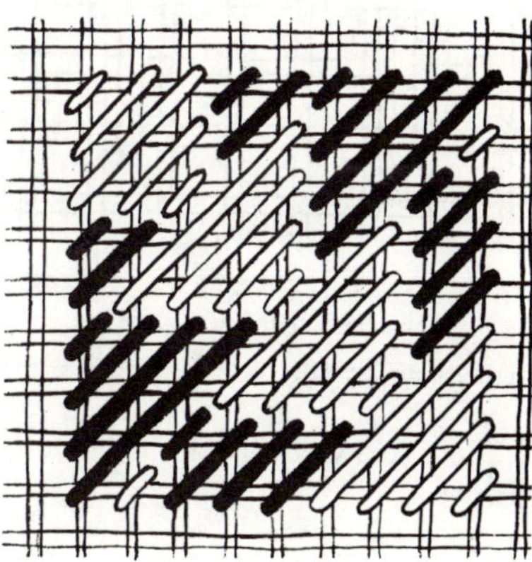

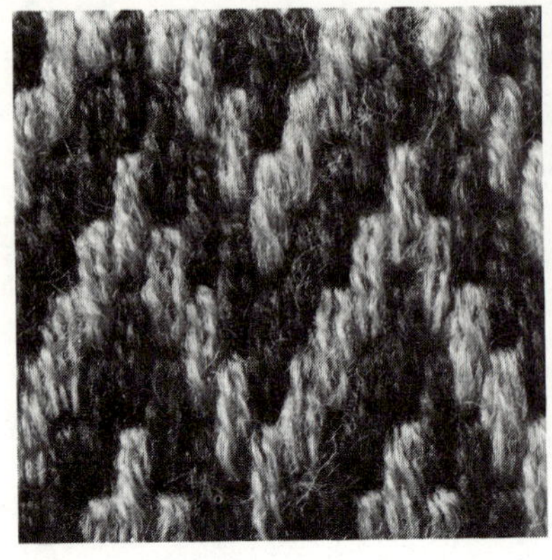

Florentine Stitch

Florentine is a category which includes unlimited zigzag designs most often formed with upright stitches worked over 4 horizontal meshes that rise and fall 2 steps. Make up your own zigzag line and draw it on graph paper to see its effect. You may want to keep the left and right sides symmetrical. The succeeding rows can follow it exactly in different shades of the color. Or they can be worked upside down, to make diamonds.

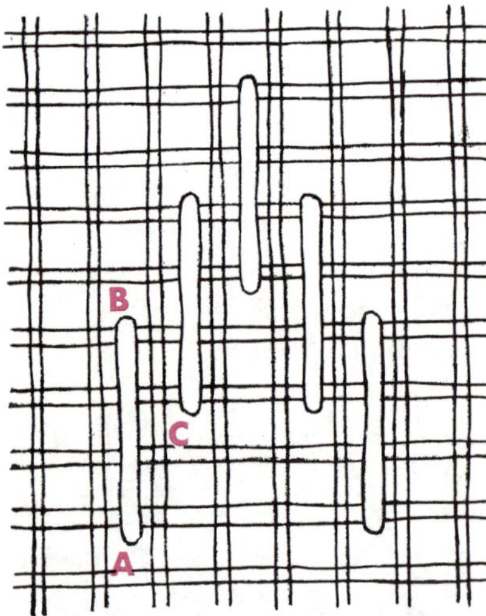

1. Work from left to right Bring needle up at (A).

2. Put it down at (B) 4 meshes above A.

3. Bring it up at (C) two meshes below and to the right of B.

Continue working in same manner from left to right.

Parisian Stitch

Parisian is a simple but very effective and durable stitch. Two colors in alternating rows are often used.

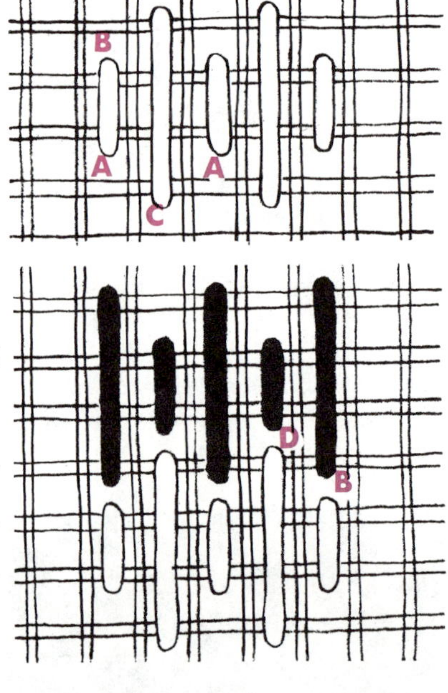

1. Starting at left, bring needle up (A).

2. Put it down (B) 2 meshes directly above A. Bring it up (C) 1 mesh below and to the right of A.

3. Put it down (D) 4 meshes directly above C. Bring it up (A).

Repeat from Step 2. For next row, bring needle up 4 meshes directly above B. Put it down (B). Bring it up 2 meshes above D. Continue from Step 2, but working from right to left.

Upright Gobelin (or Satin)

Rows of Upright Gobelin suggest tapestry. It's easy and quick to work and achieves handsome shaded or striped effects. Be sure your yarn covers the canvas and keep an easy tension. Don't use too long a stitch on pieces subject to snagging. Gobelin can be worked over 2, 3, 4, or 5 meshes. These steps are for 3 meshes.

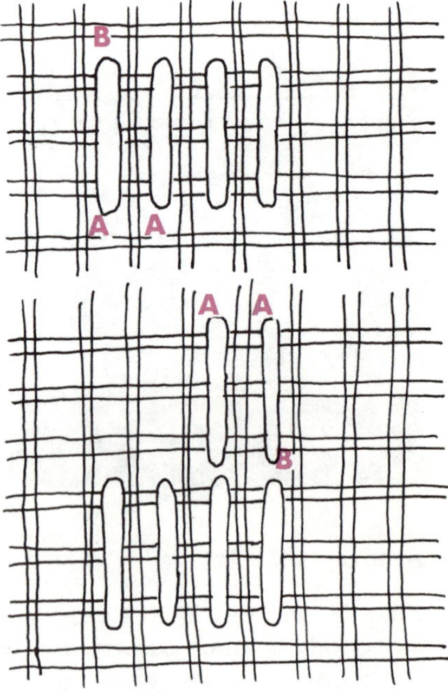

1. Work from left to right. Bring needle up (A).

2. Put it down (B) 3 meshes directly above A.

3. Bring it out (A) level with and 1 mesh to the right of A.

Repeat from Step 2. Turn the work at the end of each row.

Embroidery

What is Embroidery?

Any application of decorative stitches to a fabric may be called embroidery. Like all technical subjects, embroidery can be broken down into categories. The simplest potholder or the most elaborate tapestry will fit into one of the major categories.

There are many sub-categories of embroidery— some named for the stitch such as Cross— Stitch Embroidery.
Or named for the traditional color of the thread such as Black Work or White Work. Or the type of thread such as Crewel which is actually named for the wool yarn used for it. Or even the region where it is popular such as Ukranian Embroidery.

The simplest form of embroidery is the application of stitches to a fabric following a prepared design.

In the last few years a new form of embroidery has evolved—Creative Stitchery. This makes use of some of the traditional stitches but is much freer in conception. Often it is worked on bold fabrics on a large scale with heavy yarns never before used by needleworkers. It can even incorporate oddments such as beads, feathers, bits of glass and stone. It is limited only by the creativity and the willingness of the needleworker to experiment.

It was customary for our grandmothers to learn embroidery when they were children by executing a "sampler". The sampler demonstrated a variety of stitches and served as a reminder, for future work, of the stitches available and the effects they could achieve. They were often designed, in the nineteenth century, around a little homily that served not only to demonstrate the alphabet, but to remind the young embroiderer of attitudes and sentiments endorsed by her elders.

Modern needleworkers make samplers too, but not so conventionally designed. They are most useful tucked in the workbasket, where new stitches can be added all the time. The same stitch worked in several weights of yarn will answer later questions about stitch length and texture. The neighboring colors will suggest color choices for later work. The sampler itself may be worthy of hanging but, in any case, it is indispensable for ready reference.

Necessities

Fabrics

Since you will be putting both time and effort in your embroidery, choose background fabrics that will last for years. Also make certain that they will take the design well. Test a little sample to see if your yarn and needle will pull through easily and not rough up the surface of the fabric. Actually almost any plain or basket weave fabric can be used for embroidery. Just make sure that it will stand up to the wear it will receive. For instance, wall hangings can be made of looser weaves than chair seats or throw pillows.

Linen,because of its many fine qualities,is most often used as a background for embroidery. Cotton in homespun or hop-sacking weaves is most suitable. Certain wools are also excellent. For a really luxurious background silk is used occasionally. Velvets can be embroidered but are a little more difficult to work on. Even the lowly burlap makes a fine background for bold modern wall hangings. Just be careful when choosing synthetics or blends that they have these desirable characteristics.

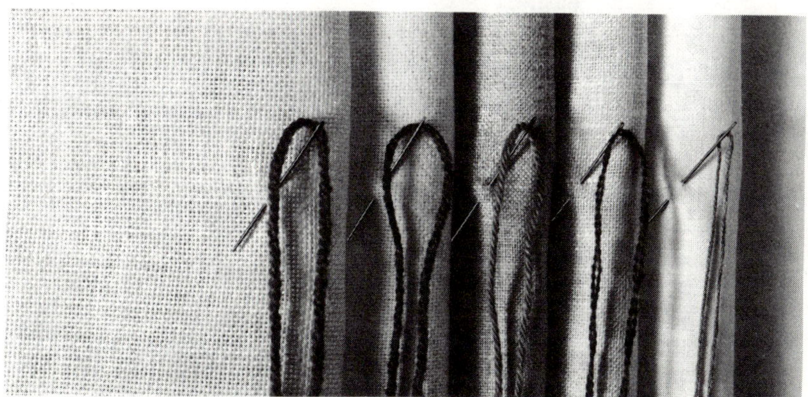

FROM LEFT TO RIGHT: COARSE TO FINE FABRICS

Hoops and Frames

Almost all needlework looks better if it is worked in a hoop or a frame. Hoops are double rings or ovals of wood or metal and come in many sizes. A wooden hoop with a screw on the outer ring that adjusts the tension is the best type to use. The hoop that is held in the hand is the cheapest. Hoops also come on stands which rest on the floor, a table or the lap. There is even a hoop rather inelegantly called the "fanny hoop" which one sits on for the support.

For really professional work an embroidery frame is desirable. This does not leave pressure marks on the fabric as does a hoop. Frames come in a variety of sizes and can usually be adjusted to larger or smaller dimensions.

If no frame is available, a sturdy old picture frame can be used. Or artists' stretchers can be purchased at any art supply store in almost any size. When assembled they make an excellent frame and if you are making a picture, it can be stretched and hung on the same strips when the work is completed.

Yarns and Threads

Almost everyone embroidered a tea towel when she was a little girl. Do you remember how you struggled to separate the strands of floss for that embroidery? The same six-strand floss is still a basic embroidery thread. There are also other lovely cotton threads available. Matte cotton has the look of the handsome Scandinavian linen threads which are hard to find here. Pearl cotton is pleasant to use and comes in sizes 1, 3, 5, 8, the smaller numbers being the heavier weights.

In the wools the most common embroidery yarn is crewel yarn which is a fine 2-ply Persian-type with a slight sheen. Generally it comes with three strands together which can be separated and used singly or in as many strands as desired. Although it is used for crewel it can also be used for needlepoint. Tapestry yarn is also used. It consists of four plys (or threads) twisted together, but it cannot be separated. Many of the interesting knitting wools can be used for embroidery but should first be carefully checked for fraying.

For the experienced embroiderer there are many unusual threads available. Silk and rayon floss which come in six strands are a bit difficult to handle but give a rich effect. Silver and gold threads add sparkle to even the most prosaic embroideries.

In any case, the yarns and threads should be geared to the background fabric, the design and the potential use of the piece of embroidery. If a piece is to be worn or to receive heavy wear such as a chair seat or pillow, only the sturdiest materials should be used. A wall hanging or a picture can incorporate novelty yarns such as raffia, plastic straw, boucle and the like.

Since very little equipment is needed for embroidery, it is sensible to get the best quality and keep it separate from the family sewing supplies. A pretty bag or box is a nice storage place.

Needles

For embroidery on most textiles, use a crewel (also known as an embroidery) needle which has a sharp point, is of medium length and has a long, easily-threaded eye. These needles are designated by number, the smaller the number, the larger the needle. Have a few sizes handy to accommodate different sizes of threads and yarns. They should be easy to thread and should make a hole in the fabric large enough to pull the thread through without tugging. However, they should not be so large that they leave holes in the fabric.

CREWEL NEEDLES SIZES 3 TO 9

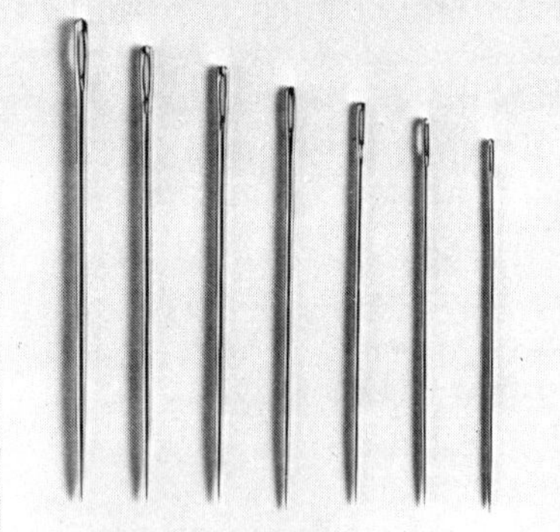

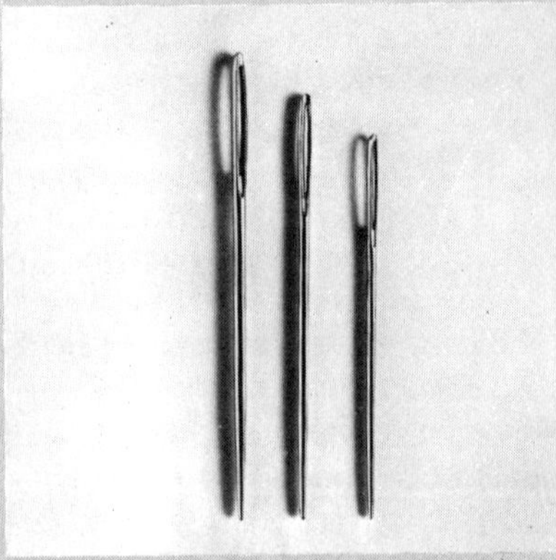

TAPESTRY NEEDLES SIZES 18 TO 22

The other major type of needle is the tapestry needle. These have blunt tips and large eyes. In this type the smaller numbers also indicate the larger needles. Use a tapestry needle for all types of canvas work and also on coarse fabrics where you want to go between the threads of the fabric rather than pierce the fibers. Also use a tapestry needle for weaving and other stitches worked on the surface of the fabric.

Thimbles

If you are doing embroidery for any length of time, you will find a thimble is a real protection. Choose a well-fitting thimble of metal (plastic thimbles are too bulky). After you become proficient, you will be doing your embroidery with both hands but even then a thimble is necessary only on the right hand (if you are right handed).

Scissors

Any fairly small, sharp pointed scissors will do for snipping threads and the preparation of embroidery. It makes one feel very professional, however, to have real embroidery scissors. These have very short blades and sharp points. In fact, they are even making reproductions of the amusing antique embroidery scissors which come in the shape of a stork. You will also need regular dressmaker's shears for cutting fabrics and finishing projects.

Preparation

Transferring Designs

For most of your projects, you will have to apply the design to the background fabric. Allow plenty of room outside the design area. Straighten the grain and cut carefully, following the grain line.

Hot Iron Transfers:

First test the transfer pattern to see how it prints on your fabric. Pin or tape scrap of your fabric, right side up, on the ironing board. Aluminum foil placed under fabric ensures a clearer transfer. Cut out a trial motif, leaving a margin. Tape, pin or baste motif, print side down, on fabric. Test the heat of your iron by pressing straight down on motif. Do not glide iron but stamp it in position. If the iron is warm enough, the print will be clear. Now test removing the stamped motif either by washing (if fabric is washable) or by using a good cleaning fluid.

PRESS TRANSFER DESIGN

TRANSFER IMPRINT

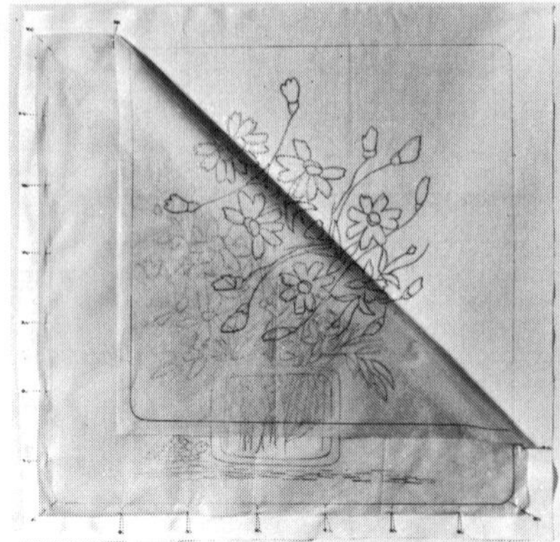

If your test has been successful, transfer the design to your fabric as for test motif.

The transfer may not be removable from some fabrics. In this case, you will have to cover all of the transfer markings with stitches.

Tracing Designs: Some transfer colors may not show up on the fabric you are using, because of the color or texture, and you will need to trace the design onto the background. You can also use a transfer design more than once with this method. First baste center line on your background

TRACING DESIGN

fabric. Also draw horizontal and vertical center lines on design. Tape fabric right side up on a hard surface. Lining up center lines, place design on fabric. Slip dressmaker's carbon paper, waxed side down, under design. Tape everything in place. Transfer design to fabric by carefully going over all lines of the design with a pencil or stylus. Be sure to

TRACED IMPRINT

bear down hard enough so that lines transfer.

Ordinary carbon paper should not be used. Use dressmaker's carbon paper which comes in dark colors for light-colored fabric and light colors for dark fabrics.

Enlarging and Reducing Designs

If you are developing your own designs, you often find that you have the perfect design but it's just too small—or too big—for your project. The easiest way to handle the problem is to take the design to a photostat house. Tell them the exact size you want your finished design and they will do it mechanically. It's well worth the few dollars it costs.

However, you can do the job yourself. Just draw in little grid lines on your design. Then on a sheet of brown paper draw the outline of the size you want your design to be. Within that outline draw in the same number of grid lines that you drew on your design. Now copy all the lines on your design to the brown paper pattern, working square by square. If your outline on the brown paper and the squares were larger than your orignal design, your new pattern will be larger. Conversely, if the outline and squares were smaller, the new pattern will be smaller.

DESIGN GRID

Setting Up Your Work

To prevent fraying, make narrow basted temporary hems, zigzag stitch or overcast all edges of your background fabric.
Now place work in hoop.
First adjust screw so that the rings of hoop fit together well; separate rings. Lay work over inside ring. Press outside ring in place. If fabric is not tight as a drum on the hoop, pull it tight, being careful not to pull it on the bias. If you do, your work may become distorted. Adjust screw again, if necessary.

Always remove fabric from hoop when you are putting away

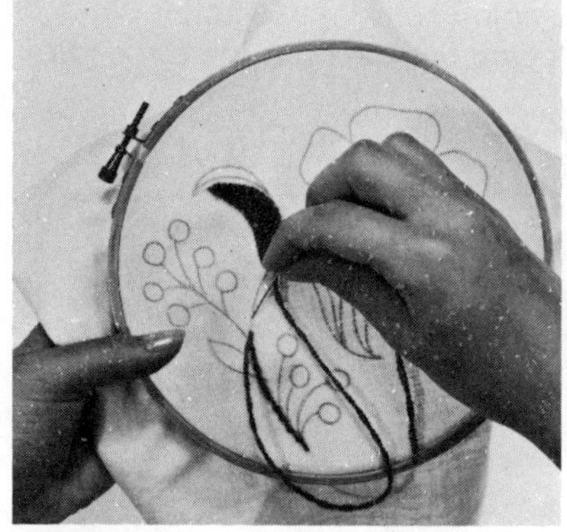

HOOP

your work. This will prevent pressure marks. And when you have to move the hoop over an area that is already embroidered, protect the work with tissue paper. Just lay tissue paper over the fabric before top ring is lowered in place. Then tear away paper from the area to be embroidered. This also prevents spoiling the surface of delicate fabrics such as silk.

If you are using an embroidery frame rather than a hoop, attach work as follows: Baste in temporary hems as above. Mark the center of top and bottom canvas strips which are on frame. Pin center of top edge of background fabric to center of top strip. Whip top edge of fabric to canvas, working from center. Repeat on bottom edge of fabric.

Now sew heavy tape along each side edge of your background fabric. Roll up the fabric on top and bottom rollers of frame. With heavy thread used double, lash the side tapes to the sides of frame. Fasten off. When the area you are embroidering is completed, cut lashing threads, roll fabric to an unworked area and relash to sides.

If you are using a picture frame or artist's stretcher strips, just thumbtack or staple work in place. Start in center of one side and work to corners, placing tacks about 1 inch (2,5 cm) apart.
Do opposite side, then the two adjoining sides.

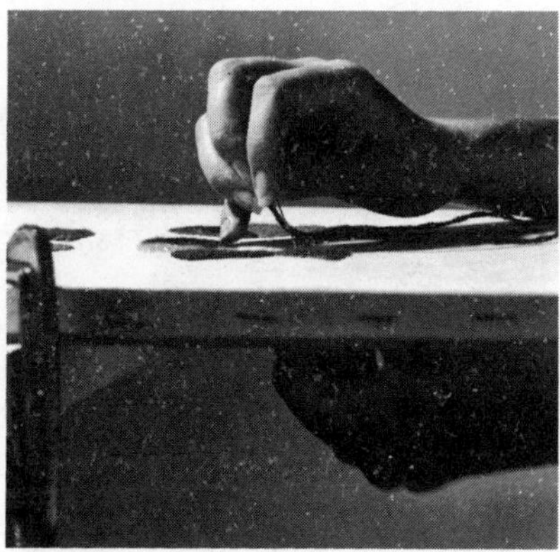

CANVAS STRETCHER

Threading Needle

Many threads will easily slip into the needle when threaded in the usual way. Soft wools may be a little more difficult to thread, however. Double these over the eye of the needle. Clasp wool near fold and slip off the needle. Now push fold through eye of needle.

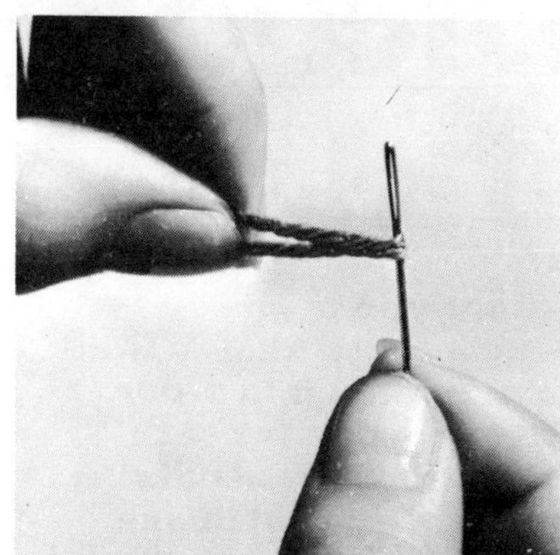

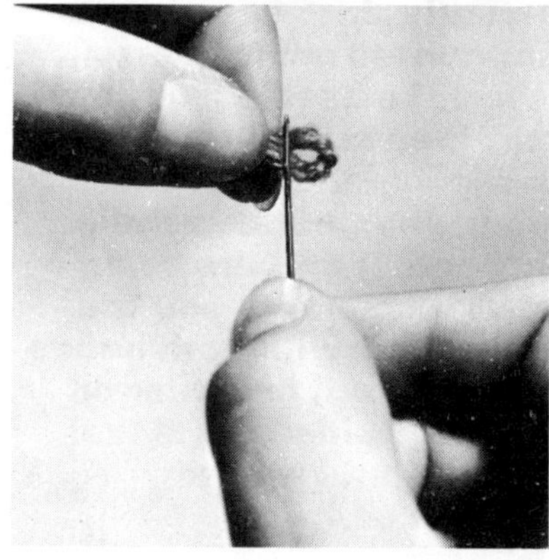

Starting and Finishing Threads

When starting a thread, hold an inch or so under the work and make the first few stitches over it so that it is anchored in place. Or make a knot in thread and begin with knot on right side of work a couple of inches from the starting place. Bring needle up at starting place and work embroidery. When work is completed, clip off knot, pull end through to wrong side, thread needle and run it under first few stitches.

Finish off threads by running them under a few stitches on wrong side. And begin new threads in a started piece of embroidery by running them under a few threads. There should never be any knots on the wrong side of the work.

Dictionary
of Embroidery Stitches

Before you begin practicing stitches, a little explanation is in order. The diagrams for each stitch show the needle going in and out in one step merely for clarity. Actually this never happens in embroidery. Insert the needle from the top, then switch your hand to the under side of the work and pull the needle through. If you are using a hoop on a stand, you can embroider with both hands —one on top, the other on the underside. This is the professional way to embroider.

Backstitch

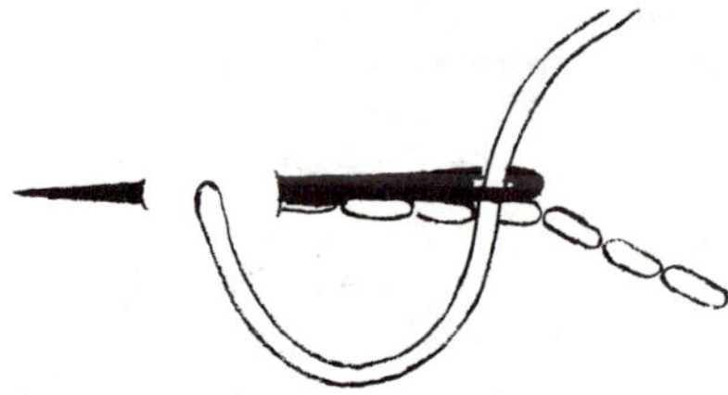

This stitch makes a nice sharp outline. When worked in close rows, it forms a solid filling. Work from right to left. Bring thread up on line and insert needle a little to the right. Now bring needle up again an equal distance ahead. Insert again at beginning of last stitch.

Backstitch, Single-Threaded

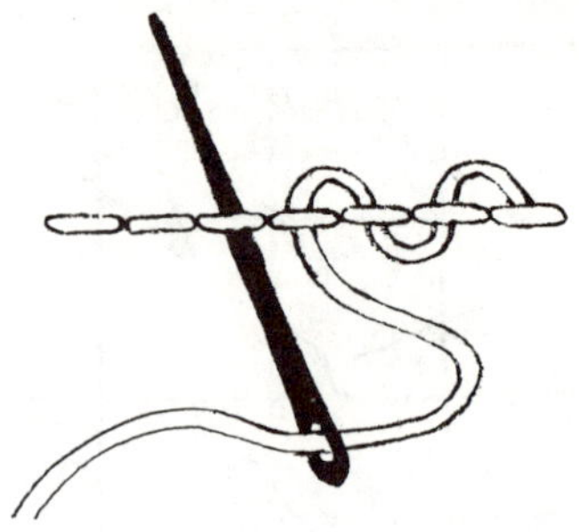

This stitch makes a more decorative line. Work a row of backstitch. With a contrasting color thread in a blunt needle, lace in and out of the backstitches. Don't pull too tight.

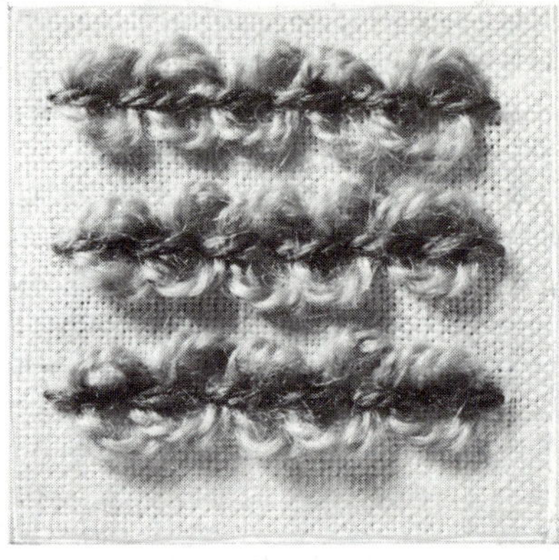

Backstitch, Double-Threaded

Work a row as in Backstitch, Single-Threaded. Complete stitch by lacing back in opposite direction.

Chain Stitch

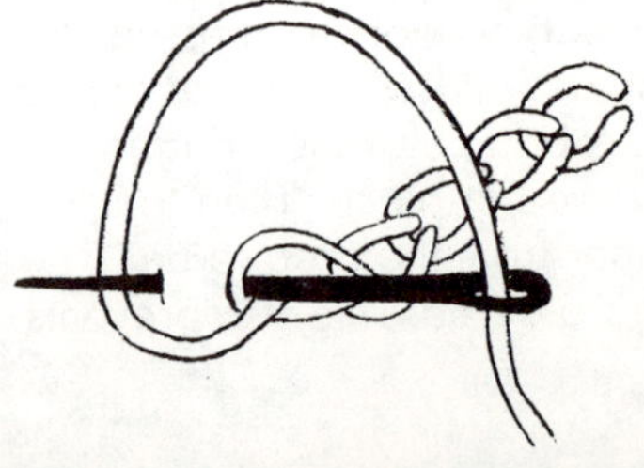

This stitch makes a decorative outline, stems for flowers or, worked in close rows, a solid filling. Work from the top down. Bring needle up at top of line. Make a loop with thread and hold it in place with left thumb. Insert needle right where thread first came up. Now bring needle out a short distance ahead on line, drawing needle over loop.

Cross-Stitch

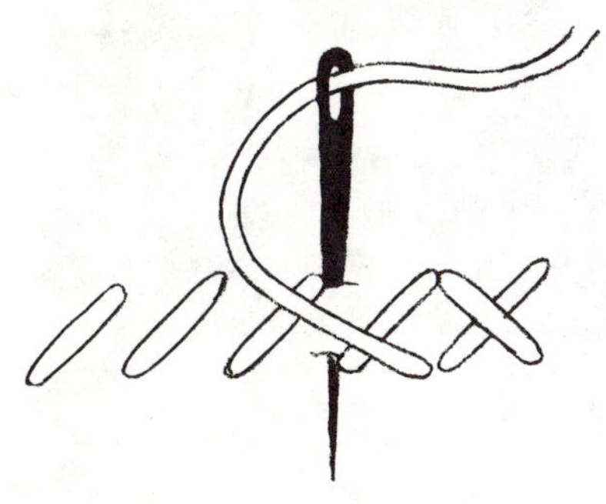

This is a versatile stitch which is used for borders and solid filling. It may be worked on canvas or evenweave linen where the threads can be counted. It can also be worked from a transfer pattern. Work from left to right. Bring needle up at lower left corner of a cross and make a diagonal stitch into upper right corner of cross. Complete row with these half cross-stitches. Now work back across row, completing each cross. Be sure that each stitch always crosses in the same direction.

Blanket Stitch

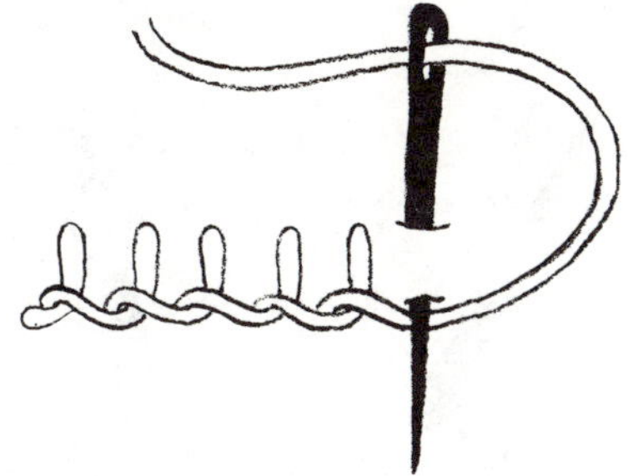

This is a multi-purpose stitch. It can form outlines, be used for filling, cover an edge of fabric or form a flower when worked in a circle. Work from left to right. Bring needle up and hold loop of thread down with left thumb. Make a vertical stitch as in diagram, bringing needle out over loop of thread.

Stem Stitch

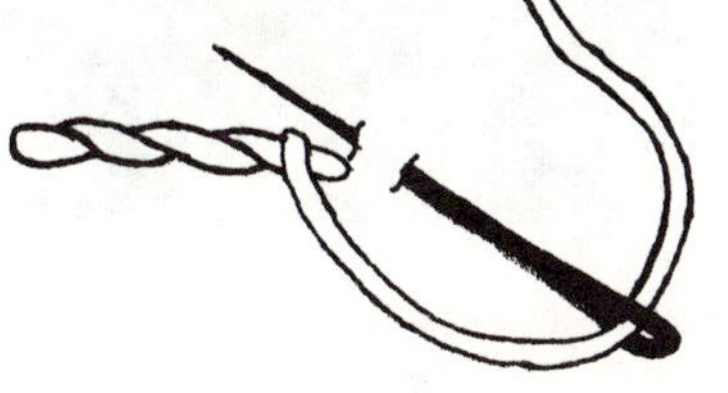

This is a basic stitch used for lines, outlines and the stems of flowers. When worked in close rows (all going in the same direction) it makes a dense filling. Work from left to right. Start at left end of guide line. Make a small stitch, slanting it slightly across guide line. Be sure to keep thread below needle throughout. If the thread is held above the needle throughout, the stitch is called Outline Stitch. Note the interesting effect you get when you make a stitch with the thread above the needle and the next stitch with the thread below the needle.

Couching Stitch

This stitch is used for lines and outlines and, worked in close rows, as a solid filling. It is worked with at least two threads used separately. Fasten one or more threads at right end of line; bring up to top of work. Hold them in place along line with left thumb. Hold them in place with tiny, evenly spaced stitches made with another thread. When row is completed, take all threads to back of work and fasten.

Holbein Stitch

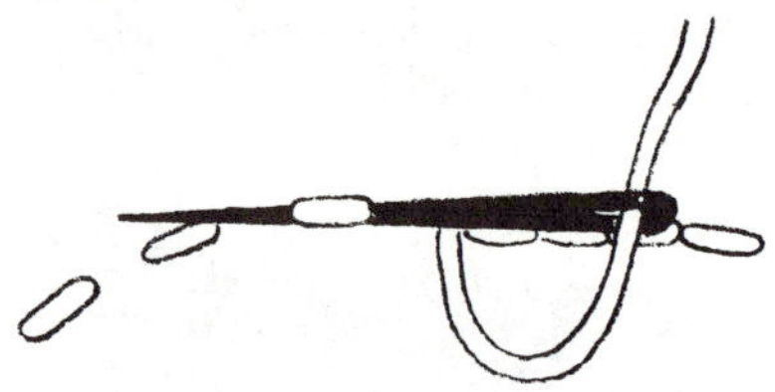

This stitch is used for outlines and lines. Along guide line work Running Stitch. Be sure that each stitch and each space between stitches is of equal size. On the return journey, work Running Stitch so that all the spaces are filled in.

Holbein Stitch, Single-Threaded

This is a more decorative form of Holbein and looks just like Backstitch, Single-Threaded. Make a row of regular Holbein. Using a contrasting color thread in a blunt needle, lace in and out of row of stitches.

Holbein Stitch, Double-Threaded

This stitch looks just like Backstitch, Double-Threaded. When you have finished a row of Holbein Stitch, Single-Threaded, work back over the row making loops in those places skipped before. This last threading may be in a different color from the first line of threading.

Leaf Stitch

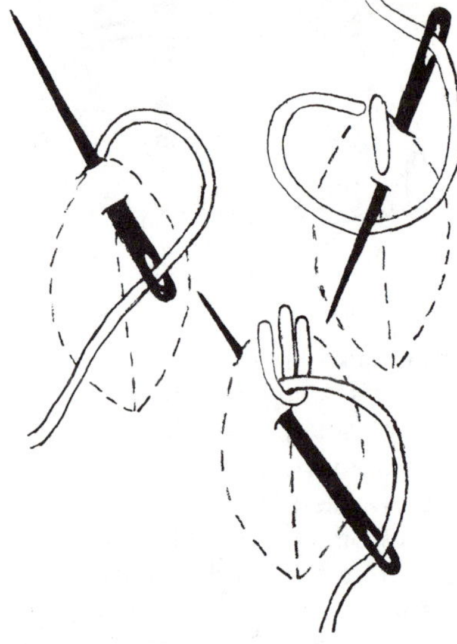

This is a pretty way of filling in a leaf shape. Starting at point of leaf, make a straight stitch part way down center.
Bring needle out on left edge. Leaving a loop of yarn, insert needle on right edge.
Now hold down loop with a small stitch over center.

Feather Stitch

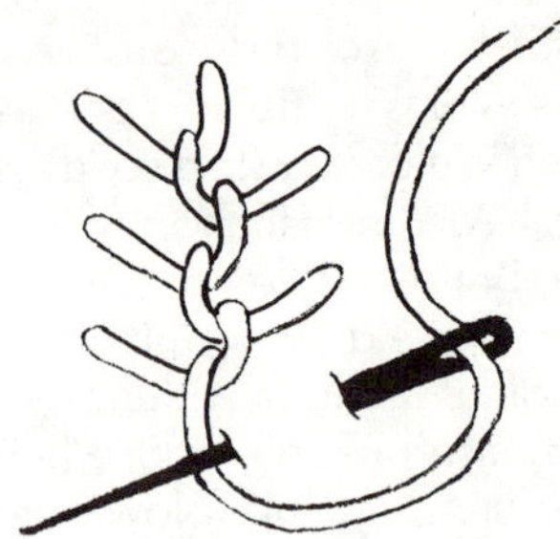

This stitch is used for borders, lines and, very occasionally, for filling. Start a little to left of guide line. Holding thread with left thumb, work a small slanting stitch at the right and a bit below where thread emerged. Needle points to the left. Pull needle through over thread loop. Make thread loop on left of guide line and work a stitch as before but with needle pointing to right. Pull needle through over thread loop.

Lazy-Daisy Stitch

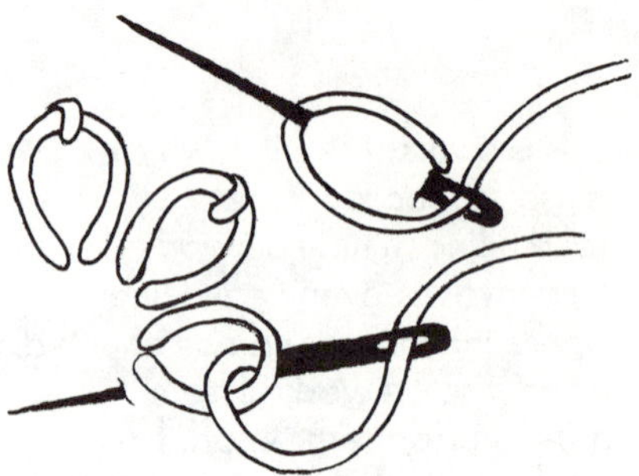

This is also known as Detached Chain Stitch. Worked in a circle, these make charming flowers. Worked separately, they may be used as a light filling. Bring thread up and hold in a loop with left thumb. Insert needle back where thread emerged. Then bring needle out the length of stitch desired and pull through over loop. Make a small stitch to anchor loop.

Coral Stitch

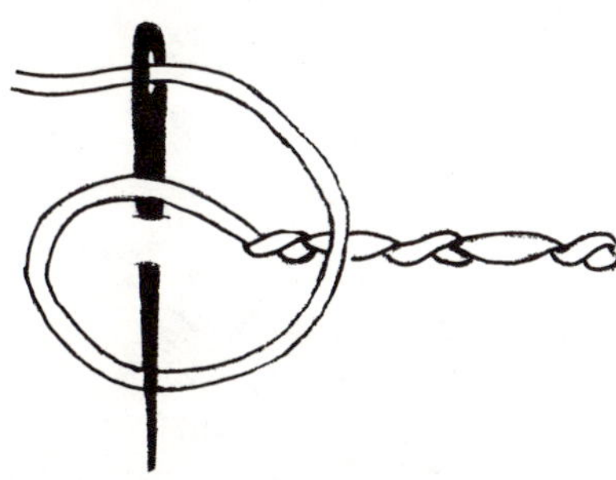

This stitch is used for straight and curved lines and outlines. Work from right to left. Start at right end of line. Anchor thread with left thumb. Going under thread, make a little stitch across line. Bring needle out over lower curve of thread.

Split Stitch

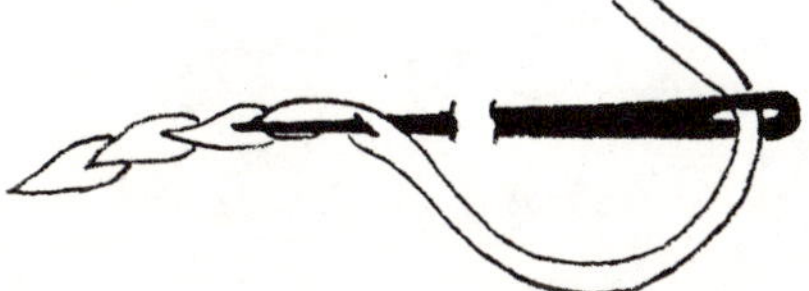

This stitch is used for lines and outlines and when worked in close rows makes a smooth filling. The method of working is similar to Stem Stitch. However, when bringing out the needle, cause it to split the thread right in the center.

Laid Stitch

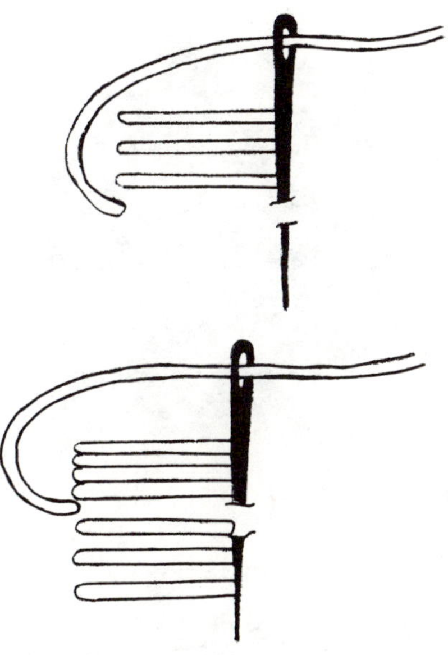

This stitch is used for a solid filling. Although it looks like Satin Stitch, it is used instead of it, when you want to save thread. Work a stitch from one guide line to the next. Take a little stitch on guide line, bringing needle out the width of a stitch away. Return to starting edge and make another little stitch. When the entire area between guide lines has been filled, work over the same area filling in all the spaces between stitches.

Straight Stitch

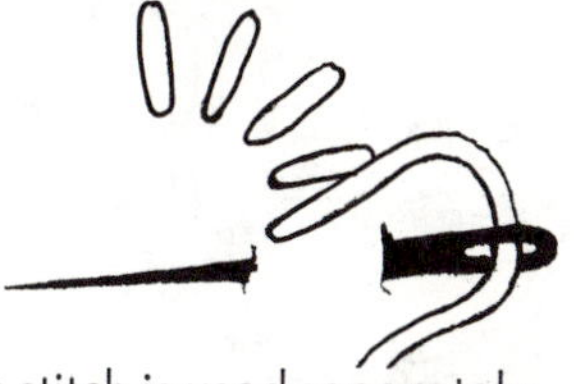

This stitch is used separately for specific effects such as a thorn on a rose. It may be worked in a circle, however, to form a flower. Just follow diagram for method.

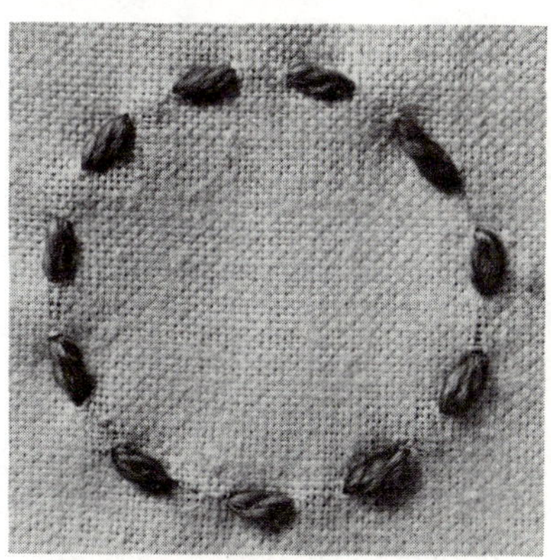

Running Stitch

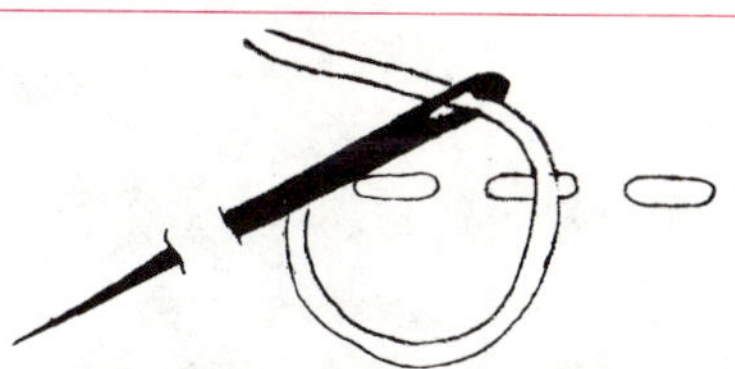

This stitch is used for lines and outlines. When worked in close rows, it makes a spaced filling. Work from right to left. Be sure that each stitch is identical in size and the spaces between are also the same. Do not make a series of stitches on the needle at one time as in doing running stitch in dressmaking.

Rumanian Stitch

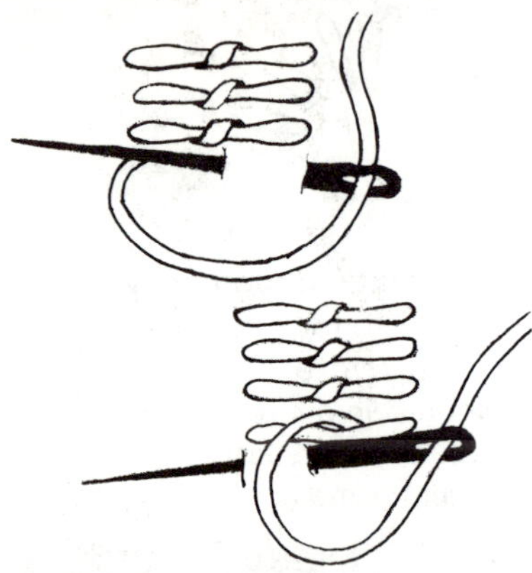

This stitch makes a neat solid border or filling. It can also be worked so that stitches are separated as in diagram. Work from the top down. Bring needle up on left guide line and make a Satin Stitch across the space. Then bring needle out just short of center and above the Satin Stitch. Now make a little slanting stitch over Satin Stitch, again bringing needle out on left guide line.

Brick Stitch

This stitch makes a solid filling. Work a row of straight stitches, leaving the width of a stitch between every adjoining stitch. Make second row of stitches in the same manner but interlock them with the first row of stitches. If you turn your work on its side, you will see how the stitches look like a brick surface.

French Knot

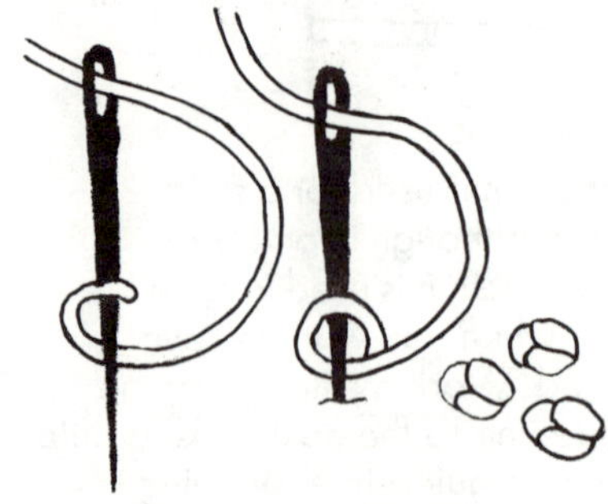

This stitch is used for dots, worked in rows for lines or worked solidly for a filling. Use number of strands required for knots of various sizes. Bring needle up, wrap thread around point of needle, then insert needle close to where needle emerged. Just be sure that it is not in exact spot where thread emerged or knot will pull through. Draw thread to wrong side, holding knot in place with left thumb.

Star Filling Stitch

This stitch is used as a widely spaced filling. First work a Cross-Stitch with the arms on the straight rather than the usual way. Then work a second Cross-Stitch over the first, making the second in the usual way. Next work a small Cross-Stitch over the first two, tieing them down.

Overcast Stitch

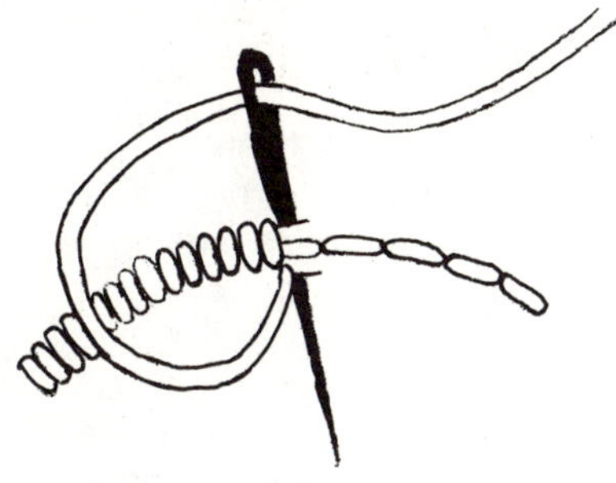

This stitch is used for raised lines, precise outlines and is frequently used in fancy monograms. First make a row of Holbein Stitch along guide line. Next make tiny close stitches over Holbein Stitches, picking up as little fabric as possible.

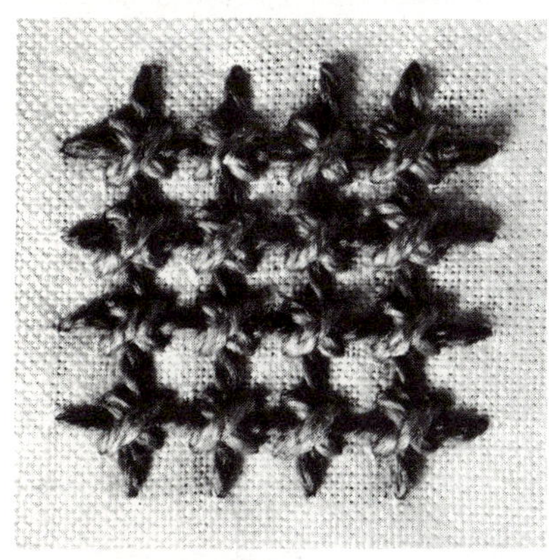

Trellis Stitch

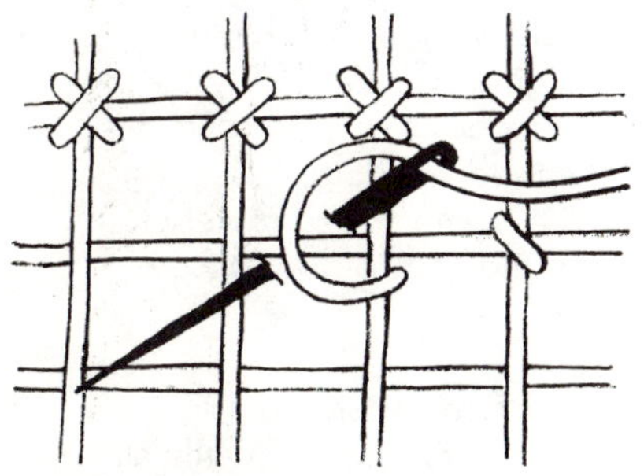

This forms a very decorative filling and can be used to fill large areas. First work long vertical stitches across the given area. Be sure they are evenly spaced. Then work long horizontal stitches over the first stitches. Tie stitches in place at each intersection with a half Cross-Stitch or a full Cross-Stitch. For an even more decorative effect try making a French Knot or Star Filling Stitch in the center of each square.

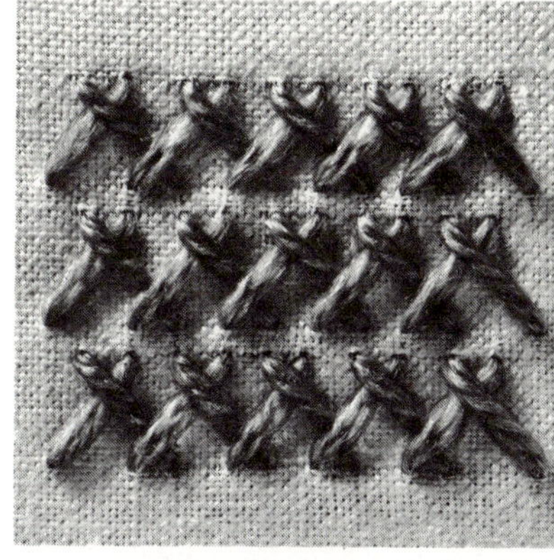

Herringbone Stitch

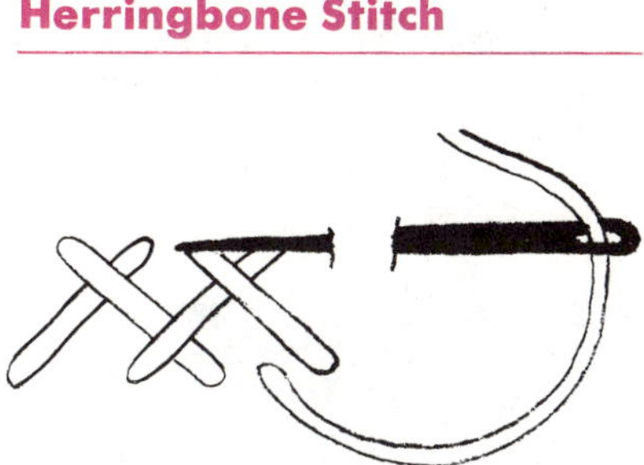

This stitch is used for borders. Work from left to right. Bring thread out at left end of lower guide line. Make a small stitch from right to left on upper guide line as in diagram. Now make a similar stitch from right to left on lower guide line. Keep stitches very even.

Satin Stitch

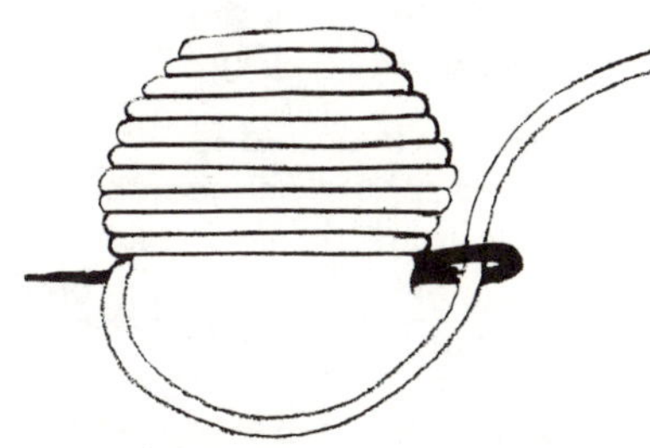

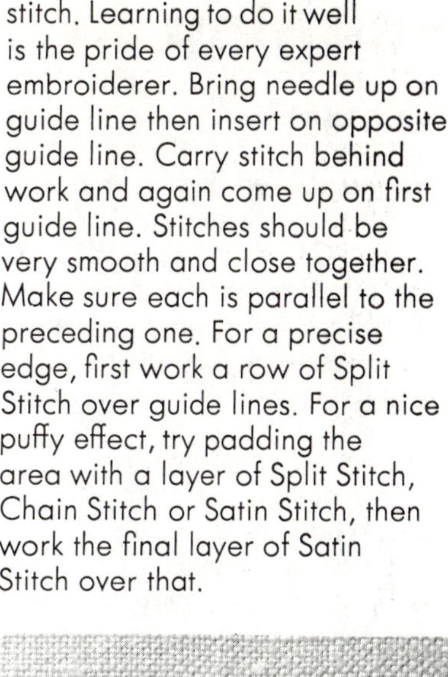

This is a basic solid filling stitch. Learning to do it well is the pride of every expert embroiderer. Bring needle up on guide line then insert on opposite guide line. Carry stitch behind work and again come up on first guide line. Stitches should be very smooth and close together. Make sure each is parallel to the preceding one. For a precise edge, first work a row of Split Stitch over guide lines. For a nice puffy effect, try padding the area with a layer of Split Stitch, Chain Stitch or Satin Stitch, then work the final layer of Satin Stitch over that.

Fishbone Stitch

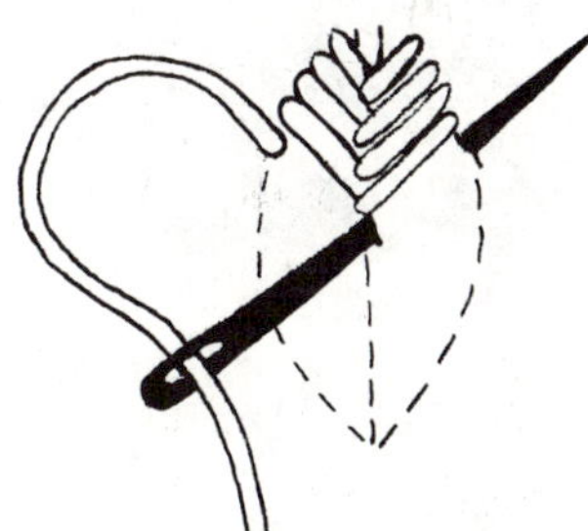

This stitch is used to fill in a small area—usually a leaf. Make a small vertical stitch at top point of area to be filled. Bring needle up on left outline. Make a slanting stitch toward center, inserting needle just below first straight stitch and a thread or two to right of center guide line. Bring needle out on right outline. Now make a slanting stitch toward center, inserting needle a thread or two to left of center line. Stitches just cross at center.

Finishing

Needlepoint

Hold the finished canvas up to the light to examine it for mistakes. Correct errors and clean soiled spots with cleaning fluid or liquid cold water soap for wool. Be sure the edges are still completely taped or hemmed.

Blocking will straighten and smooth your work. Cover a board that you can put tacks into with clean cloth or paper, on which you have marked, with a waterproof marker, the outlines of the piece. If canvas is very much out of shape, dampen back with cold water.

Place the needlepoint right side up on the board. Insert rustproof tacks, matching the edges of the needlepoint to the drawn outline and pulling, if necessary, to square the sides. Tack each side and continue tacking an inch apart.

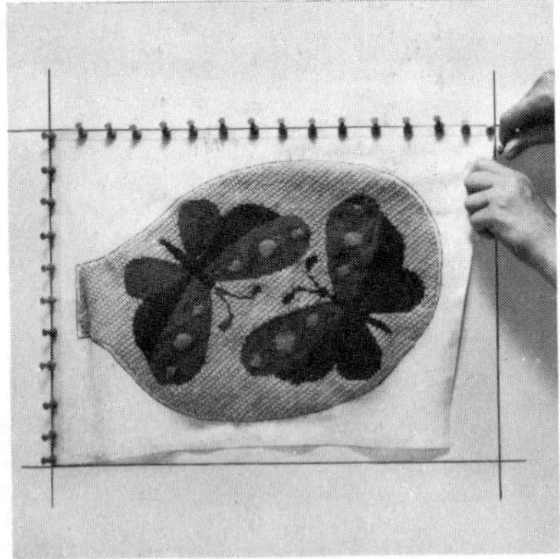

Place a very damp cloth on top of the needlepoint. Let it dry thoroughly. Remove work from the board.

After blocking, needlepoint used in tennis racquet covers, pictures, belts and other items requiring stiffness for the finished effect should be mounted. For belts, trim corners of canvas as shown to reduce bulk. Cut a heavyweight nonwoven interfacing to the size of finished article, making sure corners are square.

Place nonwoven on back of needlepoint and fold unworked canvas over edges of nonwoven.

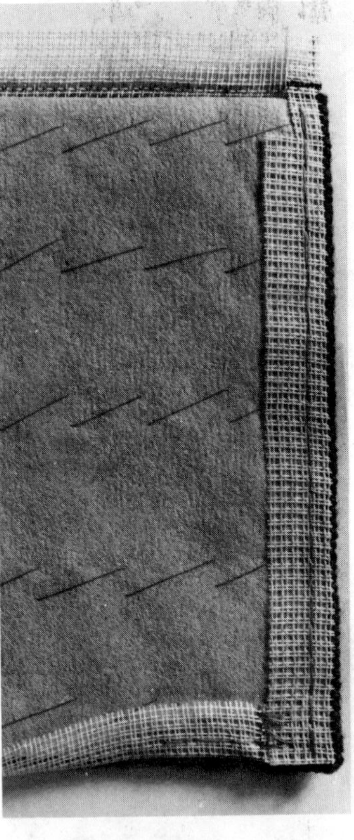

If necessary, trim unworked canvas edges to 1 inch (2,5 cm) wide.

Baste unworked canvas to nonwoven and nonwoven to needlepoint as shown, catching only back side of needlepoint. Line or finish off as desired.

Needlepoint intended for framing or hanging should be mounted on cardboard and trimmed in the same manner as for belts. Secure the unworked edges with masking tape.

Embroidery

Even with the utmost care sometimes a piece of embroidery becomes soiled in the making. If the background fabric and threads are washable, the piece can take gentle hand laundering. Wash in warm water using mild soap flakes. Do not squeeze or wring. Rinse thoroughly then remove excess moisture by rolling loosely in a bath towel.

If your embroidery cannot be washed, try removing the soil and any visible signs of the transfer pattern with cleaning fluid. Or take it to a reputable dry cleaner.

To press embroidery, pad your ironing board with a number of bath towels. Lay embroidery right side down on them. Use a steam iron or a dry iron and a damp press cloth. Press very lightly, not permitting the weight of the iron to rest on embroidery. The margins of the piece where there is no embroidery can be pressed in the usual manner.

Like needlepoint, embroidery should also be blocked to straighten the work. If your piece was made in a frame and does not need washing, block it right in the frame. Place a wet cloth over the embroidery. Allow it to dry.

If you have washed your embroidery, block it while still wet—but not sopping. Follow the same technique as blocking needlepoint. Be sure edges of embroidery are trimmed along one thread of background fabric. This will make squaring off the work easier. Cover piece with a cloth and allow to dry.

Embroidery for pictures may be mounted the same as needlepoint.

Old-time Favorites

Rows of ribbons woven in romantic fashion . . . for a delicate camisole, a pillow in soft pastels, ruffled sachets, and a breakfast-in-bed tray.

Camisole photographed at The Dairy, Central Park, N.Y.

Pillow, sachets, camisole and tray: Offray Ribbons
Tray design: Ruth J. Katz/Photos: Mort Mace

Cross-stitchery for country-style charm . . . a colorful clutch purse and a placemat, napkin and coaster set adorned with bright flowers.

Placemat, napkin & coaster: Sara Gutiérrez; Photo: Mort Mace.

Classic monograms for that personal touch . . . fancy initials for lush bath and bed linens and a basketful of boudoir beauties.

Latch hook rugs emblazoned with color . . . the free-form streams of Galaxy match a modern decor, while Boston Fern sets a more traditional tone.

Rugs: Spinnerin

Monogramming

Monogramming means, simply, embroidering initials. It's the perfect way to make gifts bearing the message that the receiver is special or to personalize your own wardrobe and linens.

Preparation

The best source of letters for monogramming is, no doubt, a transfer pattern. These patterns contain iron-on transfers for a complete alphabet, usually in three or four sizes. There's a choice of script and block letter styles. Other sources of letters include headlines in newspapers and magazines, also posters, and these can be enlarged or reduced and transferred to your fabric by following the suggestions on pages 20 and 21.

Silk buttonhole twist or two or more strands of embroidery cotton are recommended threads for monograms. A fine thread is necessary since the design is worked in a rather small area and the stitches are usually fine. Other materials for monogramming are those used in regular embroidery. The section on *Embroidery*, beginning on page 17, is a good reference for this, as well as a pattern guide on the various embroidery stitches you might use.

Design Planning

It's good to plan your idea for a monogram on paper before marking the fabric. Make open spaces large enough to be formed by the embroidery thread and stitches you will be using. When creating your design, if all letters will be the same size, the initials should be placed in the following order: First, middle and last. If you plan on a large center letter, it should be the initial for the last name.

Consider the placement of your monograms as well. Place monograms on the corner of a tablecloth and in one corner of the napkins. Or, place monograms on a tablecloth in the middle just above the place setting. Locate signatures on placemats on the upper left-hand corner. Of course, coordinated table linens should all be monogrammed in the same style with the size of the design suitable to the item. Center initials on bed linens just above the hem, on the top hem of sheets so that the design appears when the sheet is folded back.

How to Monogram

There are several ways to approach your monogram design. One, plan to work the initials themselves rather plainly, using the stem stitch and padded satin stitch, for example. Then, make the background design or the space around it fancy. You could twine floral garlands in and out of the letters, or create something abstract with a filling stitch like seeding.

A second way is to embroider letters plainly, as above, but surround them with a decorative border or enclose them in an elaborate circle or square.

A third way is to make both letters and the decorations entirely from cross-stitch, and this is very effective on gingham.

The method of monogramming is that of any embroidery, but there are a few special things to remember. When transferring your design, keep the marking lines thin so the embroidery will cover them. When monogramming pile fabrics like velvet and terrycloth, it's best to transfer your design first to cotton organdy. Baste this to the fabric and complete the embroidery. Trim the organdy close to your monogram and pull out any stray organdy threads with tweezers if necessary.

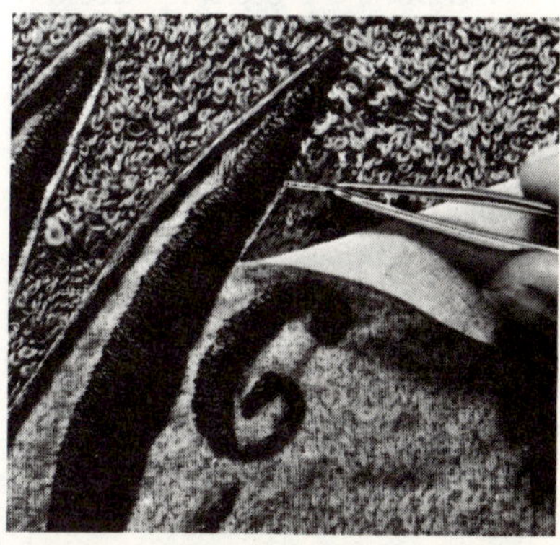

Cross-Stitching

If cross-stitching has always been a favorite of both the beginner and the expert embroidery enthusiast, maybe it's because it's so versatile. Plain or fancy, bold or dainty, cross-stitch designs can decorate almost any fabric. The fun of needlework is adding your own touch, and there are six ways here to transform your ideas into stitches. The half dozen methods tell how to take a cross-stitch design, purchased or your own, and work it on virtually any fabric from velvet to rug canvas. These methods can be adapted for other embroidery stitches as well.

Preparation

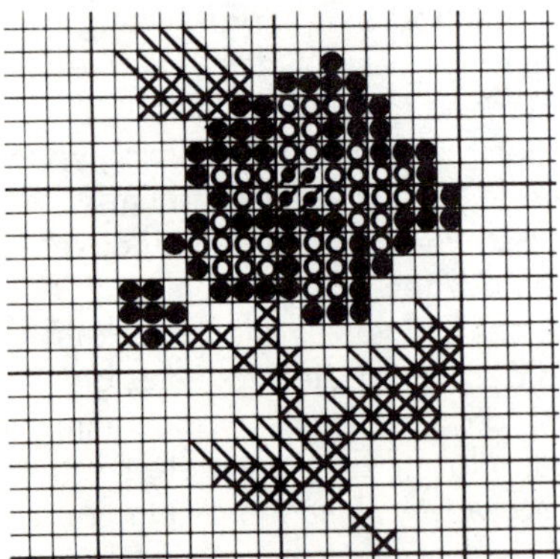

For any of the methods, begin by working out the cross-stitch design with X's or dots on a graph paper chart. The chart above shows a rose design planned in this way, for example. Colored pencils or a set of symbols can be used if there are two or more colors involved. This doesn't have to be done, of course, if you are using a purchased transfer pattern as is. To choose a suitable needle and thread, see *Embroidery*, pg. 18.

To translate any design or transfer pattern to your fabric, first draw a line through the center of the design in both directions.

Transfer these lines, marking the center of your design on your fabric with basting. Then refer to these lines as you work. Be sure design is placed an even distance from both edges of any corners.

The ways you may use cross-stitching depend on the background fabric you are using.

Six Methods

Gingham Squares: This is a good technique for beginners or for a child's first embroidery project. Use gingham or any other evenly-checked fabric for background. The gingham checks come in several sizes, from ⅛ inch to 1 inch (3 mm to 2,5 cm), so by your fabric choice, you can also enlarge or reduce a design as you stitch. With this method, a charted design can be copied without marking every stitch on the fabric. Just make a cross-stitch in each fabric check that corresponds to

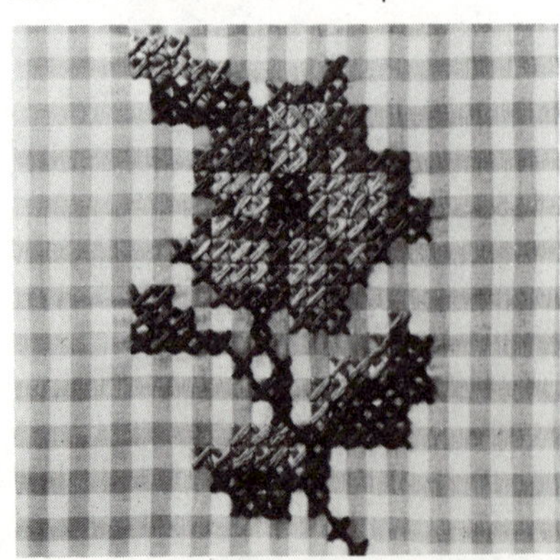

a square marked with a symbol on the chart.

Counted Threads: This is similar to the gingham method, above, but threads instead of checks are counted. Use an even,

plain weave fabric with uniform threads big enough to count easily. Linen or monk's cloth are good choices. No markings are made on the fabric, except the centers of your design. Just follow the chart and mentally divide the fabric into squares of two or more threads to work the cross-stitches. This method is used for the finest, heirloom quality embroidery.

Knits: A cross-stitch design can be embroidered on any hand-knit

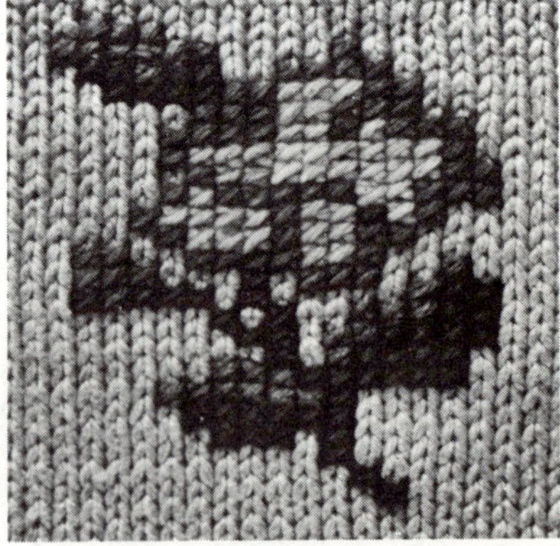

or purchased knit garment or accessory if the knitting is even and the knitted pattern is a rather simple, flat type. Follow *Counted Threads*, above, counting knitted stitches instead of fabric threads.

Canvas: This is another variation of *Counted Threads*, above, using thick rug wool on canvas or other needlepoint wools on suitable canvas. After the design is completed, fill the rest of the canvas in with cross-stitches or a suitable background stitch.

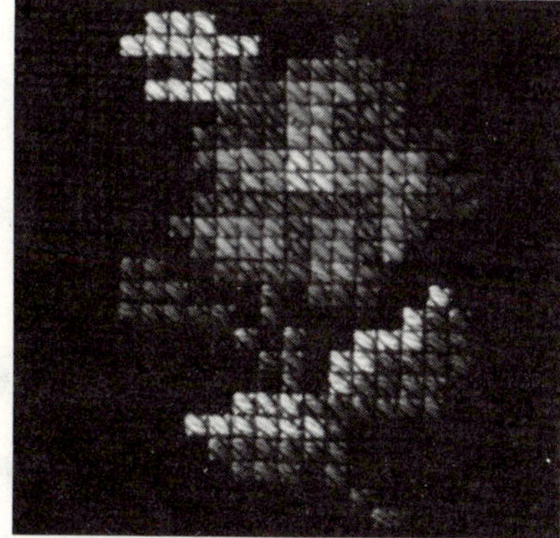

Transfers: Purchased transfer patterns can be used as is, and some helpful suggestions for working with them are in the *Embroidery* chapter. Any cross-stitch design can be enlarged or reduced and transferred with do-it-yourself methods, too; see pages 20 and 21 to enlarge or reduce a design and page 20 to transfer a design.

Temporary Canvas: For fabrics where threads can't be

counted (like felt) or are difficult to see (like fine linen) and transfers either won't work (like velvet) or would leave a permanent mark (like some synthetics), here's an ingenious way to work a cross-stitch design. Baste a piece of 10 mesh Penelope needlepoint canvas or monk's cloth to the right side of the background fabric, where you will embroider. Following the design chart, make somewhat tight cross-stitches right over the canvas threads and into the fabric. When the embroidery is completed, cut the canvas at any open spaces and trim off excess. One by one, draw the remaining canvas threads out, using tweezers if necessary.

To finish cross-stitch embroidery on fabric, carefully press as on page 28. For cross-stitch on canvas, block and finish as for needlepoint (see page 28).

Applications

With these six cross-stitch methods, you can embroider practically whatever you wish. The examples on the color pages preceding this chapter show some of the possibilities. You can also use cross-stitch for a footstool, on a pin cushion, for linen luncheon mats, on a knitted tote, or on a gingham apron. And no doubt you have ideas of your own.

Ribbon Weaving

This contemporary craft is an easy method of weaving square or rectangular pieces of "fabric" without a loom. Instead of yarn, ribbon or other trim is used, so the weaving goes quickly and the "fabric" that results is truly one-of-a-kind.

Almost any kind of ribbon, plain or fancy, will work well. Grosgrain, velvet, satin, embroidered and taffeta are some of the types well-suited for weaving. Other trims, such as braids, leather strips, lace and the fabric type of trim with a woven novelty design, can be used as well, as long as both edges are finished.

When a basic over-and-under plain weave is used, the same ribbon in two contrasting colors makes a graphic checkerboard design.

Using just one ribbon creates an interesting texture, and an assortment of trims and ribbons can be woven together for a

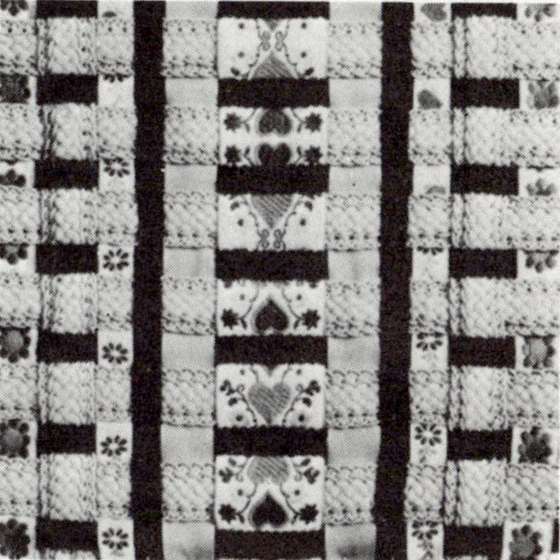

quaint sampler effect.

Your weaving may cover completely or may have "windows" where fabric shows through. This is a charming way to use scraps. There are so many more ways to use ribbons and trims in weaving that you will enjoy experimenting and creating new designs and weaving variations as you work.

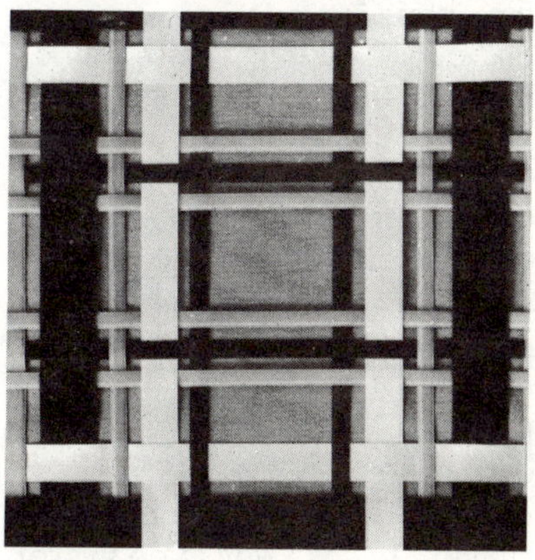

Determine Yardage

Plan your ribbon design on a piece of paper, deciding how many colors and types of trim you will use. To determine the amount of ribbon needed, first measure the width of the ribbon or the total width of several different trims you have selected. Then, decide what the final length and width of the weaving will be, keeping in mind that these dimensions should be multiples of the ribbon's width so the weaving comes out even on all sides. Figure out how many yards of ribbon, laid side-by-side in strips, will completely cover the weaving, plus ½ inch (1,2 cm) in length on two sides for seams and finishing, and double this amount to get the total yardage required. (Allow for wider seam allowances on trims and ribbons that ravel easily.) For example, if your ribbon is 1 inch (2,5 cm) wide and your finished weaving will be 11″ x 11″ (27,9 x 27,9 cm), 11 pieces of ribbon 12″ (30,5 cm) long will cover the weaving horizontally. Another 11 pieces of ribbon 12″ (30,5 cm) long are needed to cover the weaving vertically since when woven, the ribbon will be two layers thick. If you are using two colors for this design, you will need to buy 3⅔ yards (3,40 m) of each color of ribbon.

To back the weaving, muslin or broadcloth to match the color of the ribbon is a good choice. For an "open" design, choose fabric to complement your design. Buy enough yardage to back the finished article plus ½ inch (1,2 cm) on all edges for seam allowances and finishing.

Preparation

For those trims that can be washed, it's a good idea to pre-shrink all materials before cutting. An easy way to do this for ribbon or trim is to wind it around coated cardboard (the kind seam tape comes on). Immerse in a hot water bath until completely wet, then bend cardboard to allow for shrinkage. Remove when dry.

To prepare for weaving, cut a backing from fabric, the size of the finished weaving plus ½ inch (1,2 cm) on each edge for seam allowances and finishing. Cut the ribbon into enough strips to cover the backing both horizontally and vertically when the strips are laid side-by-side or in the design planned. Do not cover side seam allowances with vertical ribbons and top or bottom seam allowances with horizontal ribbons.

Weaving the Design

Some way of keeping the ribbon strips from sliding around while working your design is needed. Use T-pins or straight pins to anchor the ribbon strips in place over the backing on a cutting board or an ironing board. A piece of corrugated cardboard or a breadboard is an ideal working surface too, and these can be held in your lap. You will find it easiest to weave as you plan your design, particularly if it is complicated. If you will be fusing the ribbons in place after weaving, cut a sheet of fusible web the same size as backing and place over backing before anchoring ribbons. Then, work at the ironing board when planning the design, securing the ribbons to the board cover or to cardboard resting on the ironing board.

Line up ribbon strips side-by-side vertically so backing is completely covered, except for ½″ (1,2 cm) seam allowances on either side, or space ribbons at intervals for an open design. Anchor them at one end. Anchor one end of

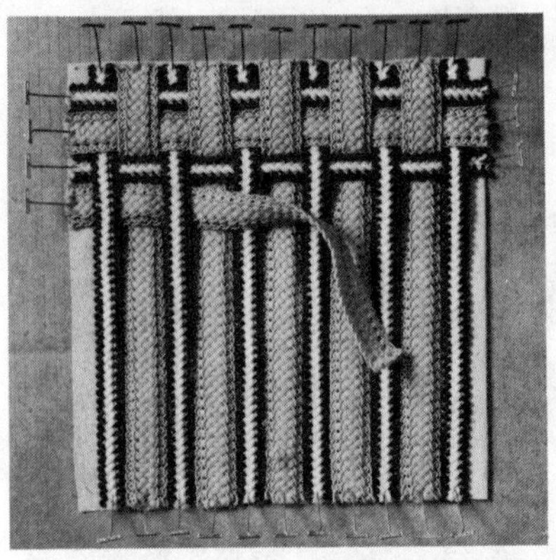

the first horizontal ribbon ½″ (1,2 cm) from top of backing and weave it over and under the vertical ribbons. Repeat with remaining horizontal ribbons, keeping them as close together as possible for a neat weave.

Fastening Weaving

To secure the weaving to the backing, there is a choice of methods calling for different materials. One method calls for stitching, and polyester/cotton or silk thread work well. Another method calls for glue and a third for iron-on fusible web.

Stitching: This method is excellent for articles with the backing covered entirely by ribbon. After weaving, pin, then baste ends of ribbon to backing to keep ribbon edges butted neatly together as you sew. Stitch ½ inch (1,2 cm) from edge around all four sides of the weaving.

Glue: For weaving with "windows" of backing showing through or other loosely woven designs, ribbons along the four edges of the design should be glued to the backing. Other ribbons within the design which tend to slide around should also be glued at intersections and to the backing.

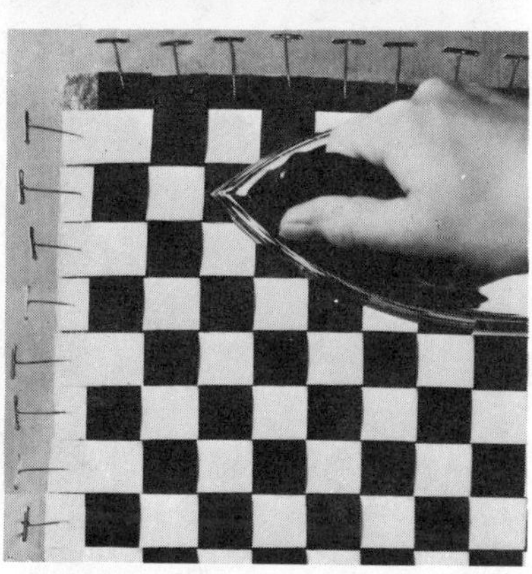

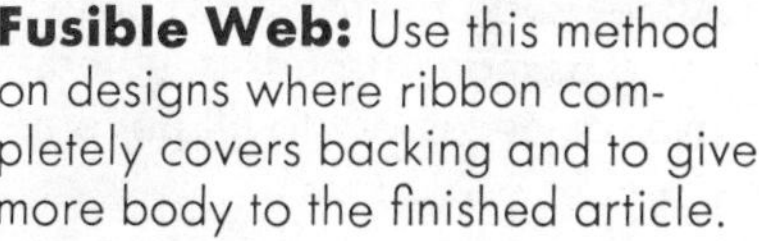

Fusible Web: Use this method on designs where ribbon completely covers backing and to give more body to the finished article.

Making sure fusible web is between ribbons and backing, use a steam iron and press cloth to fuse the three layers together carefully, following the directions given for the fusible web by the manufacturer.

Finishing

Press carefully and gingerly with a press cloth and iron, being careful not to press in ridges where the ribbons cross, then finish various craft items as follows.

Pillows: Cut a pillow back the same size as the ribbon weaving. Place back and weaving right sides together and stitch ½" (1,2 cm) from edges, leaving an opening for turning and stuffing. Trim corners, turn and stuff with polyester fiberfill. Sew opening closed.

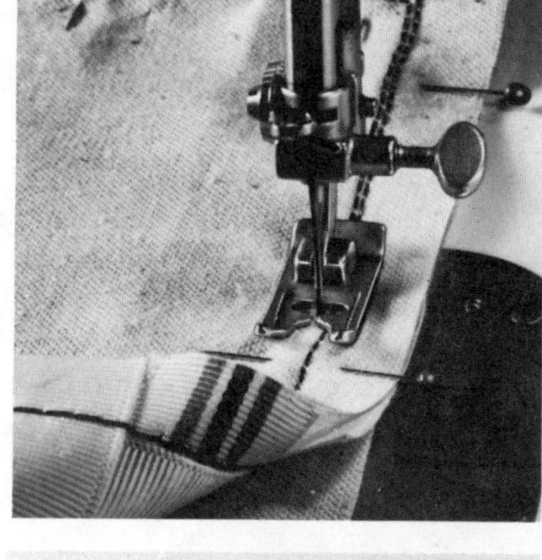

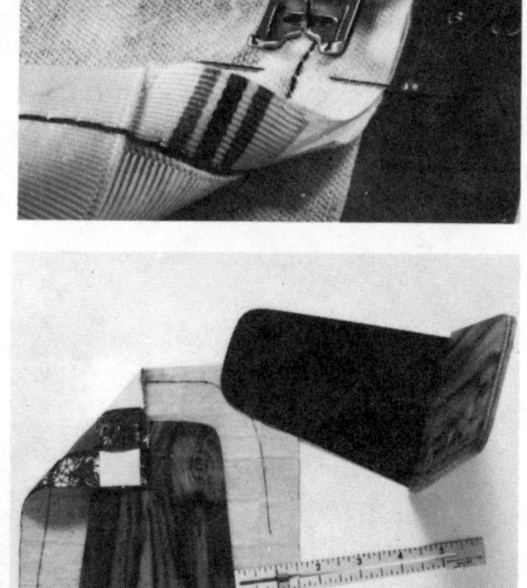

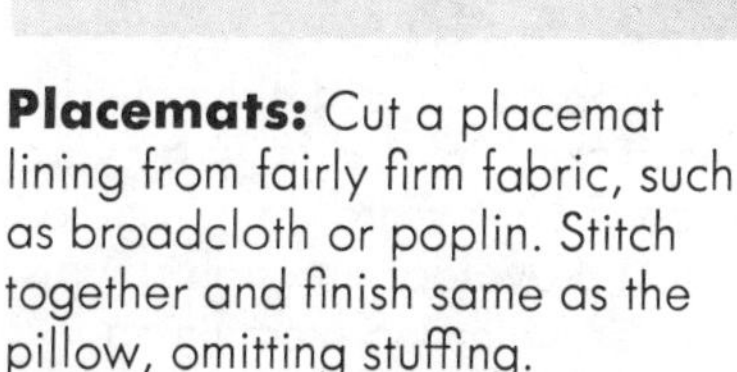

Placemats: Cut a placemat lining from fairly firm fabric, such as broadcloth or poplin. Stitch together and finish same as the pillow, omitting stuffing.

Book Covers, Mirrors, Eyeglass Cases, Etcetera: Trace outline of item on backing of weaving. Add generous seam allowances so that the weaving may be easily turned to the wrong side. Stitch ¼ inch (6 mm) inside outline, if ribbon ends are not already glued or fused in place. Cut around edges of outline and use fabric glue to secure weaving to mirror or book cover. Glue a suitable fabric or cardboard over the raw edges.

Applications

Ribbon weavings make unusual and exciting decorator pillows for around the house, mirror frames, eyeglass cases and boutique placemats, too. The effect is formal or casual depending on the kind of ribbon used and there are many possibilities. Imagine a pillow woven from suede strips for a contemporary setting, for example; or for the boudoir, think of woven lace and satin ribbon with a pastel backing. You could choose ribbons to pick up the colors in a drapery or slipcover print for a custom accent pillow, and you don't have to limit yourself to one or two colors, either. Narrow white satin ribbon, woven for a bride's ring pillow, makes a thoughtful gift, and the expectant mother might weave pastels to cushion the cradle. Red and black velvet makes a checkerboard design perfect for a most elegant game board/placemat. Think of ribbon weavings for bazaar items, too, for the work goes quickly and the results are definitely eye-catching best-sellers.

Rugs

Rug making is an extremely satisfying craft that can be created by one person or the whole family.

A rug can be made in any texture, shape or size—you can explore different dimensions with the use of bought or found-at-home materials. Hand made rugs can be made from practically anything, but the materials should be sturdy. Rug yarn is available in a wide variety of fibers and colors; jute, twine, rope or fabric strips cut on the bias also provide attractive results. Rug-making supplies can be purchased as separate components for designing your own rug or in kits. Special supplies for the techniques suggested are listed in each section.

Design and color inspirations can come from any source—pictures, tiles, nature and fabrics. Suggestions for transferring your ideas to the rug backing are found on page 7 for canvas and pages 20 and 21 for other fabrics.

There are many techniques for the crafts person to try—needlepoint, crochet, quickpoint, crewel, afghan stitch and knitting. (Instructions for these stitches are listed in other chapters, see index.) Some additional creative possibilities are crochet with loops or shag, latch hooking, rya (loop stitch) and punch needle.

Crocheted Rugs

The most commonly used crochet hook sizes for rug making are J, K and Q from smallest to largest. The size you will use is determined by the thickness of your materials and how close together the stitches will be. For example, a Q hook is used with most bulky materials.

Naturally, you can crochet any stitch that you've mastered—mixing and matching as you go in sections or shapes. However, two stitches that can be used to create a plush effect are the loop and foundation or mesh stitches.

Loop Stitch: Use a ruler or cut a piece of heavy cardboard to the exact height of the loop desired and long enough to manage comfortably in your hand. With crochet hook and yarn, ch desired length. Row 1: Sc in 2nd st from hook and in each remaining st, ch 1 to turn all rows. Row 2:

Holding cardboard behind work, insert hook in next sc, wrap yarn around cardboard from front to back, draw loop through st, yo and draw through remaining 2 lps; continue across row. Repeat rows 1 and 2 for pattern. The same technique may also be worked in double crochet (page 72).

Foundation Stitch: Single crochet is used as a canvas backing would be used to knot on yarn for a shag effect. Make a foundation ch. Row 1: Sc in 2nd st from hook, and in each remaining st, ch 1 to turn. Row 2: Sc in each sc of the previous row. Ch 1 and turn. Repeat row 2 until foundation is desired size.

Attach shag to crocheted base, using as many strands doubled over as necessary to fill pattern.

Fold strands in half. Insert a crochet hook under sc. Pull loop under sc.

Draw loose ends through loop. Pull ends tightly, forming a knot close to the base.

Continue making shag until rug is filled.

To prevent skidding, tack rug grip material or rubber jar rings to wrong side of rug.

Latch Hook Rugs

The technique of latch hooking a rug is simple and quite effective. Each knot is made with a length of yarn pulled through an open mesh canvas with a latch hook. Most of the time these lengths are uniform in size, but you can cut varying lengths for a sculptured look.

To latch a rug you will need: Penelope canvas backing, size 3½, 4 or 5 meshes to the inch (2,5 cm) depending on how thick you want your shag (the higher the number the thicker the shag); a latch (latchet) hook and yarn. You can purchase pre-cut packages of yarn or cut your own. It's easy to do: wind, but do not overlap, yarn strands around a piece of cardboard. For 3 inch (6 cm) pieces, a good working size is 1½ inches (3,8 cm) by 8 inches (20 cm). Cut along one edge only; repeat as many times as necessary. Cut your canvas one inch (2,5 cm) bigger than finished rug on all sides. Prepare the canvas by taping the edges.

Wrap 1 strand of yarn around shank of latch hook, keeping yarn ends even. Starting at the lower corner of canvas, insert latch hook under first two horizontal threads of row one and up through mesh just above it (Latch must be above threads.) Pull latch hook toward you (with latch open.

Fold yarn under hook to the left. Close latch and pull hook back through first mesh (one knot formed).
Tighten by pulling ends. Work one mesh per strand of yarn, following color pattern. Always keep knots facing you.

To finish latch hook rugs, fold 1 inch (2,5 cm) edge back and sew by hand. For a more finished edge you can apply rug binding. This is available in packages for sewing, or ironing to rug. An alternate method is to fold edges in and work latch hook stitch through double thickness, thereby eliminating hemming.

Rya Rugs

Making a rya rug is a fast uncomplicated process involving one basic stitch—a knot made with a needle—creating a very comfortable, luxurious rug. Make a test row of the rya knot before beginning your project.

You will need the following materials for your rug: sufficient woven fabric like homespun, burlap or, if available, a special rya backing which has panels of open weave alternating with close weave; also a blunt tapestry needle and yarns. To prevent raveling, bind the edges of your fabric with a machine zigzag or overcast by hand. Cut three strands of yarn about 36 inches (91 cm) long and thread your needle. Also cut a cardboard gauge about 6 inches (15 cm) long and as wide as desired loop height. Or use the fingers of your left hand as a gauge for loop height.

On the face side of your rug backing, begin in the lower left hand corner. Work stitch from left to right. Insert needle under two open weave vertical threads and draw yarn through until about 2 inches (5 cm) remains. Hold this piece under left thumb, and insert needle under next two vertical threads to the right as shown.

Pull tightly to secure knot.

Align gauge with knot.* Wrap yarn from left to right, under and over gauge. Insert needle under two vertical threads as shown.

Draw yarn through and insert needle under next two vertical threads to the right. Pull tightly to secure knot, bringing yarn under and over gauge. Repeat from * until end of yarn or row. Cut loops to form pile after completion of each row. If not working on special rya backing, leave five or six horizontal threads between each row.

Finish rya rugs in the same manner as latch hook rugs, page 39.

Punch Needle Rugs

Creating a punch needle rug is an exciting revival of our heritage. Originally known as hooking rugs, this simple technique has been passed on since colonial days. Naturally the craft has evolved—traditional rugs were made of fabric scraps, and hooked from the right side. Ours are more quickly punched from the wrong side with yarn and other fibers.

The best materials for this craft are sturdy woven backings—unbleached cotton, burlap or monk's cloth. There are some punch needles that make only one size loop while others can form short, medium or long loops depending on where you set the gauge. Always be sure your yarn pulls easily through your punch needle.

When punching a rug, it is necessary to use a frame; you have far more control over your work and it won't stretch out of shape.

Cut your woven fabric about 2 inches (5 cm) larger than area to be framed. Stretch and tack securely in place. With wrong side of backing facing you and threaded punch needle in your hand, leave a 3 inch (7,5 cm) end and punch needle through fabric.* Carefully remove needle point from fabric, move a couple of threads away and punch needle through backing. Repeat from * Do not raise needle from surface of fabric.

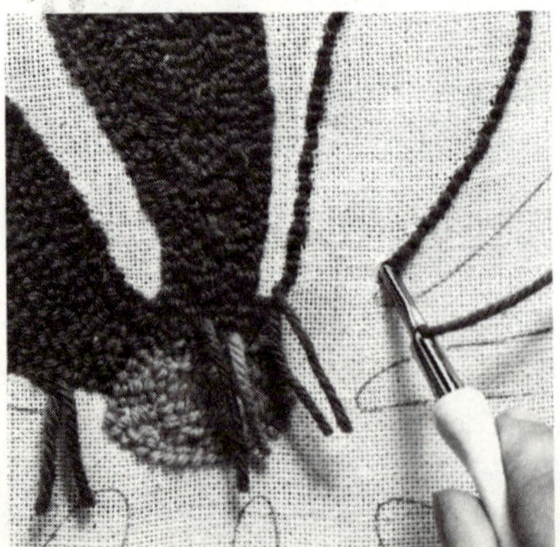

In working your design, you can punch randomly or in straight rows or both. Another variation is produced by clipping the front loops with long, narrow scissors. When changing or ending yarn lengths—pull them to the right side of your work and leave a length about 1 inch (2,5 cm) long. When finished , trim all ends to height of loops.

To keep all loops in place, you must protect the backings with a latex rug adhesive. Before removing rug from frame, coat the back of your work and let dry. Remove work from frame, turn edge and hem in place. Apply rug binding if desired.

Quilting, Patchwork and Appliqué

Traditional techniques with modern interpretations in basic brights . . . the appliquéd barn wall hanging can serve double duty as a crib quilt; the ruffled patchwork quilt and pillow will light up any setting.

Barn wall hanging: Liz Dominick/ Quilt & pillow: Shirley Botsford/ Photo: Mort Mace/Photographed at the home of Dr. & Mrs. J. Hyman, Suffern, N.Y.

The crown jewel of a rich needlework heritage . . . hand quilting, combined with patchwork, makes this magnificent Twinkling Stars quilt sure to become a cherished heirloom.

Quilt: Stearns & Foster/ Photo: Mort Mace at the home of Dr. & Mrs. J. Hyman, Suffern, N.Y.

Appliqué a country kitchen . . . coordinated pot holder, placemat and chair seat cover with checkered and calico leaf motifs.

Pot holder, placemat & chair seat cover: Liz Dominick/Photo: Mort Mace

Quilting

Patchwork, Applique

Quilting, which generally includes patchwork and appliqué, is the oldest American craft. The Pilgrims made the very first crazy quilts when they sewed together the tatters of their bedclothing. The sewing of patches into larger pieces of fabric continued throughout the gradual building of America.

Because of the pressing needs of daily life, little thought was given to art, only to things which had a purpose. But even the early pioneer women could express their inner sense of beauty and order through their appliqué and patchwork quilts and hand sewing. Thus the art of quilt making became highly refined and somewhat competitive, as well as forming the nucleus of the social life of that time.

Although the reasons for making quilts may have changed, the pleasure derived from the arts associated with quilting has not diminished at all. And now appliqué and patchwork, either alone or combined with quilting, are being applied to many unique end uses. You will find no limit to the imaginative ways patchwork, appliqué and quilting can spark your home and your wardrobe!

Terms

Quilt—(1) Anything made of two pieces of material with filling between and held together with stitches. (2) The act of fastening three layers of materials together to firmly secure the filling.

Backing (Lining)—The bottom layer of a quilted piece of work, usually of white or a pastel, although it may be printed or colored.

Patchwork—The art of piecing together fabrics of various patterns, shapes and colors.

Quilt Top—The main piece of material used in a quilt. It is the upper portion of the quilt and may be appliquéd, embroidered, or patchwork, or any combination of the three.

Filler—The middle layer of a quilt, made usually of cotton or a polyester batting.

Block—One complete pattern in a quilt.

Crazy Quilt—A patchwork made up of many different sizes, shapes, colors and textures of materials put together like a jigsaw puzzle. Often parts of the piece are outlined with different embroidery stitches.

Appliqué—To lay pieces cut from one fabric onto another fabric and sew in place.

Binding—The material used to finish the edges of a quilted piece of work.

Tools

One of the nicest things about this craft is that you need few exotic tools—if you sew at all, you probably have most of them.

For Marking and Cutting

A metal straight-edge is absolutely the best tool for getting accurate straight lines. Choose one about a foot (30,5 cm) long, calibrated like a ruler. A T-square or triangle is also important for forming accurate angles. A compass and protractor will aid you in making perfect circles and hexagons, pentagons, etc. Remember, also, that you may use the straight grain or threads of your fabric as a guideline for marking some fabric pieces.

Sharp, hard-leaded pencils and tailor's chalk are best for making fabric and cardboard patterns. Cardboard, from either shirts or shoeboxes, is necessary for making stiff patterns (called templates). Very fine sandpaper is also recommended for templates because it will not slip on the fabric. See pages 20 and 21 for supplies to enlarge or reduce designs you wish to copy.

Single-edged razor blades (with a holder) and mat knives are best for cutting cardboard. They are available at art supply stores. You may use good paper shears instead, if you can cut good angles with them. You must have good, sharp fabric shears which close perfectly all the way to the point, especially for appliqué.

For Sewing

Needles have many different names, and come in many sizes. "Sharps" and "Embroidery" needles are the same except that embroidery needles have a larger eye. They are available in the same lengths and thicknesses. "Quilting" needles are the right length and thickness for quilting. Choose a needle of medium length and try it to see if it suits you; you may prefer a longer or shorter one. While you're at it, get a good thimble and get used to using it—it's a godsend when you're doing lots of hand sewing.

Thread should match the fiber content of the fabric whenever possible. However, synthetic thread is available in many more colors than cotton or silk, so you may find yourself preferring it for the color. Try to choose one that is cotton-wrapped, since it will abrade your fabric less. You will sometimes want to outline your patches with embroidery stitches, and for this you will need embroidery floss. It comes in many beautiful colors, and is usually made up of six strands twisted together. For most stitches, you should use three or more strands. (Check the section on *Embroidery* for more information on embroidery threads and stitches.) A 18 to 25 inch (45,7 to 50,8 cm) length of thread is recommended, no matter what kind of thread you are using. A longer length tangles, and is weakened by being repeatedly drawn through the fabric.

A fusing agent is extremely helpful in positioning, especially when appliquéing. It can be used on almost all types of materials and will prevent edges from fraying on ravelly fabrics. If applied to the edge of an appliqué, it may eliminate the need to turn under a seam allowance or to apply embroidery stitches. Follow product instructions for use.

Frames or hoops are used to hold the work taut while being quilted. You may find a frame somewhat unwieldy, since it's at least as long as one side of the quilt and stands on the floor. If you cannot buy one, it can be made from 2 x 2 inch (5 x 5 cm) wood to resemble the

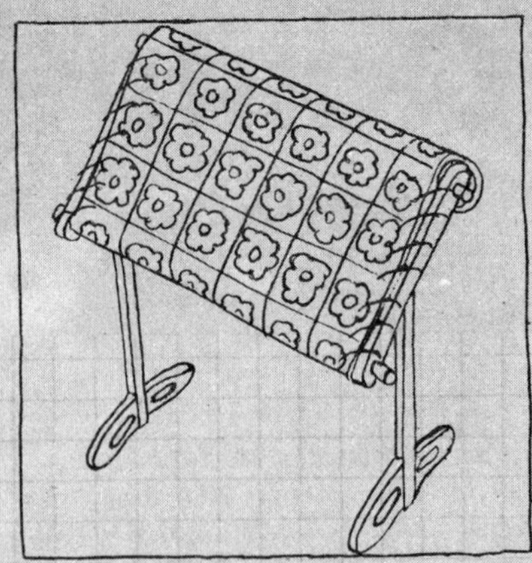

illustration. The long bars should fit securely into the short bars at the corner. Nail twill tape to the two long bars and then sew the top and bottom of the quilt to this tape. Roll one end of the quilt up until you have reached the width of the short bars. Roll until quilt is taut, then lock long bars in position. To hold

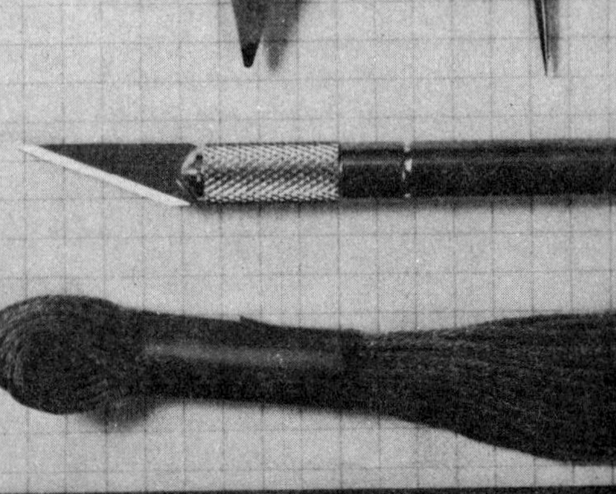

ends of quilt taut, sew them over short bars with heavy duty thread, as shown. Quilt will be held securely for hand-quilting.

Embroidery hoops 22 inches (55,9 cm) in diameter are more easily managed and are large enough to accommodate a good section of the quilt at a time.

Quilt binding is pre-packaged strips of cotton bias, 1 inch (2,5 cm) wide finished, which comes in assorted colors and may be used for finishing off quilts and pillows.

Fabrics

Now that you know what you need to work with, what are you going to work on? There was a time when woven fabric, either cotton, wool, or linen, would have been the only answer. This is no longer the case, however; many synthetics, even knits, are perfectly acceptable patchwork and appliqué material. Consider also unusual fabrics like satins, taffetas, velvets, fake furs, vinyls and leathers. Do not overlook ribbons as a bright possibility. Try different combinations for interesting effects.

Although the list of possible materials has grown longer since colonial days, there are still two rules which should be followed: make sure the fabric has a close, or tight construction and a soft texture, and use only fabrics which have the same general qualities in each piece of patchwork. For example, if you plan to wash your finished patchwork, make sure all materials in it are washable. Also, if you combine very delicate fabrics with very sturdy ones, the delicate ones will wear out long before the others.

All fabrics should be color-fast. Test, reds especially, by washing a sample in hot water, drying and ironing it. Most fabrics sold today are color-fast. If one seems not to be, you can set the dye by adding vinegar to boiling water and soaking the fabric in it for a few minutes.

Of course, many of us decide to make something out of patchwork when our scrap basket is overflowing with remnants too big to throw out (no matter how small!). And part of the special joy of patchwork is the memories of friends or good times it can bring back by containing a familiar scrap of fabric. But you can also buy fabric specifically for a patchwork project, and what a lot of fun that is, too! Old garments may be used if you're quite certain the fabric has not been weakened by repeated laundering or dry-cleaning. Remember that patchwork and appliqué, particularly if they are quilted, will last for many years, so don't put in a "weak link" like an exhausted old fabric.

Filler

A filler is the middle layer in a quilted piece which adds warmth and dimension to the finished piece. The best choice is polyester batting, because it is washable and dry-cleanable and does not bunch or mat. The fiberfill comes in sheets which can be unrolled in one piece for easy handling. A polyester fleece, sold by the yard, may also be used for filling in small or large pieces.

Backing or Lining

The lining for any of your patchwork should be of the same quality as the top. A percale sheet is a good choice for cotton and cotton-type fabrics. Plan to buy enough fabric to equal the size of the top unless you want to bring the edges of the lining to the right side for a binding. In that case, it should be 2½ inches (6,4 cm) larger all around.

Preparation and Assembly

The most difficult part of patchwork and appliqué is deciding on your design. There are literally thousands of known designs for either method. When you buy a pattern for an appliqué or patchwork quilt, complete instructions are included and fabric yardages have been accurately figured according to the size and type of the design. However, you may want to alter the size or change the number of blocks or fabrics used.

If you are using simple patchwork squares, plan your design carefully on graph paper in miniature with fabric or colored marking pencils before beginning to work.

For Patchwork and Appliqué

Once you have decided what you are going to make, here are the steps you follow to make patchwork or appliqué:

1. Estimate how much of each fabric you need. In order to do this, you must first decide on the size of your finished piece. Obviously, if you are going to make only a small pillow top, you will not need to do a great deal of figuring. However, for a larger project, you will want to buy economically.

After deciding on the size, multiply the length by the width for the total area. This will give you x number of square inches (or centimeters). From your design you will see how many fabrics you are going to use and what portion of the total area each fabric occupies. For example, if you are making a patchwork quilt with no border that is made up of a design of three pieces of fabric, each being used equally, it is obvious that each fabric would be one-third of the total area. Add 1/4 inch (6 mm) to each side of the patch for seam allowances. Then multiply the total patch widths by the total patch lengths for the entire quilt. Divide the total area by three for the base area in inches for each fabric. To find out how many yards of each fabric, divide the width of the fabric you are purchasing into the fabric area. (Ex.: If the fabric area is 2250 square inches and the fabric is 45" wide, you will need 50" of fabric, or about 1 5/8 yards.)

2. Count the number of different shapes there are in your design and how many of each piece you must cut. With this in mind, you should make your cardboard patterns, or templates, for each section. If there are a great many pieces to be cut of one shape, it is a good idea to make more than one template for that shape.

First use your graph paper to enlarge or reduce your pattern to the desired size. Add 1/4 inch (6 mm) seam allowances on all sides of the pattern at this point. Trace the pattern onto the stiff cardboard or sandpaper and cut it out with your mat knife or single-edged razor blade.

3. Use your template to trace the correct number of shapes onto the lengthwise grain of each fabric. You may cut up to four thicknesses of fabric at one time. Trace the shapes onto the wrong side of the fabric leaving 1/2 inch (1,2 cm) between each shape, then put pins through the four layers to hold them in place for cutting.

4. Cut out each shape exactly on the traced lines.

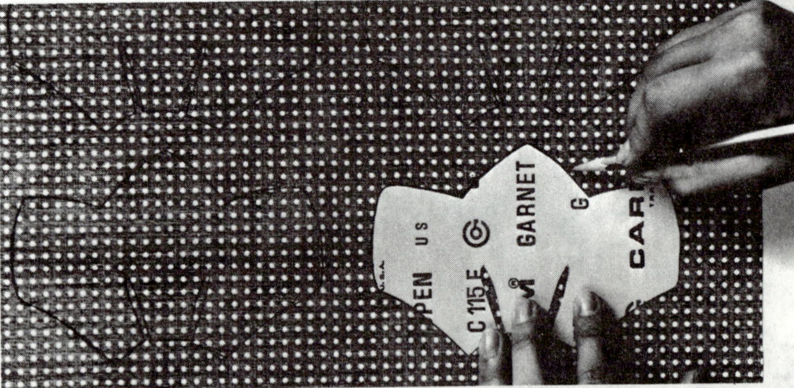

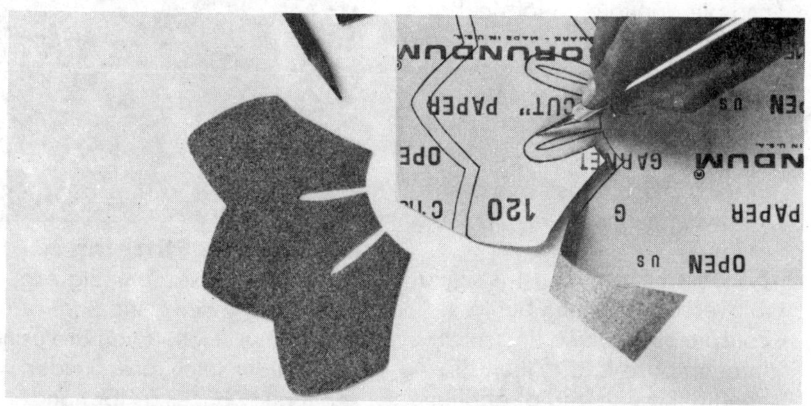

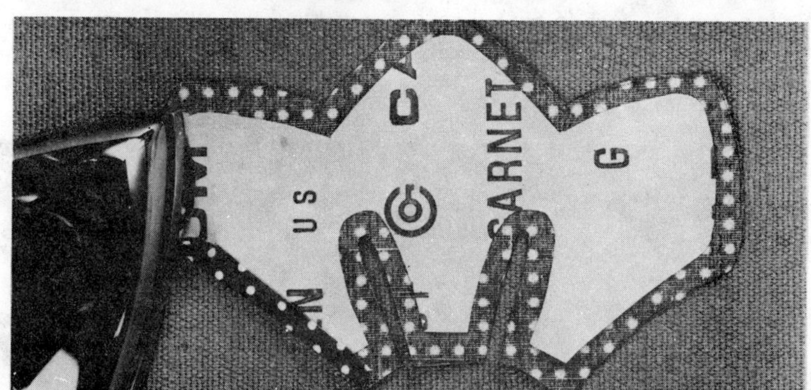

5. After cutting out all the pieces, make a second template without seam allowances. Place the template in the center of the cut shape on the wrong side and press back the seam allowances over the pattern, thus making a distinct and accurate guideline for stitching. Clip the seam allowance to the marked design, where necessary.

6. Complete patchwork or appliqué blocks. (See *Stitches* for specific directions). Make patchwork blocks by joining from the center out. Sew blocks together in strips. The strips are sewn together and completed according to *Finishing* directions.

STITCHES

Patchwork and appliqué can be sewn either by hand or machine, and appliqué may often be fused.

For Patchwork

More intricate patchwork designs are put together by joining the pieces of each block from the center out, then putting the blocks together. The traditional way of joining is by hand with right sides together, using a small running stitch. Press seams open. Blocks are also joined to one another from the center out. Each block may be assembled by machine instead of handstitching. Again, work from the center out to form the block. Remember to

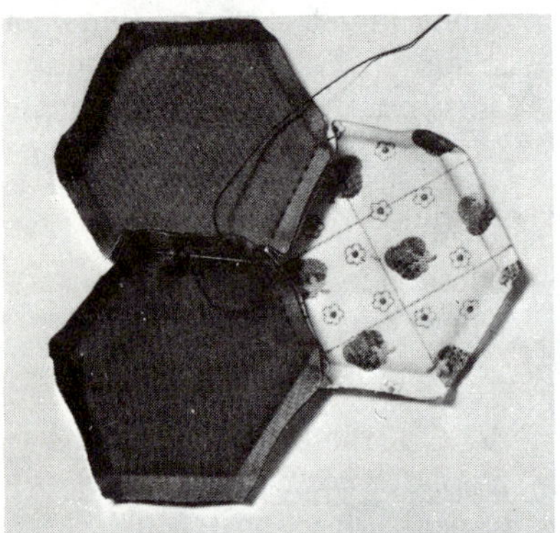

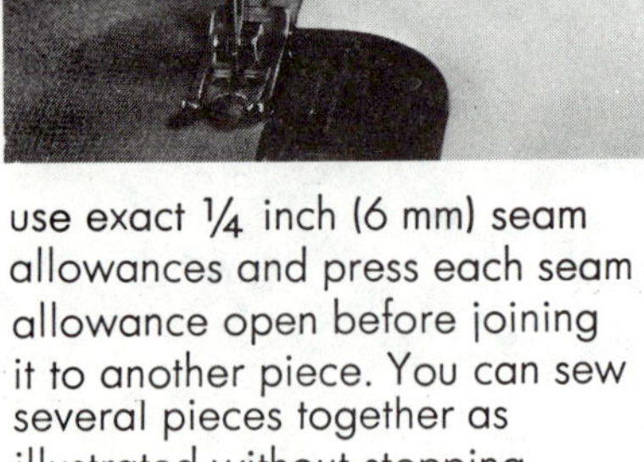

use exact ¼ inch (6 mm) seam allowances and press each seam allowance open before joining it to another piece. You can sew several pieces together as illustrated without stopping the machine.

For Appliqué

First crease under seam allowance and pin appliqué to fabric. Baste or fuse appliqués in place. Use a thread which closely matches the fabric of the appliqué. Without knotting take a few stitches on the base fabric to secure the thread. Then choose one of the following methods.

1. Blind Hemming is similar to overcast hemming but less conspicuous. Take a tiny stitch through base fabric, then slip needle through fold of appliqué for about ¼ inch (6 mm); then take another tiny stitch through base fabric. Do not pull stitches tight.

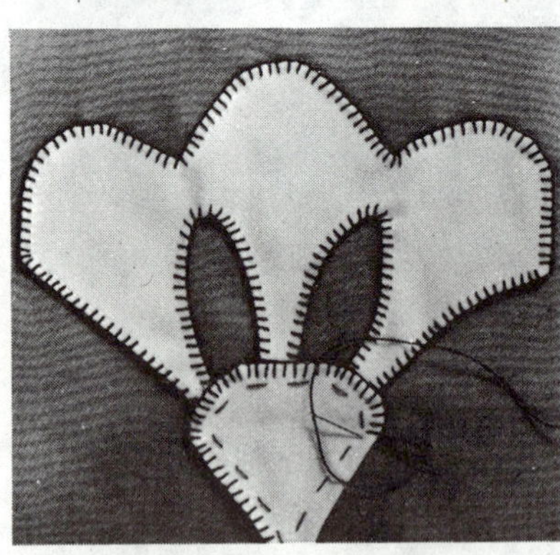

2. Embroidery Stitches may also be used to hold the appliqué in place. (See pages 22-27.) It is a wise idea to hand-baste or fuse the edges of the appliqué in position first.

3. Machine Stitching may be done, using a straight, zig-zag, satin (a very dense zig-zag) or a decorative stitch. If you are using the straight stitch, press under seam allowances as for hand-stitching. If you are using an overedge stitch, trim seam allowances, as the stitch will cover the raw edges.

4. Fusing Appliqué can be quickly done with the aid of a fusing agent. If the fusing agent extends all the way to the edge of the appliqué fabric, and product directions are followed, the edges of the appliqué will be held securely and should not ravel.

Finishing

Once you have completed your patchwork or appliquéd design, you must finish it off. If you decide to quilt the piece, finish the raw edges afterward.

QUILTING

To prepare for quilting, you must first place the quilt top, the batting, and the lining together. If the piece is large, you may have to work on the floor. Lay the lining flat, smoothing it out. Place the batting on top of the wrong side of the lining and make sure it is also free of wrinkles. Then lay the top over the other two layers, being careful to place it exactly in

position without disturbing the other layers. An easy way to do this is to fold the top in half lengthwise, then crosswise, and place one corner of the top to the matching corner of the other two layers. Unfold the quilt top and match the next corner—half the top is now in position. Gently unfold the other half, and the quilt top should be all neatly matched to the bottom!

You must baste all three layers together by hand before either hand or machine quilting. Start at center of quilt and baste out to center of each side through all three layers, using a long stitch. Then, again starting at center, baste diagonally to each corner. Baste around all outside edges.

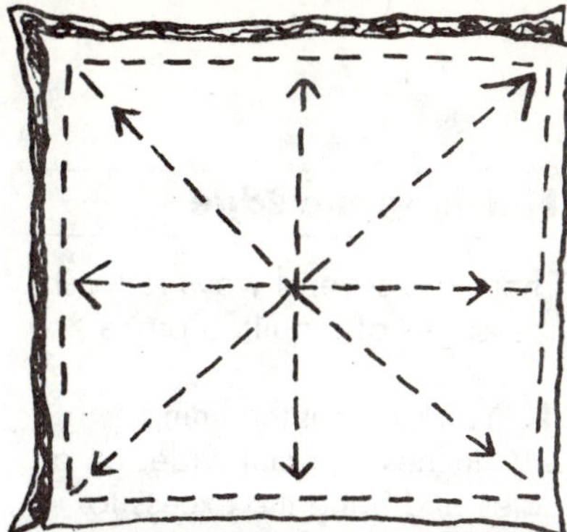

A fusing agent is a handy alternative to basting. Use narrow strips between all three layers in the same places you would baste. Fuse in place according to manufacturer's directions.

Hand Quilting

First prick the design of the quilting onto your fabric with a needle or draw it with chalk if you are not following the outline of the top. Push the needle from underneath straight up through the three layers of

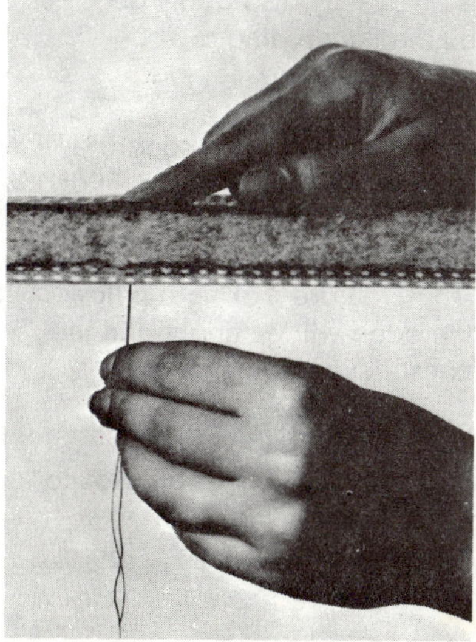

material (top, batting, and lining). Draw thread through, then push needle straight back through ⅛ inch (3 mm) away from first

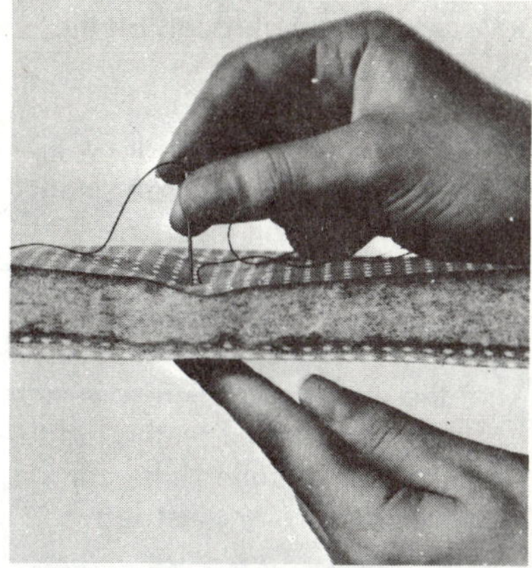

stitch. It will help to position a finger at the exact spot where the needle should come through each time. The finished stitch looks similar to a running stitch, but you must not try to take "bites" of fabric as you would if you were doing a running stitch.

Machine Quilting

This is a great time-saver for large projects. It should be used for emphasis primarily on designs with simple lines. Stitch over appliqué or patchwork seams, being careful to avoid shifting of fabric layers. Do not stitch over design lines close together or puffy quality of quilt will be reduced. For a curved design, hand-baste along the exact lines of your quilting before stitching.

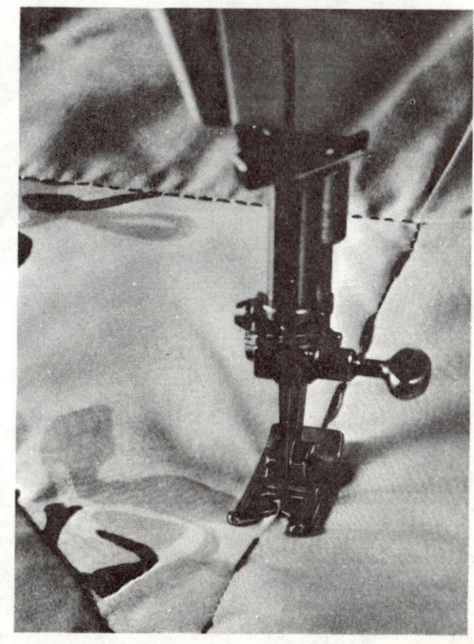

TUFTING

For a fun, quick way to finish off your quilt, try yarn tufting. Just sew tufts of yarn through all the layers at intervals.

Thread a large-eyed needle with yarn and take two or three small stitches through all layers at each marked spot. Cut the yarn, leaving 2 inch (5 cm) ends.

Knot the yarn ends twice so 1 inch (2,5 cm) tufts remain on the right side. Longer or fuller tufts can be made if you prefer—just leave

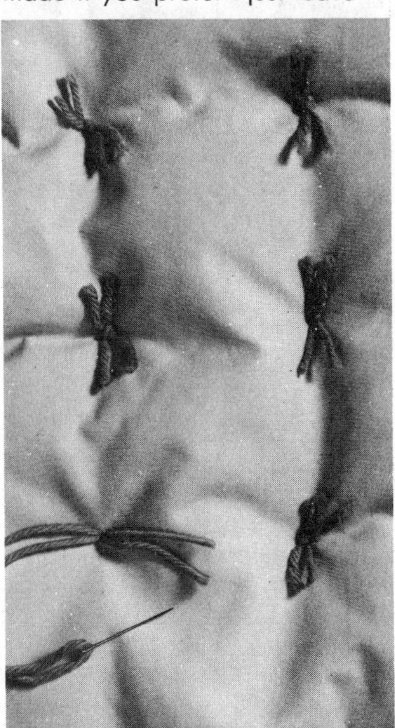

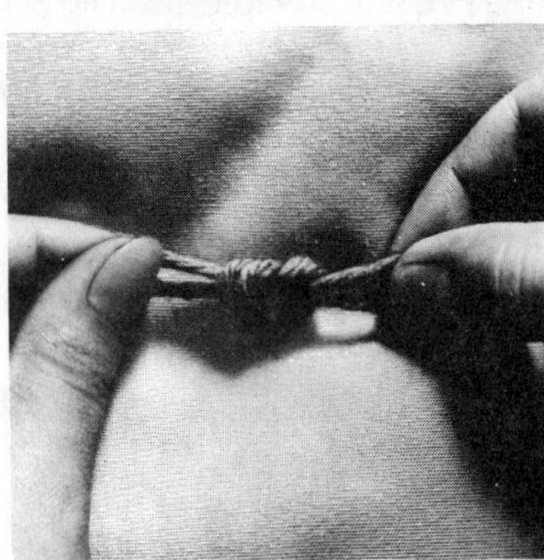

longer yarn ends or take more stitches at each marking. Narrow ribbon can replace the yarn tufts. Leave longer ends and tie in a bow.

Finishing the Edge

There are several ways to finish the edges of a quilted piece:

1. You may cut the lining 2½ inches (6,4 cm) wider on all sides and bring the excess to the right side of the piece to form a border. To do this, simply turn under the raw edges ¼ inch (6 mm) and hem to quilt top, mitering corners.

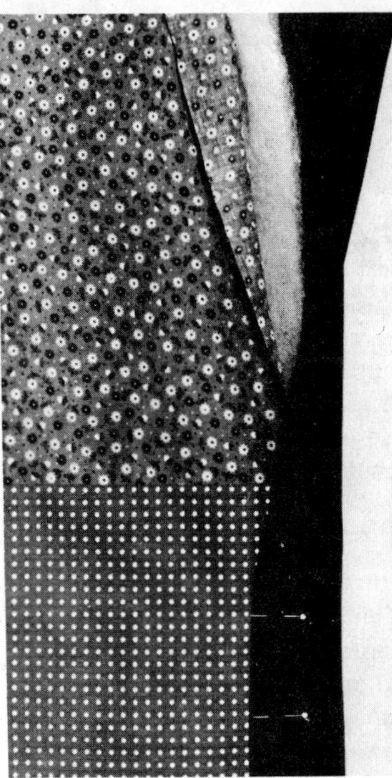

2. You may also apply quilt binding according to your favorite binding method.

3. You can apply a separate border, which you can quilt or not, as you choose.

4. If you are making a pillow, the edge will be finished in the construction of the pillow.

5. You can allow ½ inch (1,2 cm) more fabric all around the top and lining. Turn raw edges in and slip-stitch closed.

Applications

Patchwork and appliqué is by no means limited to making bed covers.

Try making an appliquéd wall hanging . . . or take one single block from a stunningly intricate old patchwork pattern and mount it on a solid background for a not-to-be-beaten center of interest in a room. Use the same idea to make pillows for the floor or furniture in wonderful fabrics—furries, leathers, vinyls. Make patchwork or appliqué draperies . . . appliqué place mats and napkins . . . stuff and pad an appliqué on a towel.

Make entire garments of patchwork—try vests, belts, ties, shirts, bags. Let your imagination run riot with color and fabric texture. Use appliqué to cover a worn spot on your favorite jeans, to give personality to a basic dress or new jeans. Appliqué a pocket onto a shirt.

Use quilting to highlight collars, cuffs, pockets, yokes. For special interest, try quilting in a contrasting color. Quilt around a design on a print fabric for chair seats, pillows, cushions, detail areas of garments. Add a special touch to an outfit by quilting the skirt and making a blouse out of matching fabric, not quilted. Or quilt a blazer fabric and make matching unquilted pants.

Use a combination of all three to make dolls and stuffed toys for your favorite children. Make a patchwork hat and quilt the brim for body. And why not make a patchwork or appliqué quilt? It's something to be treasured for generations and will give you a great deal of pleasure in the making. Have some real fun and make Victorian Crazy Quilts out of silks, satins and laces and outline each patch with different embroidery stitches.

Blue sweater design: Marcia Whalen/Photos: Mort Mace

Knit treats for the young or the young-at-heart . . . an irresistible doll with a cascade of dark curls, and a pair of wild and wooly horses.

Doll: Ursula von Wartburg/ Photo: Mort Mace

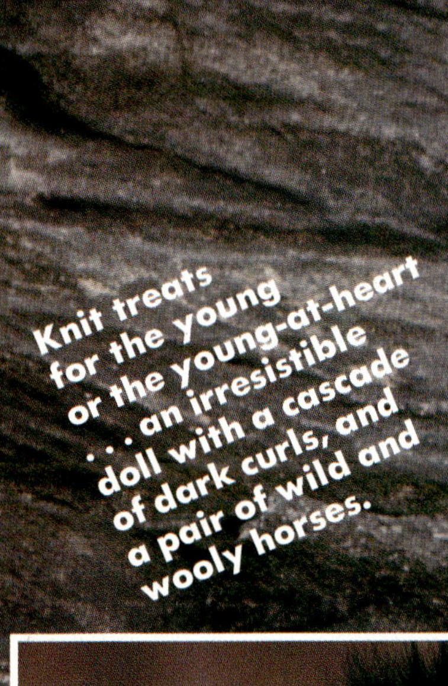

Horses: Ursula von Wartburg/Photo: Mort Mace

Crew-neck pullovers that are perfect companions for cold weather days . . . hers in a bold patchwork pattern, his in neutral Nordic stripes.

Sweaters: William Unger & Co./Photo: Mort Mace

Sweaters: Columbia-Minerva/Photo: Mort Mace

Knitting

How to Knit

Knitting goes back at least to the time of the Egyptians and if the present interest in knitting yarns and patterns is any indication, knitting will proceed at least as many years into the future.

It has reigned as the most popular of all home crafts through the ages principally because it is easily and quickly mastered; because it fulfills a basic need for warm clothing and household effects and because it offers the imaginative woman an endless variety of patterns, designs and textures.

Knitting is simply the interlacing of lines of loops made by two needles. Out of this interlacing, a knitter can produce baby bootees no larger than a postage stamp or a rug to cover a baronial hall.

The knitted sweater remains for many men the measure of a woman's love and any hand-knitted item the measure of high style.

Abbreviations and Terms

beg	**begin or beginning**
dec	**decrease**
dp	**double pointed**
inc	**increase**
k	**knit**
pat	**pattern**
p	**purl**
psso	**pass slipped stitch over**
rnd	**round**
sl	**slip**
st	**stitch**
tog	**together**
yo	**yarn over**

*** — Asterisk:** means repeat the instructions following the asterisk as many times as specified, in addition to the first time.

Even: When directions say "work even," this means to continue working without increasing or decreasing in the pattern you have been using.

( ) — Parentheses: mean do what is in the parentheses the number of times specified. Example: (k 1, p 1) four times, means four times altogether. Parentheses are also used to set off changes in size when more than one size is given for a garment.

"Place a marker in work": means to mark with a safety pin or strand of contrasting color yarn a certain point on the piece itself to use as a guide in making future measurements.

"Place a marker on needle": means to place a safety pin or special stitch marker on the needle between the stitches. It is slipped from one needle to the other to serve as a mark on future rows.

Multiple of stitches: A stitch pattern often has to be worked on an exact number of stitches. When directions say "multiple of," it means the number of stitches must be divisible by this number. For example: "multiple of 5" would be 10, 15, 20, etc.; "multiple of 5 plus 4" would be 14, 19, 24, etc.

Needles and Yarns

There are many types of needles and yarn available for knitting. Knitting needles are made of plastic, aluminum and wood. They come in a wide range of sizes, types and lengths. Single pointed straight needles are used when you work back and forth in rows. Double pointed needles are used in sets of four for working tubular knitting such as socks and mittens. Circular needles are usually used for knitting skirts or other tubular garments when you work in rounds. They are also used when a straight needle is not long enough to hold a large number of stitches. Small needles are used for thin yarn and larger needles for heavy yarn.

Use the same size needle that your directions call for, then test your gauge (see below) to determine if you need larger or smaller needles.

Yarns are made of many materials. They differ as to twist, size, texture and weight. You can purchase many different weights of wool, plus synthetics, mohair, metallics, angora, cotton and blends of all kinds.

Any item you intend to make will specify the yarn used in the original and to obtain the best results you should use this yarn. If you have to substitute be careful that you obtain the correct gauge and texture.

As dye lots vary, always buy enough yarn to make the entire article.

Gauge

To have your article the correct size, it is very important to knit to the gauge specified in the directions. Gauge means the number of stitches and rows per

GAUGE = 4 STITCHES PER INCH (2,5 CM)

inch. Using the needles and yarn specified, make a practice swatch 3 or 4 inches (7,6 or 10,2 cm) square of the stitch given. Place flat on table and measure the number of stitches and rows you have per inch. If your number does not correspond to the gauge given, try different size needles until correct number is achieved. If you have more stitches per inch use larger needles; if you have fewer stitches use smaller needles.

To Start Knitting

For practice pieces use knitting worsted weight yarn and No. 6, 7 or 8 knitting needles. Try each step or stitch until you are familiar with it.

How to Cast On

There are two methods of casting on. Try both of them to see which you prefer and which looks best for the item you are making.

First Method

Use only one knitting needle. Make a slip knot on needle leaving a long end (allow about 1 inch for each stitch).

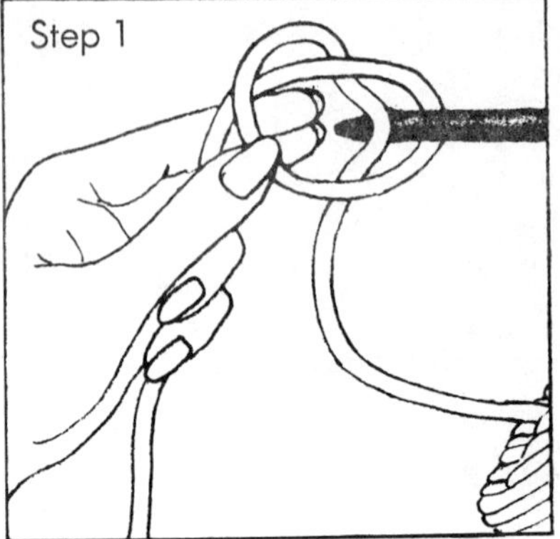

Step 1

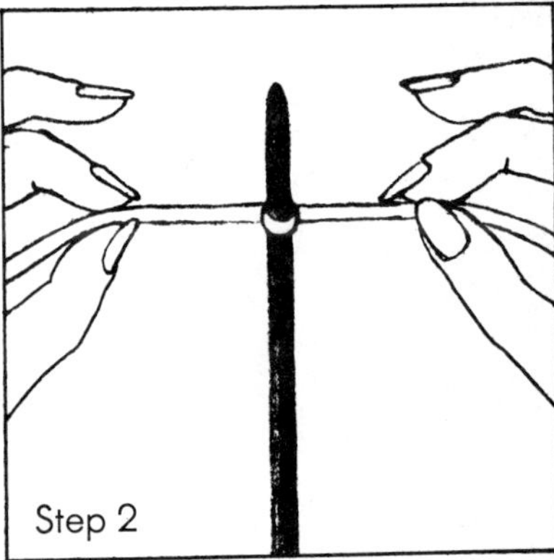

Step 2

Pull both ends of yarn in opposite directions to tighten the loop on the needle.

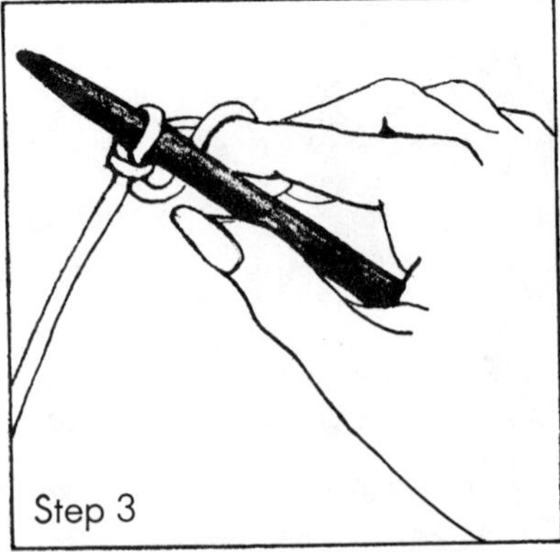

Step 3

Hold the needle in your right hand as shown.

Or like this.

Whichever is more comfortable for you. Move the loop near the point of needle.

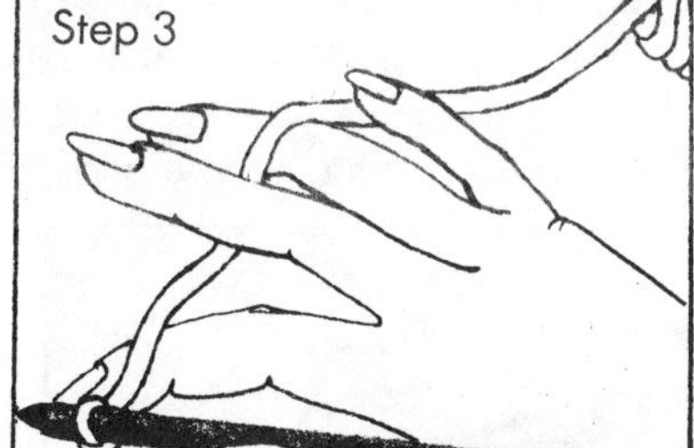

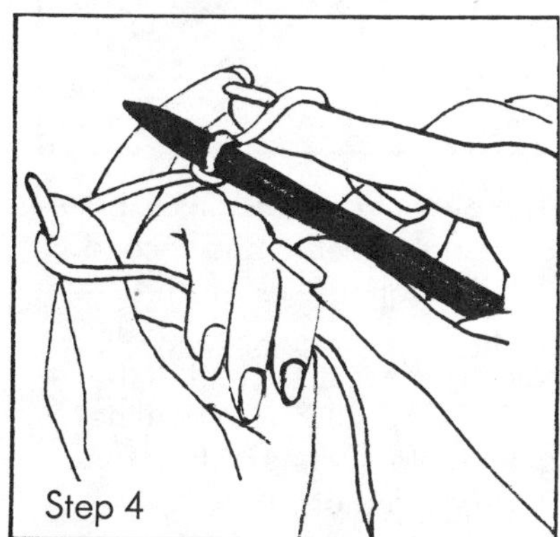

Loop yarn from skein over fingers as shown. Loop the free end of yarn around your left thumb.

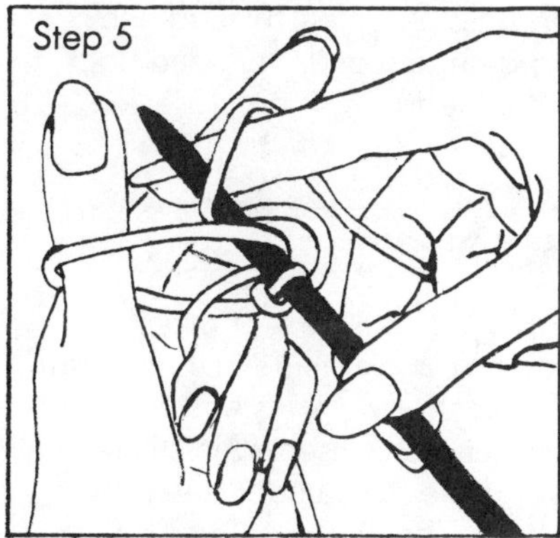

Insert needle in loop. Wind yarn in right hand over needle.

Draw yarn through loop on thumb.

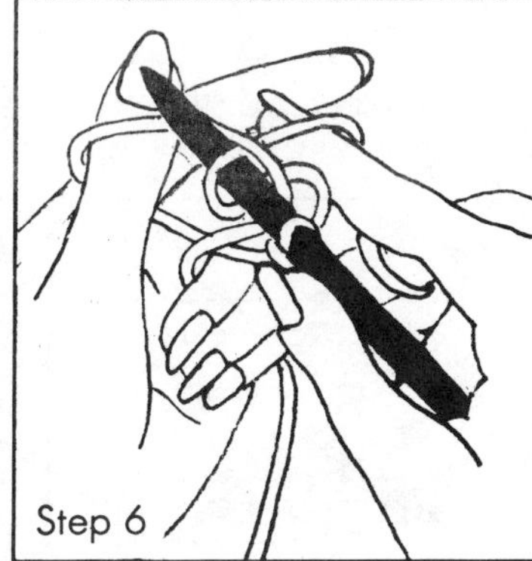

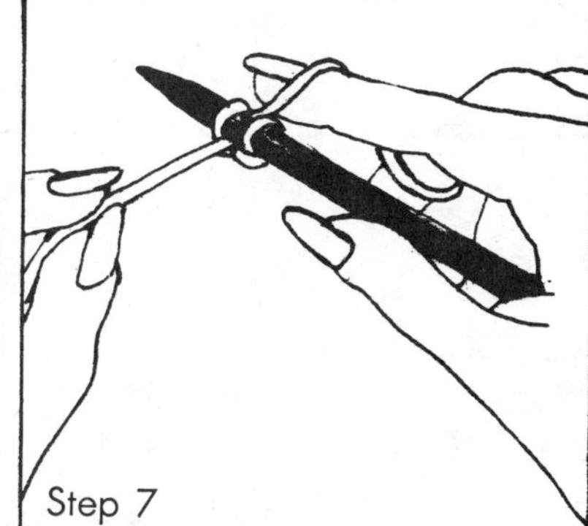

Slip loop off thumb and pull the free end of yarn to tighten the stitch on the needle. One stitch is cast on.

Practice until you can cast on evenly—not too loose or too tight. With this method, some people cast on over two needles or use a larger size needle than the main part of garment to insure a loose edge with enough stretch.

Second Method

Use two knitting needles. Make a slip knot on needle. (See Steps 1 and 2 of *First Method).*
Hold needle in left hand. Hold second needle in right hand with yarn in working position. Insert point of right needle in loop on left needle. With index finger of right hand, bring yarn over the point of right needle. Draw yarn through loop.

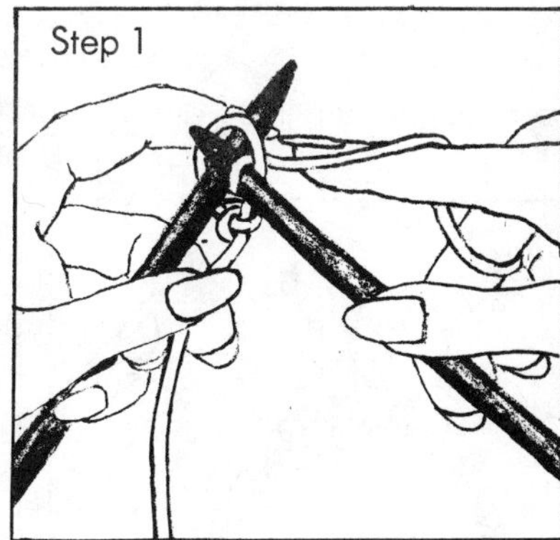

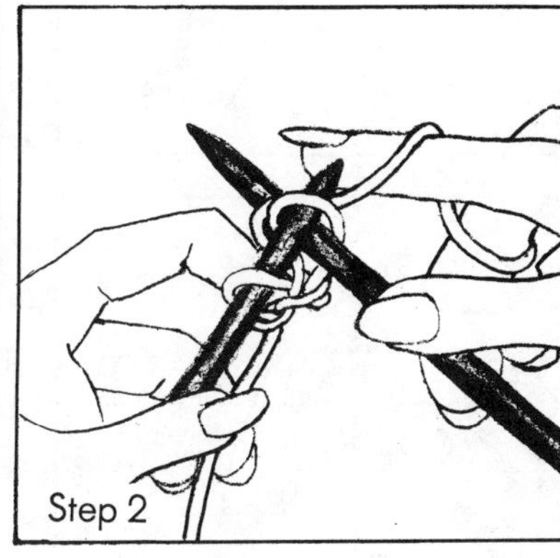

Insert left needle in loop. Bring yarn over point of right needle and draw yarn through loop.

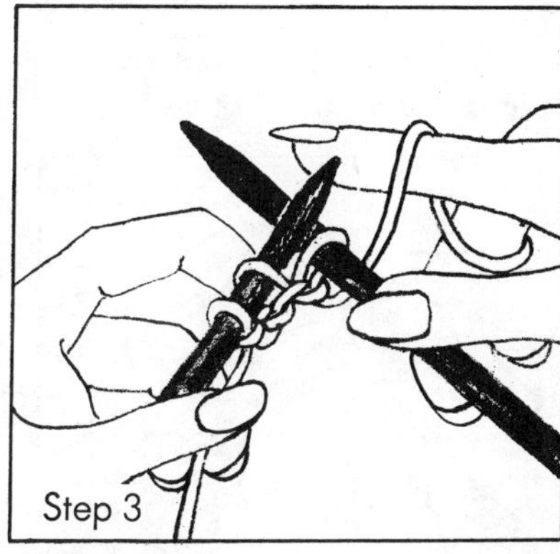

Two stitches are cast on left needle.

Repeat step 2 until you have the desired number of stitches. For last stitch, insert left needle in loop and remove it from right needle.

BASIC STITCHES

How to Knit

Cast on 20 stitches for practice piece. Hold needle with cast on stitches in your left hand. Hold second needle and yarn from skein in your right hand. The yarn from skein should be in back of your needles.

Insert right needle into front of first stitch.

Step 1

Step 2

Wind yarn from your right hand under and over point of needle.

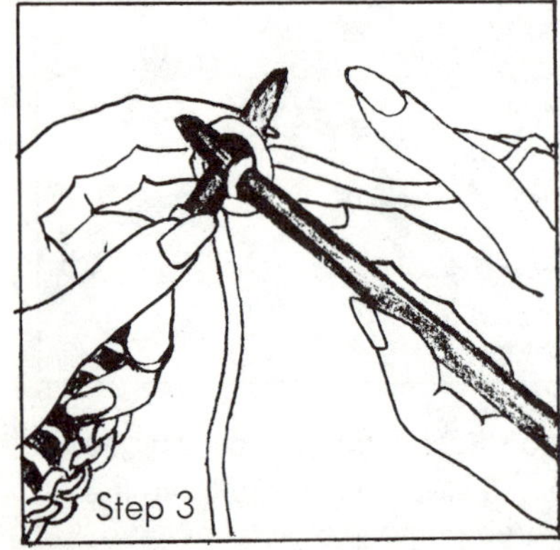

Draw right needle and yarn through stitch.

Slip the stitch just made off left needle. One knit stitch made.

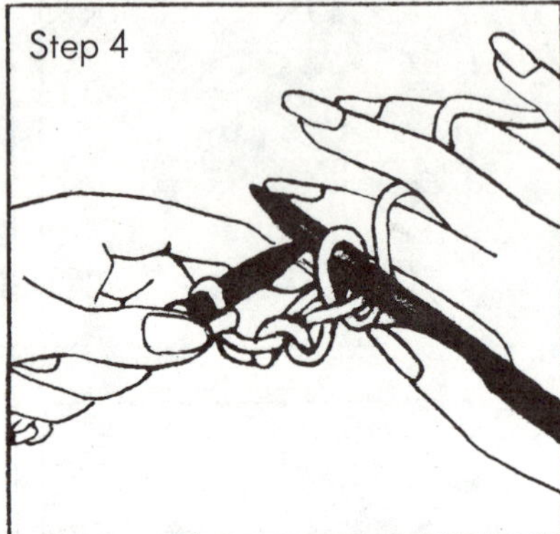

Repeat in each stitch across until all the stitches have been knitted off left needle. Push work along left needle so the stitch to be worked is near tip. At the end of row, turn work so needle with stitches is in your left hand. Continue working rows of knit stitch in this manner until you are familiar with this stitch. When you knit each stitch in each row it is called garter stitch.

To Bind Off

When you have finished your swatch, you are ready to learn to bind off. It is necessary to bind off in knitting to prevent your stitches from raveling. It should be done rather loosely. Slip the first stitch off the left needle onto the right needle without knitting it. Knit the next stitch. Insert the left needle through the front of the first stitch on the right needle and

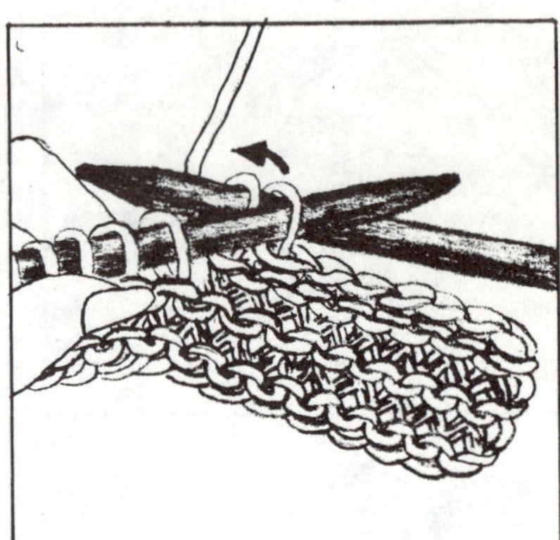

slip it over the second stitch, bringing the right needle and second stitch through the first stitch.

Then slip the first stitch off left needle. One stitch is left on the right needle. Knit next stitch and slip preceding one over it.

Continue across until you come to your last stitch. Cut yarn about 5 inches (12,7 cm) from needle. Draw loose end through last stitch and pull to tighten. Thread end into a needle and work end back through edge. Cut off close to work.

How to Purl

Cast on 20 stitches for practice piece. To make this stitch, the yarn is in front of work instead of back and needle is inserted in stitch over, instead of under, left needle. The wrong side of a purl stitch is a knit stitch.

Hold needle with stitches in your left hand. Hold second needle and yarn from skein in your right hand. Insert right needle through the front of the first stitch on left needle from right to left.

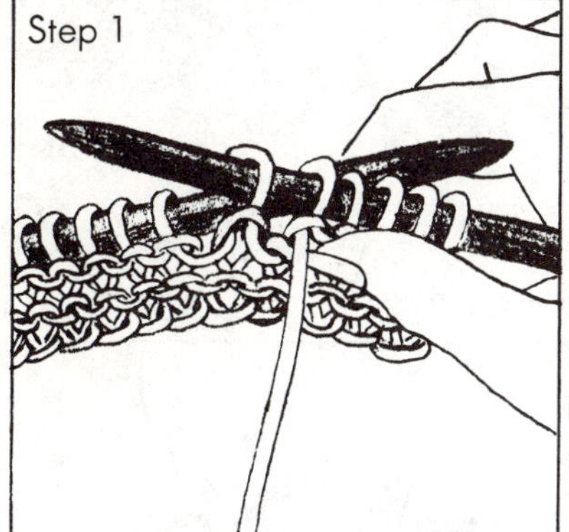

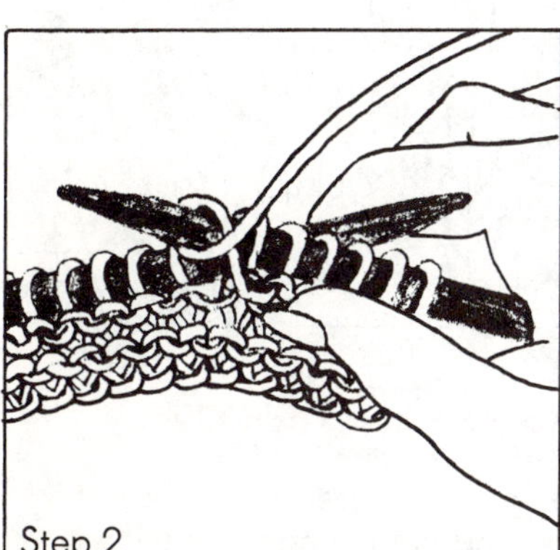

Wind yarn over and under point of needle.

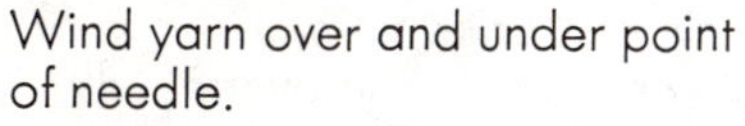

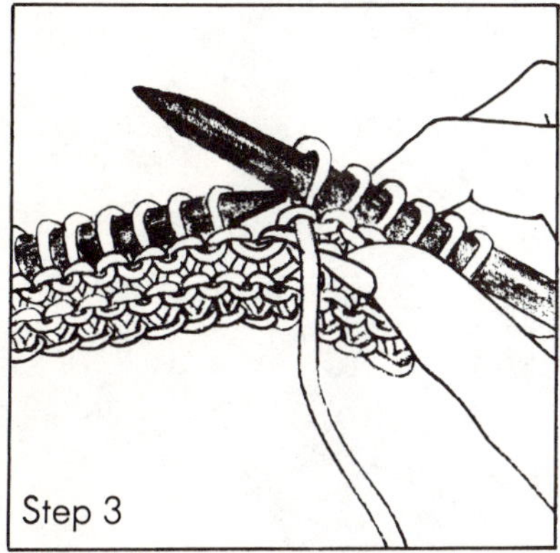

Draw yarn through stitch. Slip the stitch off left needle. One purl stitch made. Continue to purl each stitch across row. The purl stitch is never used alone so to practice the stitch proceed to stockinette stitch.

Stockinette Stitch

Turn work. Knit next row. Purl next row. Repeat these two rows for stockinette stitch. Continue to work until you feel familiar with the stitch. Bind off. If you bind off on a purl row, purl the stitches instead of knitting them.

In stockinette stitch the knit side or smooth side is usually the right side of work.

The purl side is the rough side. You have now learned the two basic stitches from which all knitting is derived.

Ribbing

Ribbing is a combination of knit and purl stitches. Knit one, purl one or knit two, purl two are the most common. Because of its elasticity it is usually used for neckbands, waistbands and wrists.

Cast on 22 sts for practice piece. 1st row: K 2, * p 2, k 2; repeat from * across.

2nd row: P 2, * k 2, p 2; repeat from * across. Repeat these two rows. It is easier to work ribbing if you identify the stitches and simply knit the knit stitches and purl the purl stitches.

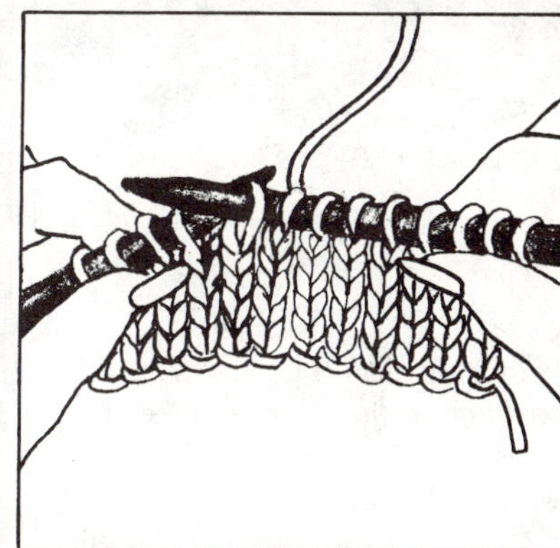

MORE BASICS

How to Slip a Stitch

With yarn in back of work and holding needle as if to purl, slip stitch from left needle to right without working it.

How To Increase

To increase on a knit row, knit the stitch in the usual manner but do not slip the stitch off the left needle. Knit again in the same stitch by inserting the needle into the back of the stitch. Now slip the stitches off the needle.

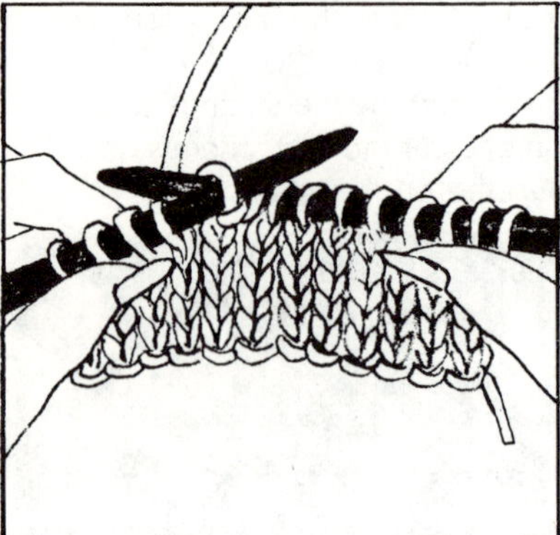

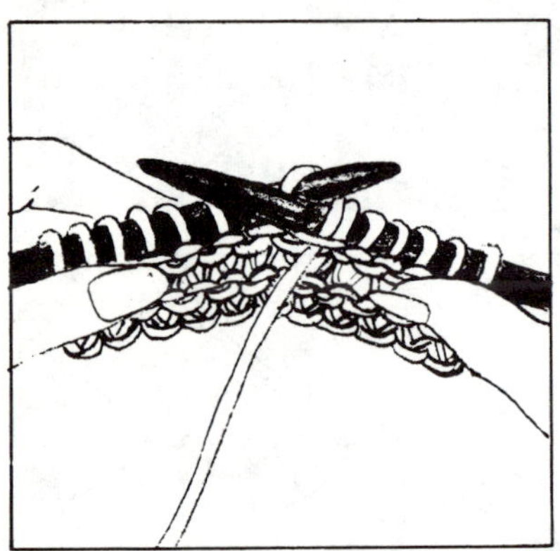

To increase on a purl row, purl the stitch in the usual manner but do not slip the stitch off the left needle. Purl again in the same stitch by inserting the needle into the back of the stitch. Now slip the stitches off the needle.

How To Decrease

To decrease on a knit row, knit two stitches together by inserting the right needle through two stitches.

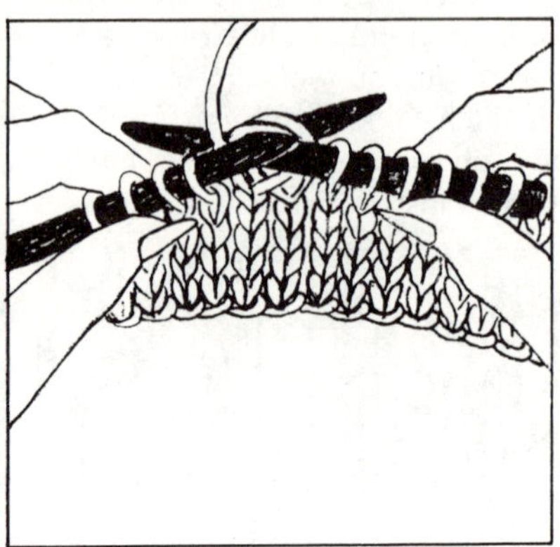

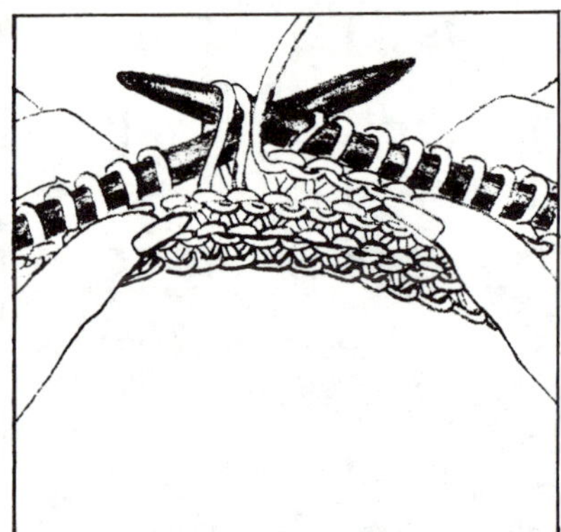

To decrease on a purl row, purl two stitches together by inserting the right needle through two stitches.

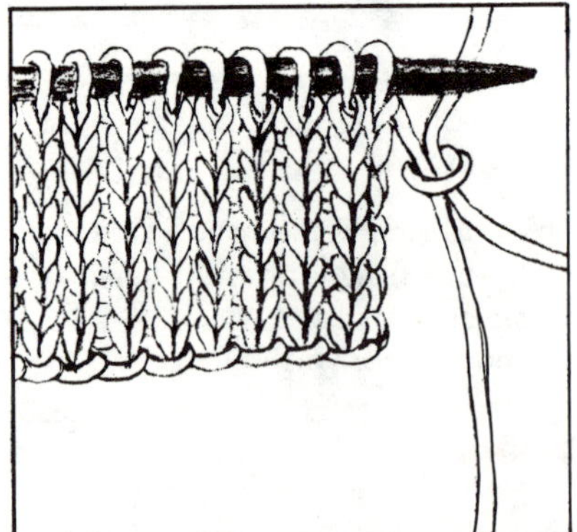

How To Attach Yarn

When your skein of yarn runs out or when you have to change colors, you attach a new skein. If possible join the new yarn at the beginning of a row. Simply tie the new yarn and fasten ends securely.

To attach new yarn in the middle of a row, thread the new yarn in a needle and weave it back through the old yarn for several stitches. Leave short end of yarn on back of work and cut off when project is finished.

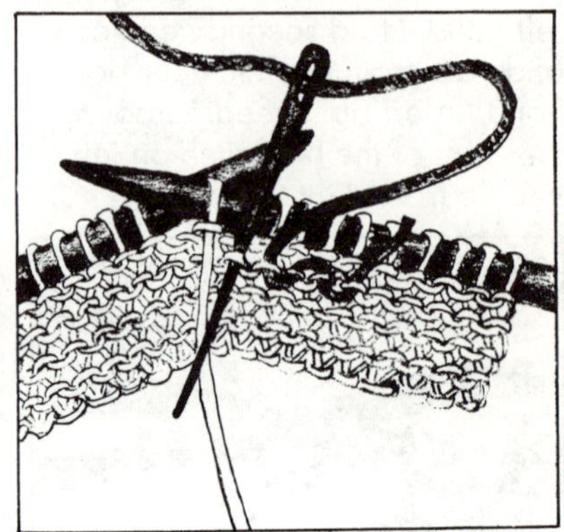

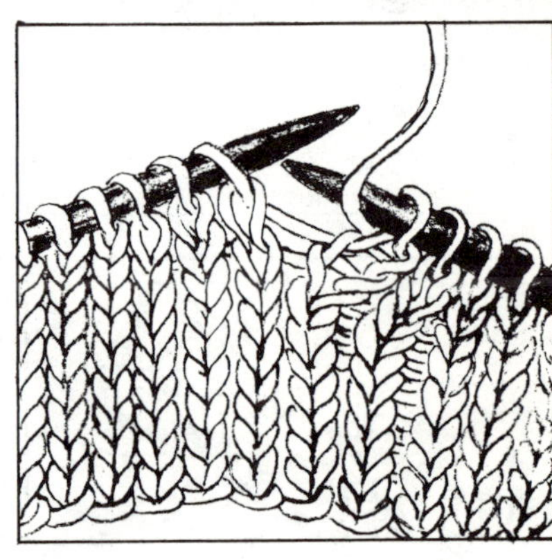

To Make A Yarn Over

Yarn over increases a stitch and is used in lace patterns since it produces a hole in the work. On a knit row, bring yarn under tip of right needle, up and over needle, then work next stitch.

On a purl row, bring yarn over right needle, around and to front again, then work next stitch.

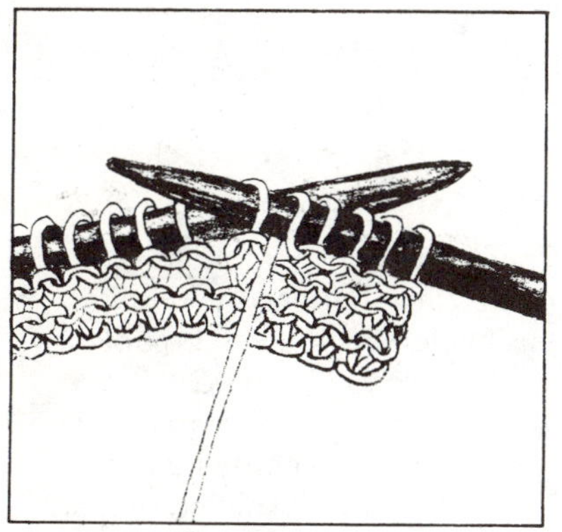

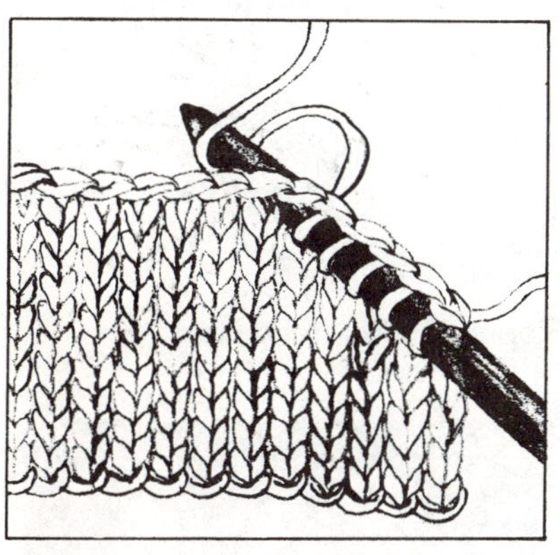

How To Pick Up Stitches

Directions often say pick up stitches along an edge of a piece that is already knitted. Usually neckbands and front edges are worked with picked up stitches. With right side of work facing you, attach yarn to work where picking up is to start. Work with yarn and only one needle. Insert point of needle through knitting a short distance from the edge, wrap yarn around needle as if to knit and draw loop through piece. Continue in this manner across edge, spacing stitches evenly.

Duplicate Stitch

Duplicate stitch is used to work a design on top of knitting. Thread a large-eyed needle with contrasting color yarn. Draw yarn from wrong to right side through center of lower point of the knit stitch. Insert needle at top right-hand side of same stitch. Then holding needle horizontally, draw through to top left side of stitch. Insert again into base of same stitch. Keep work loose so it completely covers the knit stitch.

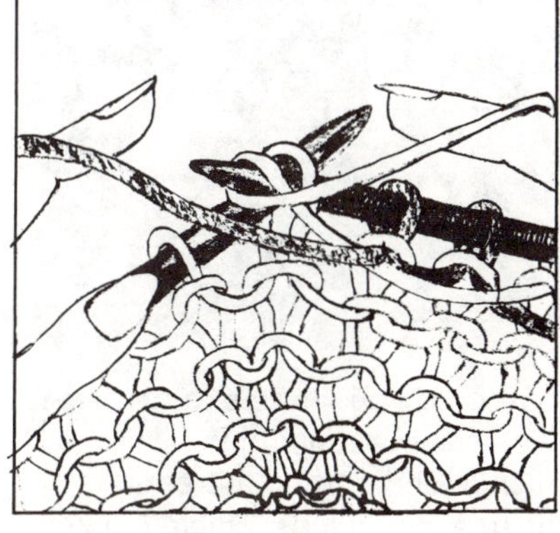

To Change Color in Knitting

When color appears in a definite line or block, you attach a color as it appears in the design. When changing colors, simply twist yarn by bringing new color under yarn you are working with. This prevents holes in the work.

Fair Isle Knitting

This term is used for a pattern where two colors are used in the same row of knitting and the color changes every few stitches. It is usually used in stockinette stitch and you carry the yarn not being used on the wrong side of work throughout the whole pattern.

The color yarn used most is held in right hand and the second color is held in the left hand. If yarn is carried more than three stitches, catch the carried yarn so you won't have long loops on the back. Catch yarn as follows:

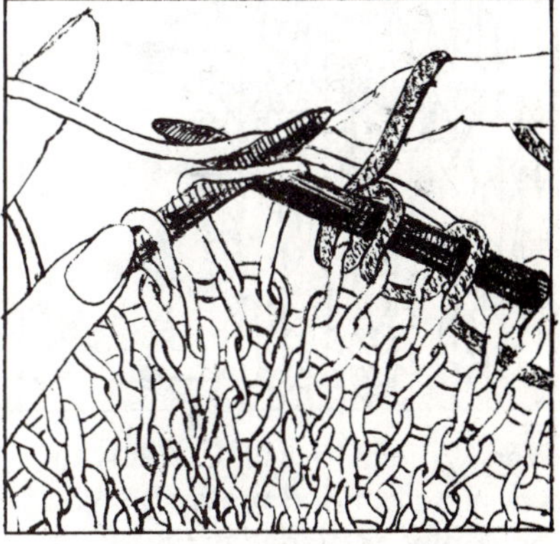

* Insert right needle in usual manner but before picking up yarn to work this stitch, slip right-hand needle under the carried yarn, work stitch in usual manner, dropping carried yarn as stitch is completed. Work next stitch in usual manner. Repeat from * across.

Finishing Knitting

Work all loose ends into a solid part of the knitting to fasten it securely. Thread end into a needle and weave it through work. Cut off close to work. If yarn end is not long enough to thread into a needle use a crochet hook to work the end in and out of the knitting.

Blocking

Blocking is the pressing or steaming of knitted pieces. Man-made fibers such as orlon or nylon often do not need blocking. The yarn label or directions will say, "do not press," or "steam press lightly." Also some mohairs and bulky yarns or designs with a raised pattern should not be blocked because they will lose their texture.

To block other materials, lay each piece separately on a padded surface, wrong side up. Using rustproof pins, pin the edges to the correct measurements,

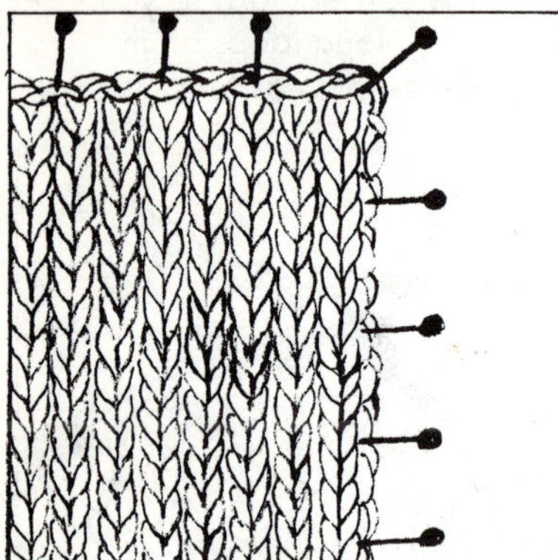

every 1/4 inch (6 mm). Cover with a damp cloth and press lightly. Leave pieces pinned until dry.

Joining

Right sides facing, pin edges to be sewn. Some people prefer to baste edges together and try on before sewing. Thread a tapestry or yarn needle with matching yarn. There are several methods of joining. Use an

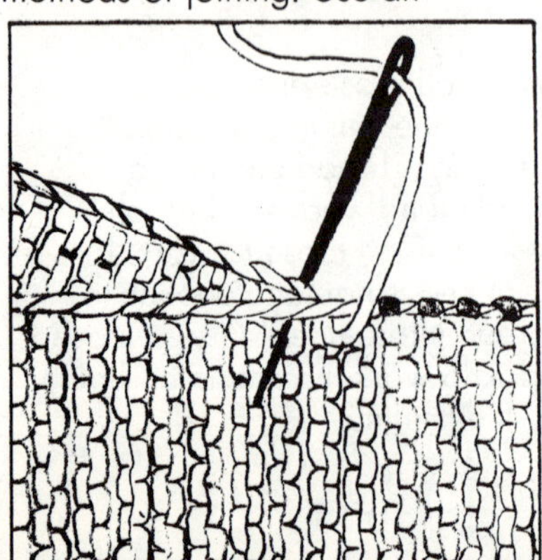

overcast stitch worked over straight edges or a backstitch worked slightly in from curved or uneven edge. You can also crochet your pieces together with slip-stitching or use the

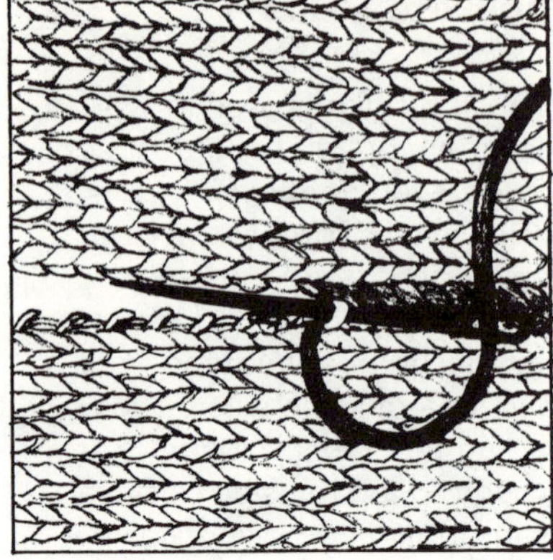

duplicate stitch for an invisible seam. Always leave stitches loose enough to match elasticity of knitting. Steam seams and edges lightly.

ADDITIONAL STITCHES

Moss or Seed Stitch

This stitch is good practice for you to identify knit and purl stitches.

In ribbing you made straight lines of stitches by knitting the knit stitches and purling the purl stitches. But in moss stitch you knit the purl stitches and purl the knit stitches. The stitch is reversible so it is often used for scarfs, baby blankets and afghans where both sides are seen.

Cast on 21 stitches or any uneven number of stitches for practice piece.

1st row: * K 1, p 1; repeat from * across, ending k 1. Repeat this row for pattern. Continue to work the stitch until you are familiar with it and remember you are knitting the purl stitches and purling the knit stitches. Bind off in pattern.

Cable Stitch

There are many variations of cable stitch but once you learn this basic one you will be able to work any cable with ease. You will need a double-pointed knitting needle or a cable needle which is sold with knitting supplies. Cast on 24 stitches (multiple of 10 stitches, plus 4) for practice piece.

1st Row: * P 4, k 6; repeat from * across, ending p 4.

2nd Row: * K 4, p 6; repeat from * across, ending k 4.

Repeat 1st and 2nd rows.

5th Row: * P 4, slip next 3 sts to dp needle and hold in back of work, k next 3 sts, then k the 3 sts from dp needle (cable twist made); repeat from * across, ending p 4.

6th Row: Repeat 2nd row.

7th Row: Repeat 1st row.

8th Row: Repeat 2nd row.

Repeat first through 8th rows for pattern.

Practice the stitch until you are familiar with it. Bind off in pattern.

Crochet

Lacy looks that are quickly crocheted . . . a sweater and scarf to top off a turtle-neck, an elegant shawl for an evening out, and an "antique" collar in purest white.

Sweater & Scarf: Columbia-Minerva

Collar: Coats & Clark

Shawl: William Unger & Co /Photos: Mort Mace at The Dairy, Central Park, N.Y.

Floral afghan & crib coverlet: Transworld Feature Syndicate

Geometric throw: Coats & Clark/Photo: Mort Mace

Cool as sea breezes . . . a loose V-neck pullover, crocheted in beige with bands of white.

Sweater: Spinnerin

Crochet

How to Crochet

Where knitting uses two needles, crocheting is needlework done with one hook. Its principle is the simple drawing of one loop through another.

Once you master the basic stitches, you will find crocheting is fast and easy.

The variety of yarns and hooks of differing sizes will enable you to render textures as filmy as a spider's web or as solid as a rug. Crochet designs are infinite and so versatile you can turn out everything from berets to afghans.

Abbreviations and Terms

beg	**begin or beginning**
ch	**chain**
dc	**double crochet**
dec	**decrease**
hdc	**half double crochet**
inc	**increase**
lp(s)	**loop(s)**
pat	**pattern**
rnd	**round**
sc	**single crochet**
sk	**skip**
sl st	**slip stitch**
sp	**space**
st(s)	**stitch(es)**
tog	**together**
tr	**treble crochet**
yo	**yarn over**

*** — Asterisk:** means repeat the instructions following the asterisk as many times as specified, in addition to the first time.

Even: When directions say "work even", this means to continue working without increasing or decreasing in the pattern you have been using.

( ) — Parentheses: mean do what is in the parentheses the number of times specified. Example: (ch 1, dc in next dc) four times means four times altogether. Parentheses are also used to set off changes in size when more than one size is given for a garment.

Hooks and Yarns

There are a great variety of hooks and yarns available to the crocheter.

Hooks are made of steel, plastic, aluminum and wood. They come in many different lengths and sizes. The steel hooks are usually used for cotton thread or fine wool work. Hooks of plastic and aluminum are suitable for wool, synthetics, mohair, etc. They are sized in varying ways by different manufacturers. Some size them by letter, some number and some both letter and number. If you can't find the hook specified for the article you are making, ask your saleswoman for the correct one. Wooden hooks come in large sizes only and are used for jiffy work or rug making. Afghan hooks are longer (about the size of knitting needles) and are made especially for the afghan stitch.

Use the same size hook that your directions call for, then test your gauge (page 70) to determine if you need a larger or smaller hook. Yarns and threads are made of many materials today. Years ago they usually had only light, medium and heavyweight wool and the cotton threads. But now you can purchase all these plus synthetics, mohair, metallics, jute, angora and blends of all kinds. Textures vary from nubby to smooth, bulky to lightweight. Usually lightweight yarns and cottons need the smaller hooks to make baby items and the more delicate designs used in tablecloths and bedspreads. The heavier weights are best for afghans, sweaters and other wearing apparel. The heaviest weights are used for bulky sweaters and rugs.

An item you intend to make will specify the yarn used in the original and to obtain the best results you should use this yarn. If you have to substitute, be careful that you obtain the correct gauge and texture.

As dye lots vary, always buy enough yarn to make the entire article.

Gauge

To make your article the correct size, it is very important to crochet to the gauge specified in the directions. Gauge means the number of stitches and rows per inch. Using the hook and yarn specified, make a practice swatch 3 or 4 inches (7,6 or 10,2 cm) square of the stitch given. Place flat on table and with a ruler measure the number of stitches and rows

GAUGE = 3 STITCHES PER INCH (2,5 cm)

you have per inch (2,5 cm). If your number does not correspond to the gauge given, try different size hooks until correct number is achieved. If you have more stitches per inch (2,5 cm) use a larger hook; if you have fewer stitches use a smaller hook.

Make a practice swatch of each new stitch until you are familiar with it. To practice, use knitting worsted weight yarn and an H or I hook.

BASIC STITCHES

To start the first loop, make a loop at end of yarn and hold in place with thumb and forefinger of left hand; hold hook in right hand as you would a pencil. Draw working yarn through loop.

Step 1

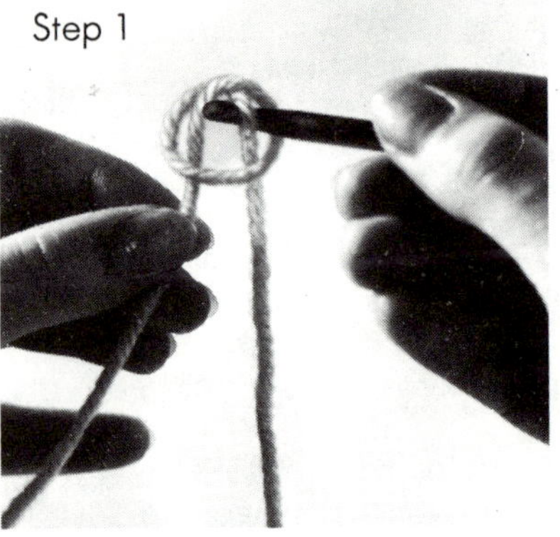

Step 2

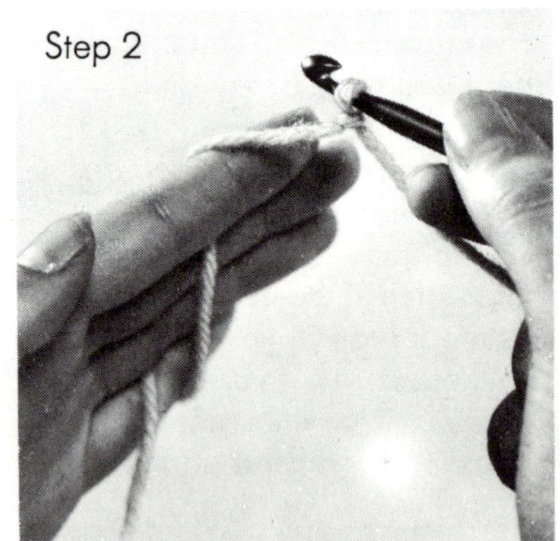

Pull short end and working yarn in opposite directions to bring loop around hook.

To hold yarn, measure down working yarn about 4 inches (10,2 cm) from loop on hook. Having palm of hand facing up, insert yarn between ring finger and little finger of left hand. Weave thread around little finger, then under and over other fingers.

Chain Stitch

Pass hook under yarn and catch yarn with hook; draw yarn through loop on hook. This makes one chain.

Step 3

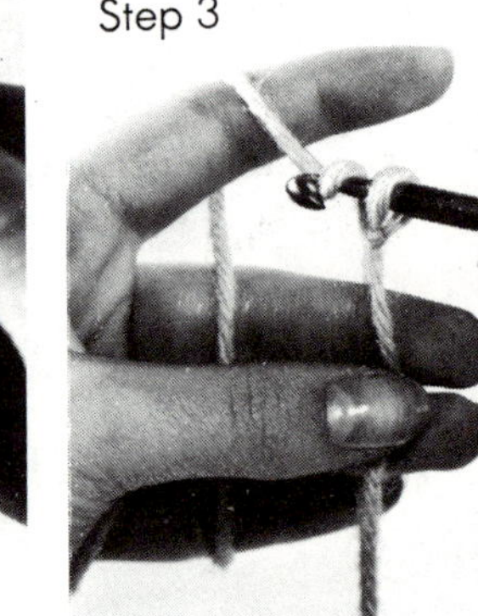

Step 4

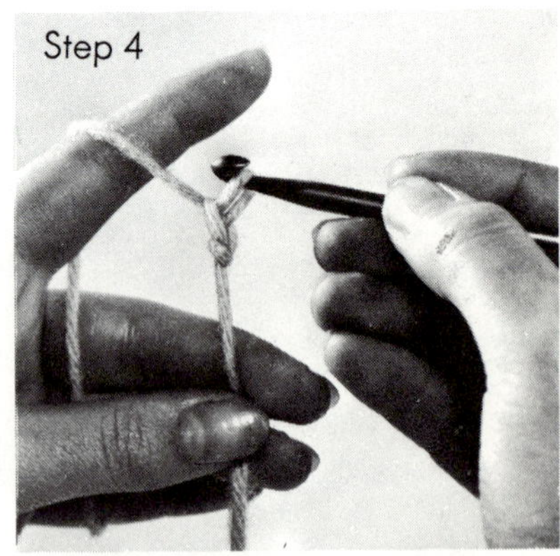

Repeat until you have as many chains as needed. One loop always remains on hook. Keep thumb and forefinger of your left hand near stitch in work to control tension. Practice until your chains are uniform — not too loose or too tight.

Single Crochet

Make a starting chain of stitches for practice piece.

Insert hook under the two top threads of second chain from hook,

Step 1

draw yarn through. There are now two loops on hook.

Step 2

Step 3

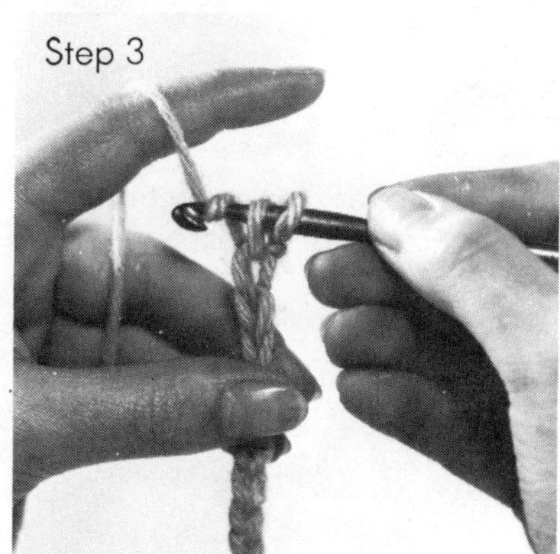

Yarn over hook and draw through the two loops.

One loop remains on hook. One single crochet completed.

Step 4

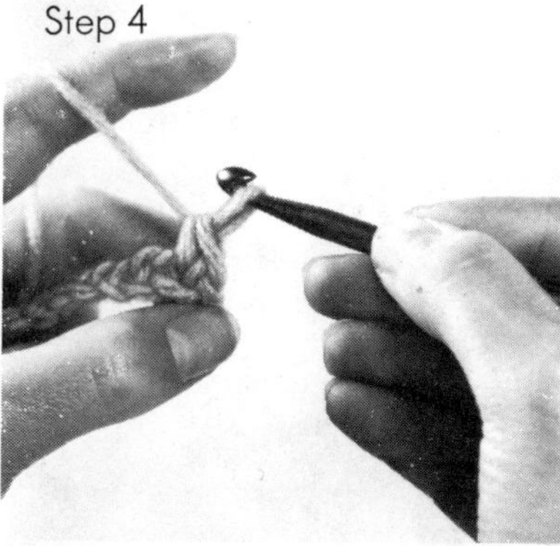

Step 5

For the next single crochet, insert hook under the two top threads of next chain and repeat. Continue in each chain across. At the end of the row, chain 1.

Turn work so reverse side is facing you. Insert hook under the two top threads of first single crochet. Repeat Steps 1 through 5. Continue working single crochet in this manner until you are familiar with this stitch.

Step 6

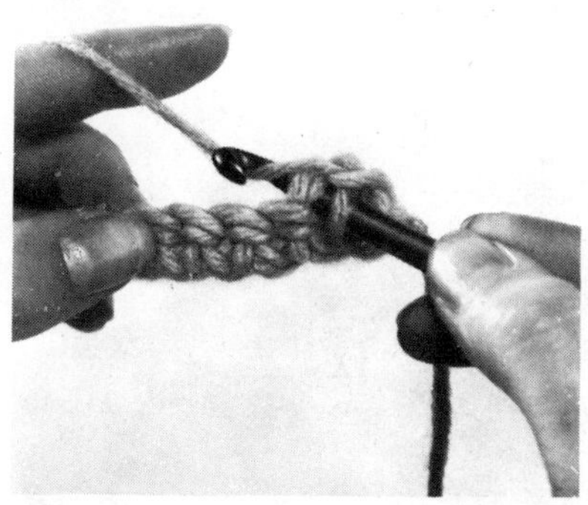

Note: In all crochet pick up the two top loops or threads of each stitch unless otherwise specified.

Double Crochet

Make a starting chain of 20 stitches for practice piece.

Yarn over, insert hook under the two top threads of 4th chain from hook.

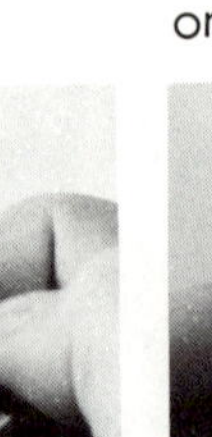

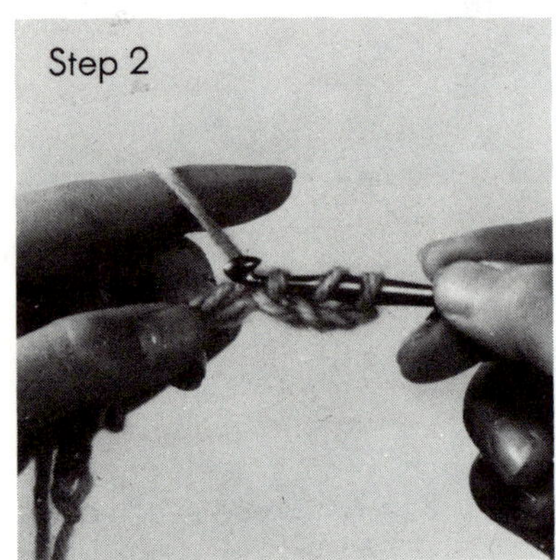

Yarn over, draw through stitch. There are now three loops on hook.

Yarn over, draw through two loops. You now have two loops on hook.

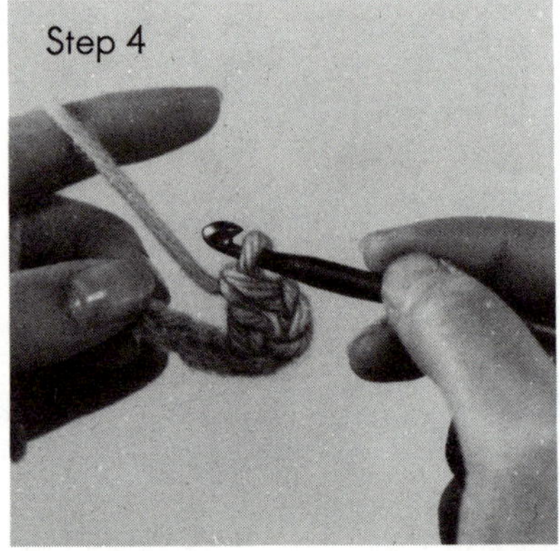

Yarn over, draw through two loops. One loop remains on hook. One double crochet completed. For next double crochet, yarn over, insert hook under the two top threads of next chain. Yarn over and draw through this chain. There are now three loops on hook. Repeat Steps 3 and 4. Continue working a double crochet in each chain across. At the end of the row, chain 3 to turn. This turning chain is always counted as the first double crochet of next row. On 2nd row, skip first double crochet, work double crochet in each stitch across, double crochet in turning chain. Chain 3 and turn. Repeat the 2nd row until you have mastered the stitch.

Half Double Crochet

To make half double crochet, repeat through Step 2 of double crochet.

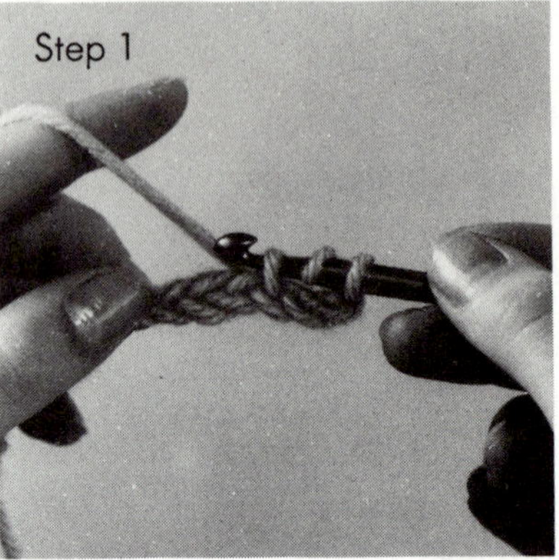

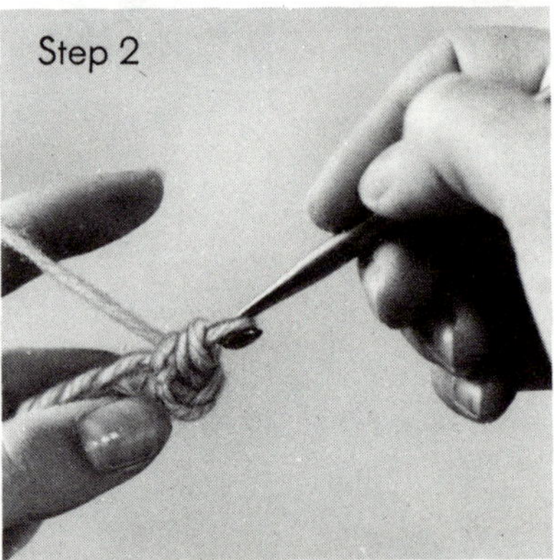

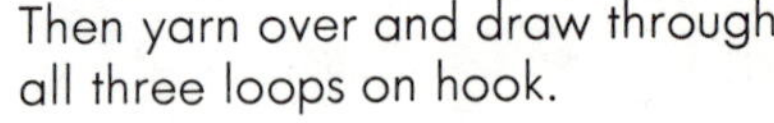

Then yarn over and draw through all three loops on hook.

Treble Crochet

Make a starting chain of stitches for practice piece.

This stitch is similar to double crochet but start with yarn over twice (instead of once). Insert hook under the two top threads of 5th chain from hook, yarn over, draw through stitch. There are now four loops on hook.

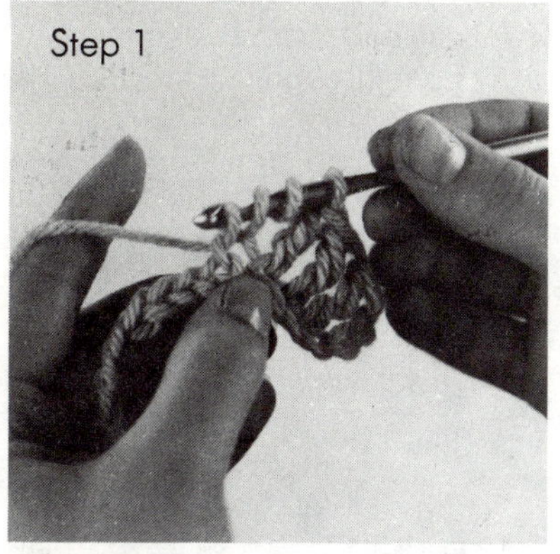

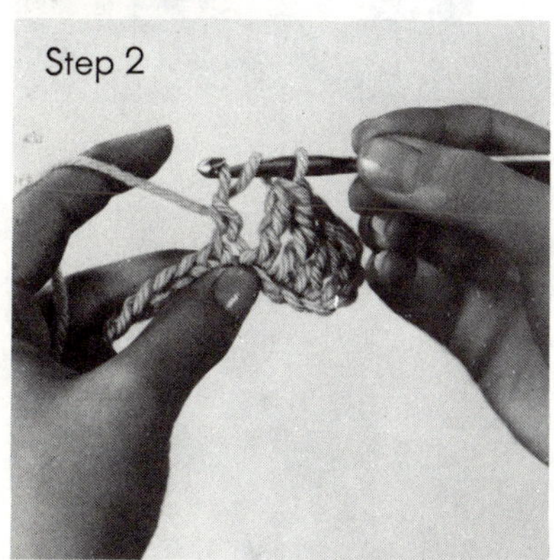

Yarn over, draw through two loops (three loops on hook).

Yarn over, draw through two loops (two loops on hook).

Yarn over, draw through two loops. One loop remains on hook. One treble crochet completed. At end of row chain four to turn. Continue as for double crochet but yarn over hook twice to make each stitch.

Slip Stitch

When directions say "join" always use a slip stitch.

Make a starting chain of 10 stitches. Insert hook through the two top threads of first chain made.

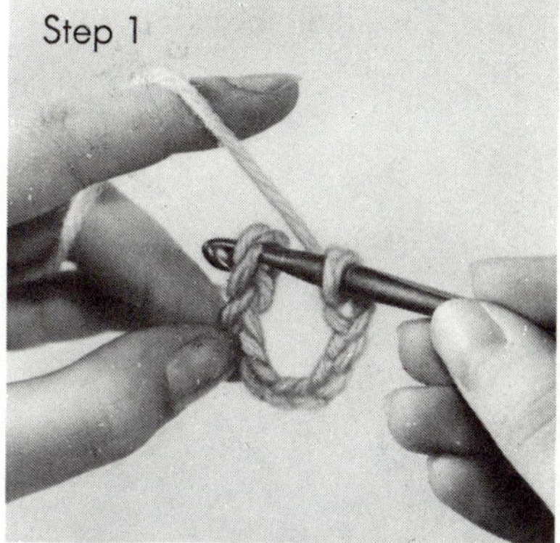

Yarn over and with one motion draw through stitch and loop on hook. This stitch is also used for straight rows of crochet and is often used as an edge stitch.

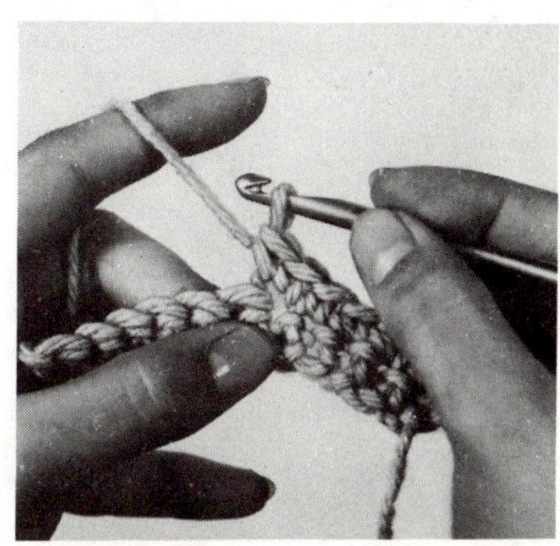

To Increase

Work two stitches in one stitch.

To Decrease Double Crochet

Work one double crochet to a point where two loops are on hook. Begin next double crochet in next stitch until there are four loops on hook.

Yarn over and draw through two loops, leaving three loops on hook.

Yarn over and draw through all three loops on hook. One loop remains on hook. One decrease made.

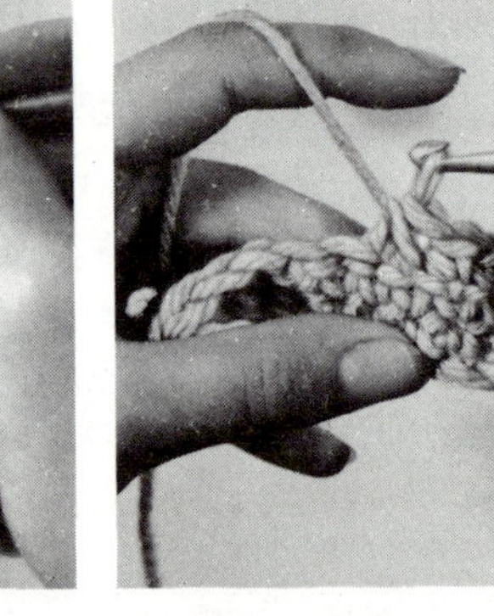

To Decrease Single Crochet

Work one single crochet to a point where there are two loops on hook. Draw up a loop in next stitch. Yarn over and draw through all three loops at once. One decrease made.

Finishing Crochet

Cut off yarn leaving about 6 inch (15,2 cm) end. Yarn over and draw yarn through last loop.

Pull yarn end to tighten and fasten the end. Thread end into a needle and work it back through edge. Cut off close to work. Work all other loose ends into a solid part of crochet to fasten it securely. If yarn end is not long enough to thread into a needle, use crochet hook to work the end in and out of the crochet.

Blocking

Blocking is the pressing or steaming of the crocheted pieces. Man-made fibers such as polyester or nylon often do not need blocking. The label on your yarn will usually tell you, or directions will say, "do not press," or simply, "steam press lightly". Also some mohairs and bulky yarns or designs with a raised pattern should not be blocked because they will lose their texture.

To block other materials, lay each piece separately on a padded surface, wrong side up. Using rust-proof pins, pin the edges to the board to the correct measurements. Cover with a damp cloth and press lightly. Leave pieces pinned until dry. After garment is assembled, steam seams and edges lightly.

Assembling

Right sides facing, pin together edges to be sewn. Some people prefer to baste edges together and try on before sewing. Thread a tapestry or yarn needle with matching yarn. There are several methods of joining. You can use an overcast stitch worked over the edges or a backstitch worked slightly in from the edge.

Backstitch is best for curved edges or if the edges are uneven.

You can also crochet your pieces together with slip stitching. Whatever method you use, leave stitches loose enough to match elasticity of crochet.

ADDITIONAL STITCHES

Afghan Stitch

The name implies this stitch is used only for afghans but it is very effective for baby clothes, sweaters, scarfs and other garments. Because afghan stitch forms squares, it is often embroidered with cross-stitch when completed. You will need a longer hook than regular crochet, called an afghan hook, in order to hold a number of stitches on the hook at one time.

To practice you can use a regular crochet hook. Make a starting chain of stitches for practice piece.

1st Row: Draw up a loop in second ch from hook, retaining all loops on hook. Draw up a loop in each ch across.

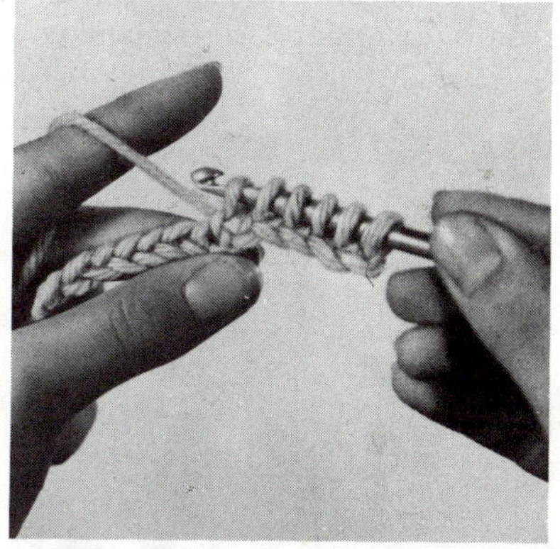

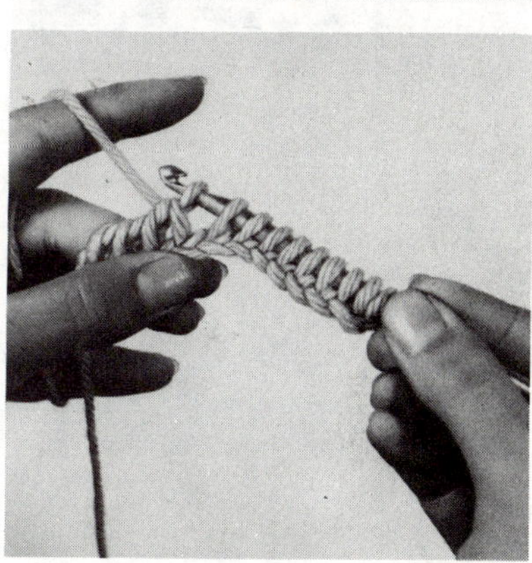

Now work off loops as follows: Yarn over, draw through one loop, * yarn over, draw through 2 loops; repeat from * across. One loop remains on hook. This is the first stitch of next row. Do not turn.

2nd Row: Retaining all loops on hook, draw up a loop in 2nd vertical bar (the front thread of the upright stitch) and in each vertical bar across to within last vertical bar. Insert hook in front thread of last vertical bar and the st directly behind it and draw up a loop. This gives a firm edge to this side. Work off loops as in first row. Repeat 2nd row until you

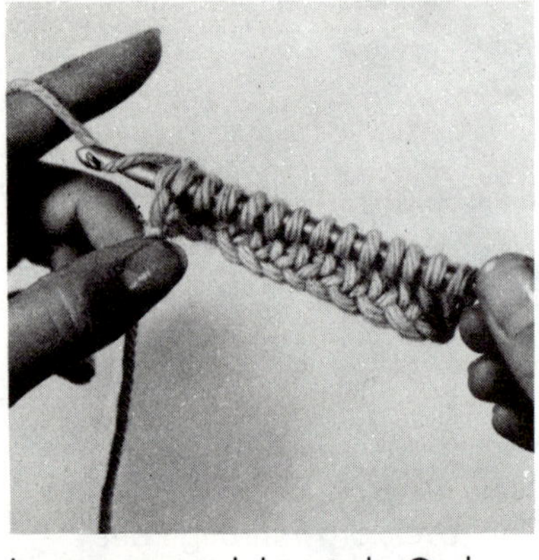

have mastered the stitch. On last row make a sl st in each vertical bar to keep edge from curling.

Granny Square

This stitch was used mostly for afghans or any straight sided item. Now you see it used for everything—skirts, hats, ponchos and even afghans again. It's fun to do, you can carry the squares around with you easily when making them and it's great for using leftover yarn. You can make the squares all of one color or change colors every round but it is usual to end the last round with the same color.

This square was made with one color. If you wish to make each round a different color, break off at end of each round and attach new color to any ch-3 corner sp for next round.

Starting at center, ch 5. Join with sl st to form ring.

1st Rnd: Ch 3, work 2 dc in ring (the ch-3 counts as one dc), ch 3, (work 3 dc in ring, ch 3) 3 times. Join with sl st to top of ch-3.

2nd Rnd: Sl st between each dc to next corner sp, ch 3, in same sp work 2 dc, ch 3 and 3 dc, (ch 1, work 3 dc, ch 3 and 3 dc in next corner sp) 3 times; ch 1. Join to top of ch-3.

3rd Rnd: Sl st between each dc to next corner sp, ch 3, in same sp work 2 dc, ch 3 and 3 dc, (ch 1, 3 dc in next ch-1 sp, ch 1, work 3 dc, ch 3 and 3 dc in next corner sp) 3 times; ch 1. Join to top of ch-3. Break off.

Shell Stitch

There are many varieties of shell stitch but once you learn this basic one others will be easy to follow. As the stitch is reversible, it is excellent for scarfs, afghans or any item where both sides will show.

Make a loose starting chain in multiples of 6 plus 3 extra for turning.

1st Row: Work 2 dc in 4th ch from hook (half shell made), sk 2 ch, sc in next ch, * sk 2 ch, work 5 dc in next ch (shell made), sk 2 ch, sc in next ch; repeat from * across, ending 3 dc in last ch (another half shell made). Ch 1, turn.

2nd Row: Sc in first dc, * sk 2 dc, work 5 dc (shell) in next sc, sk 2 dc, sc in center dc of next shell; repeat from * across, ending sc in top of half shell. Ch 3, turn.

3rd Row: Work 2 dc in first sc, * sc in center dc of next shell, shell in next sc; repeat from * across, ending 3 dc in last sc. Ch 1, turn. Repeat 2nd and 3rd rows for pattern.

PROJECT INSTRUCTIONS

TEA COZY AND TRAY COVER

(shown on page 2)

Sizes: Tea Cozy—12 x 15" (30,5 x 38 cm);
Tray Cover—24 x 15" (61 x 38 cm)

MATERIALS: 7/8 yd. (0,80 m) linen at least 45" (115 cm) wide; 3/8 yd. (0,35 m) fabric for tea cozy lining; quilt batting; J. & P. Coats Deluxe Six Strand Floss: 2 skeins each #109 Dark Willow Green and #1 White; 1 skein each #124 Indian Pink, #120 Crimson, #140 Signal Red, #5-A Chartreuse, #215 Apple Green, #216 Avocado, #223 Sun Gold, #51-C Gold Brown and #81 Dark Brown; 1 yd. (0,95 m) decorative cord.

DIRECTIONS: Cut two pieces of linen, each 13½" (34,2 cm) high x 16" (40,5 cm) wide, for front and back of tea cozy; cut one piece 25¼ x 16¼" (64,1 x 41,1 cm) for tray cover.

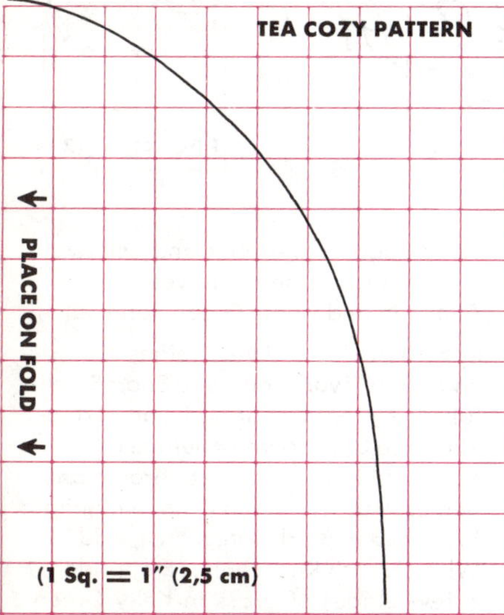

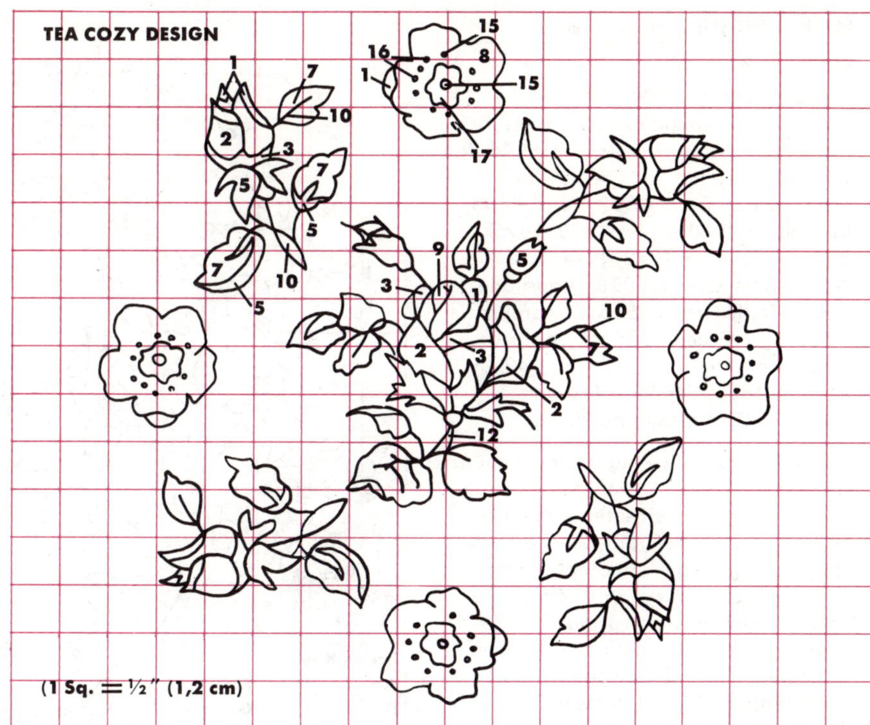

Tea cozy: Enlarge and transfer tea cozy design onto front section of tea cozy 3½" (9 cm) from lower edge and centered from side to side. Work embroidery with three strands of floss. Use the photograph on page 2 and the diagram above as guides for stitch and color placement. Stitches are shown on pages 22-27; Long and Short Stitch is on page 79. Press and block embroidery as directed on page 28.

Enlarge tea cozy pattern, left. Cut out front and back, adding ½" (1,2 cm) seam allowance around curved edge and 1" (2,5 cm) hem allowance at lower edge. Be sure to center embroidered design on front. Using same pattern, cut two pieces each of lining and batting, omitting hem allowance. For front, sandwich batting between lining and outer fabric, matching curved edges; baste around all edges. Repeat for back. With right sides together, pin front to back, matching edges. Stitch around curve ½" (1,2 cm) from edge. Trim seam and notch curve. Clean-finish lower edge of linen; then turn up along hemline and slipstitch to lining. Turn right side out. On outside, sew decorative cord along seam, forming a loop at center top.

Tray cover: Enlarge tray design. To transfer design to linen, have one short edge of fabric facing you; place design 2½" (6,3 cm) from that edge and 1¼" (3,2 cm) from sides. Transfer design to other short edge the same way. Using three strands of floss, work embroidery, following the diagram below and the photograph on page 2. Finish embroidery as directed on page 28. Clean finish raw edges. Turn up 3/8" (1 cm) hem all around, mitering corners if desired; slipstitch or machine-stitch in place.

Color and Stitch Key

Long and Short or Satin Stitch
1—Indian Pink
2—Crimson
3—Signal Red
4—Chartreuse
5—Dark Willow Green
6—Apple Green
7—Avocado
8—White

Stem Stitch
9—Indian Pink
10—Dark Willow Green
11—Apple Green
12—Avocado
13—Gold Brown
14—Dark Brown

French Knots
15—Sun Gold
16—Gold Brown

Straight Stitch
17—Chartreuse
18—Dark Brown

FLORAL PICTURE (shown on page 2)

Size: 16 x 16" (40,5 x 40,5 cm)

MATERIALS: 20 x 20" (51 x 51 cm) piece of homespun-type embroidery fabric; Coats & Clark's Red Heart® Persian Type Needlepoint and Crewel Yarn: 1 skein each Lt. Coral #852, Coral #843, Cranberry #810, Violet #650, Royal Blue #740, Blue #742, Pale Blue #781, Blue Green #028, Aquatone #032, Bottle Green #505, Chartreuse #550, Fern Green #555, Lt. Mustard #457, Canary #458, Mustard #427, Apricot #853, Copper #416 and Brown #405; tapestry needle.

DIRECTIONS: Following the instructions on pages 20 and 21, enlarge and transfer the design to the center of the fabric. Using one strand of yarn, work embroidery, referring to the photograph on page 2 and the diagram shown here. Stitch diagrams are on pages 22-27, 78 and 79. Letters on design diagram indicate stitches to be used. In addition, work leaf and flower stems in Stem Stitch, varying occasionally with Backstitch or Chain Stitch. Work small leaf and flower veins in Straight Stitch and large veins in Backstitch. Work dots and small circles in French Knots. Work large center flower in Copper and Lt. Mustard, with Bottle Green, Chartreuse and Cranberry center. Work the large flower directly above it in Violet, Pale Blue and Royal Blue, with Mustard and Lt. Mustard center. Work the large flower to the left of these two in Lt. Coral, Coral, Apricot, Royal Blue and Lt. Mustard. Work the large flower to the right in Coral and Cranberry. Outline the two pointed lilies in Apricot, using Pale Blue, Blue Green and Coral for their centers.

Two flowers are worked in Blanket Stitch—the one near center top in Violet, Canary and Aqua; the one on the left in Royal Blue, Blue and Pale Blue, with a Chartreuse base. For remaining flowers and leaves, use the photograph on page 2 as a guide. Work the bowl in Brown, Apricot and Copper and the base in Brown, Violet and Canary.

FINISHING: Press and block the completed embroidery (see page 28). Frame as desired.

FLY STITCH

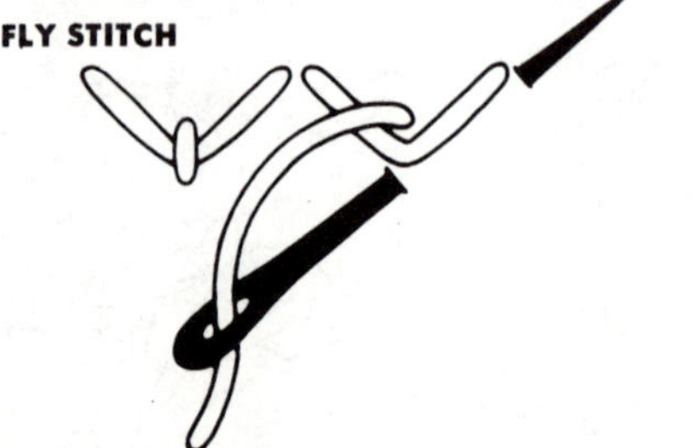

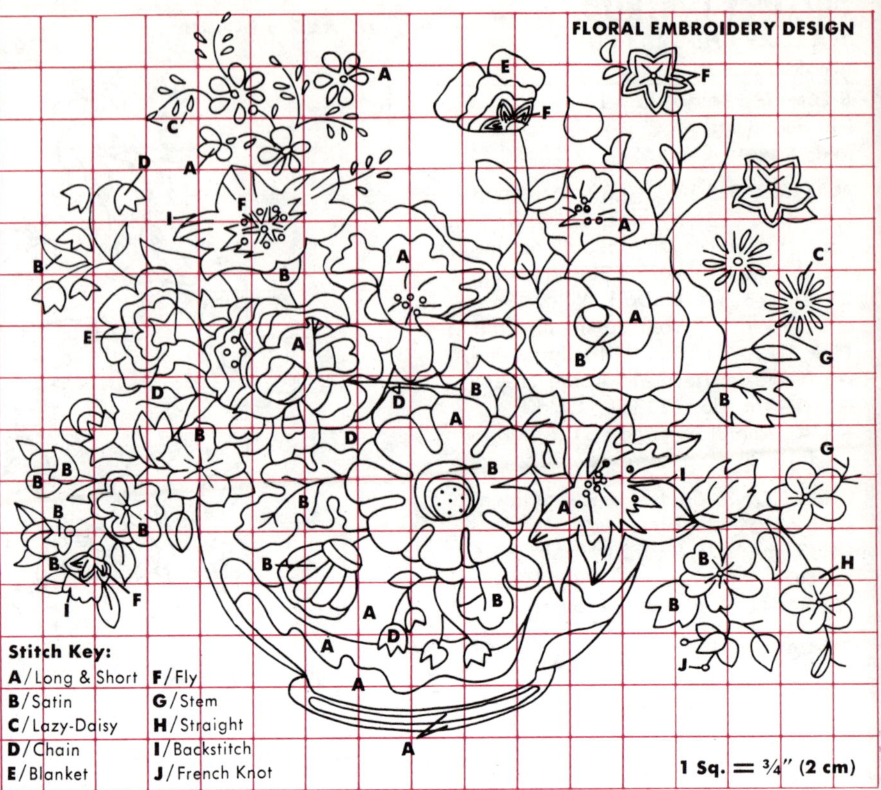

RABBIT PILLOW (shown on page 3)

Size: 14 x 14" (35,5 x 35,5 cm)

MATERIALS: 1 yd. (0,95 m) medium-weave cotton fabric; Paterna Persian Yarn: 1 skein each Kelly Green, Lt. Avocado, Apple Green, Yellow, White, Black, Orange, Gold, Lt. Beige, Dk. Beige, Med. Brown and Dk. Brown; six-strand embroidery floss: 1 skein each Avocado, Med. Pink, Dk. Pink, Lavender and Purple; thread to match fabric; 1⅝ yds. (1,50 m) ¼" (6 mm) diameter cable cord; 12" (30,5 cm) zipper; 14" (35,5 cm) square knife-edge pillow form.

DIRECTIONS: Cut pillow top 15 x 15" (38 x 38 cm). Enlarge and transfer rabbit design (see pages 20 and 21) to center of top. For embroidery, use 4 strands of floss or 1 strand of Persian yarn. Using the photograph on page 3 as a guide, work embroidery as follows (stitches opposite and on pages 22-27):

Grass—Avocado Stem Stitch, Kelly Green Straight Stitch and Apple Green Backstitch.

Ferns—Avocado Stem Stitch with French Knot at tip of each leaf.

Flowers—Tiny wildflowers: White French Knots. Clover blossoms: Med. Pink and Dk. Pink Straight Stitch radiating from stem; stems and leaves in Apple Green Backstitch and Lazy-Daisy Stitch. Violets: Lavender Straight Stitch radiating from center; add Purple veins and Yellow French knot centers. Leaves: Lt. Avocado and Apple Green Satin Stitch.

Rabbit—Using Browns, Beiges, Gold and White, work Long and Short Stitches, following contours of body, head and ears. Use Dk. Brown to outline and define, filling in with Med. Brown and Beiges. Use White and Gold to highlight. Work eye in Black Satin Stitch; add White French Knot center. Embroider a few blades of grass in Kelly Green Straight Stitch, overlapping rabbit's body. Work tail closely in Cut Turkey Work, starting in center with White and continuing around with Gold, Lt. and Dk. Beige. Trim tail carefully to leave a nicely shaped tuft.

Butterfly—Upper wings in Orange Satin Stitch, outlined in Black Blanket Stitch; lower wing in Yellow Satin Stitch, outlined in Black Stem Stitch; body in Black Straight Stitch; head a single Black French Knot.

FINISHING: Press and block pillow top as directed for embroidery, page 28. For back, cut two fabric pieces, each 8 x 15" (20,5 x 38 cm). Cut enough 1½" (3,8 cm) wide bias strips to fit around top when pieced. Make welting by encasing cord in bias strips and stitching with zipper foot; trim seam allowances to ½" (1,2 cm), if necessary. Matching raw edges, pin welting to right side of pillow top, overlapping and tapering ends into seam allowance at bottom edge. Machine-baste, using zipper foot. For pillow back with zipper, join two long edges with a ½" (1,2 cm) seam, stitching only 1½" (3,8 cm) at each end. Machine-baste the zipper opening. Following package instructions, insert a centered zipper. *Open zipper.* With right sides together, pin pillow top to back. Using zipper foot, stitch a ½" (1,2 cm) seam all around. Turn right side out and insert form.

CUT TURKEY WORK

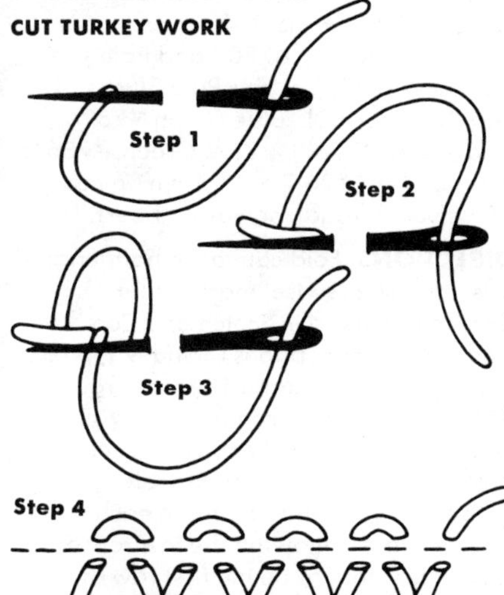

LONG AND SHORT STITCH

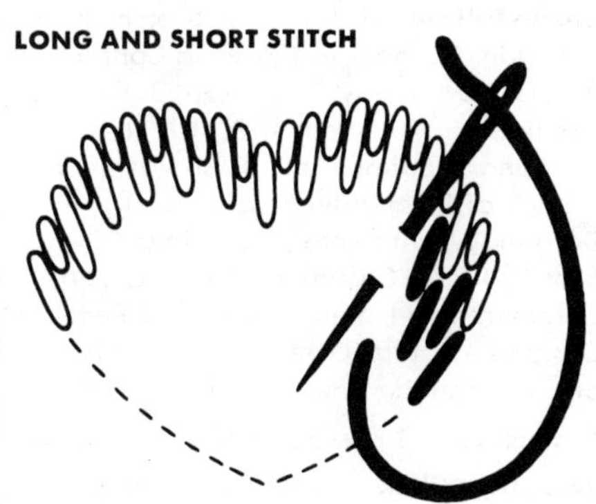

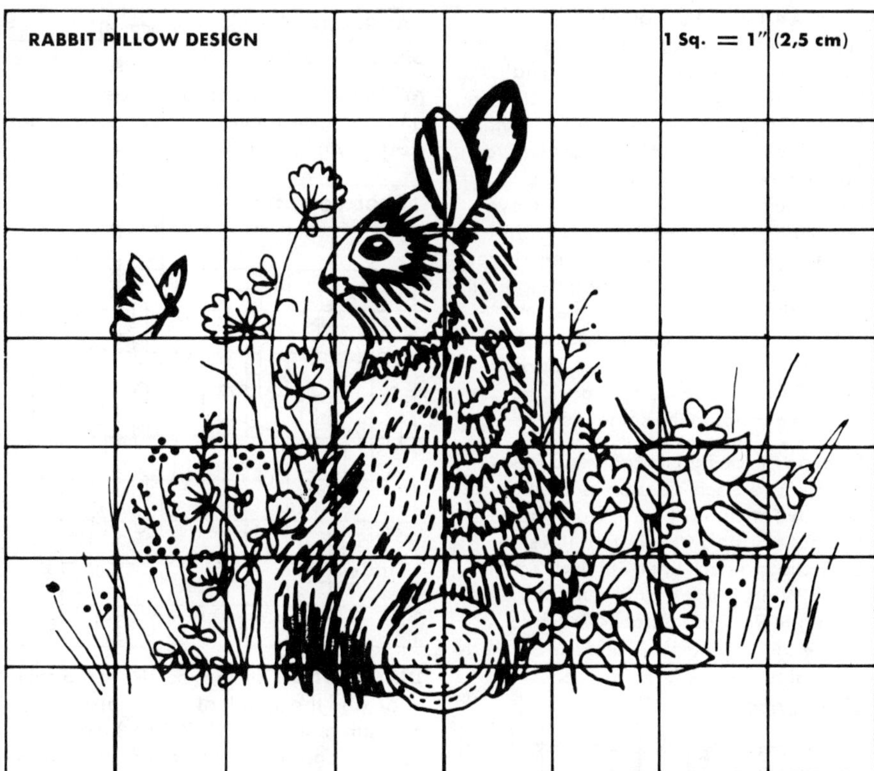

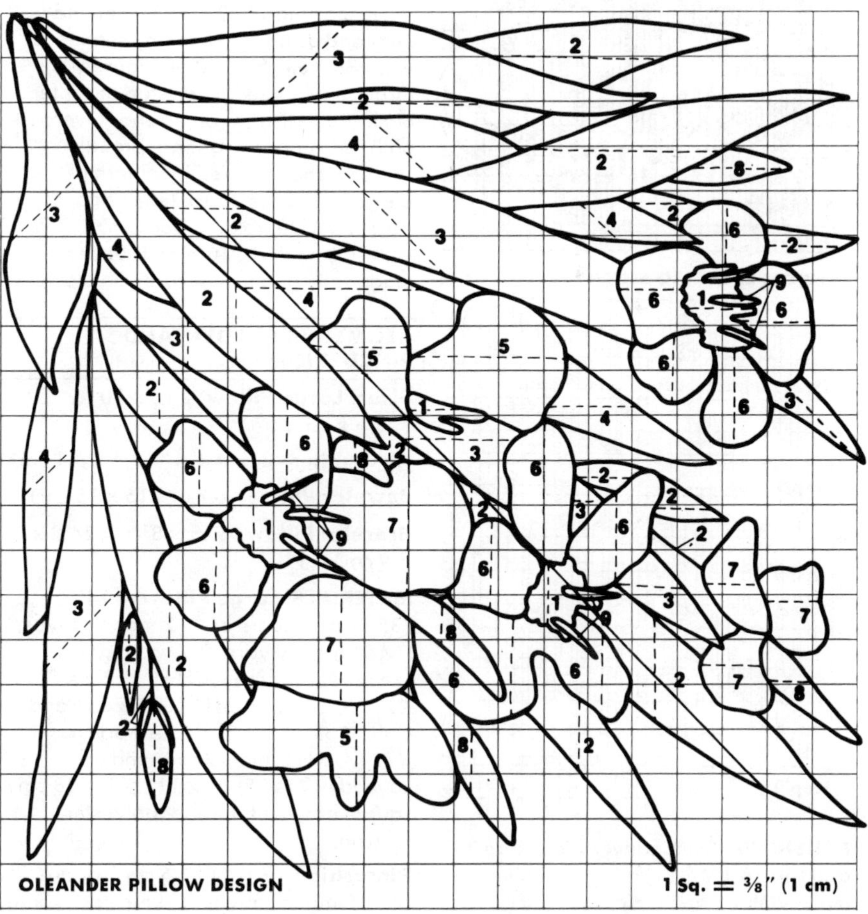

Color Key **1**/Yellow **2**/Pale Olive **3**/Medium Green **4**/Pine Green **5**/Peach **6**/Pale Pink **7**/Medium Pink **8**/Darker Pink **9**/Red

OLEANDER PILLOW (shown on page 3)

Size: 16 x 16" (40,5 x 40, 5 cm)

MATERIALS: ⅝ yd. (0,60 m) #14 mono canvas; Paterna Persian Yarn: 5 skeins White; 4 skeins Pale Olive, 3 skeins Medium Green, 2 skeins Darker Pink, and 1 skein each Pale Pink, Medium Pink, Yellow, Peach, Red, and Pine Green; ¾ yd. (0,70 m) velvet; 2 yds. (1,85 m) ¼" (6 mm) diameter cable cord; 14" (35,5 cm) zipper; thread to match velvet; 16" (40,5 cm) square knife-edge pillow form.

DIRECTIONS: Cut canvas 20 x 20" (51 x 51 cm). Mark off 16 x 16"

(40,5 x 40,5 cm) design area in center; tape edges. To divide canvas into quarters for the design, fold it in half lengthwise and then crosswise, creasing firmly. Open the canvas. Using a waterproof marker, mark the creases *between*, not on top of, the parallel threads. Place the canvas in front of you at eye level with one corner facing you. Shift it until you can clearly see the ridges formed by the mesh, running diagonally across the canvas. Using a ruler and marker, mark the diagonal through the intersection of the other marked lines. Turn the canvas and mark the other diagonal in the same way.

Enlarge the design to transfer it (see page 7) to each quarter of the canvas. With two strands of yarn, work the design in Satin Stitch. Dotted lines on diagram indicate Satin Stitch direction. Work White background (unnumbered areas) in Random Bargello Stitch so it extends one mesh beyond the marked-off design area.

SATIN STITCH

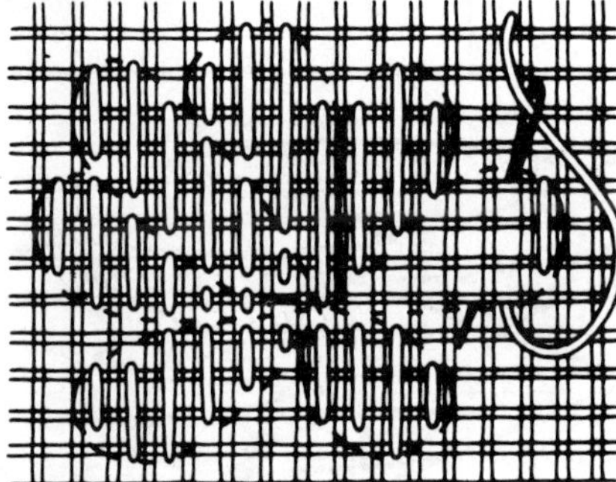

RANDOM BARGELLO STITCH

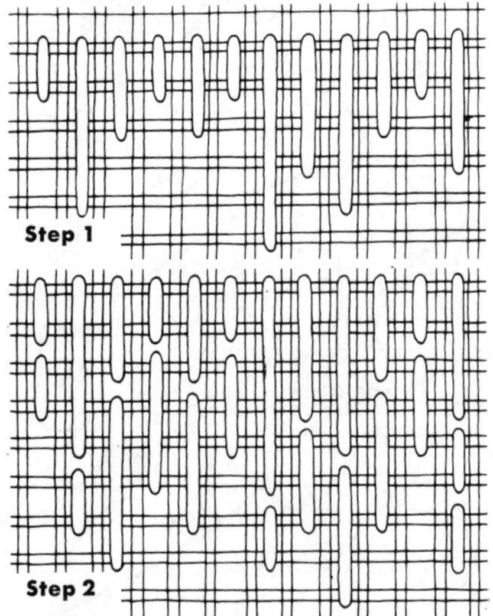

FINISHING: Block canvas (see page 28) and trim to 17" (43 cm). From velvet, make welting and a zippered back as directed for Rabbit Pillow, Finishing (page 78), but cut the back pieces 9 x 17" (23 x 43 cm); assemble pillow.

BARGELLO BELT (shown on page 4)

Size: 7/8" (2,2 cm) wide

MATERIALS: #12 mono canvas; remnants of tapestry yarn; 1" (2,5 cm) wide clasp-style belt buckle.

BARGELLO STITCH

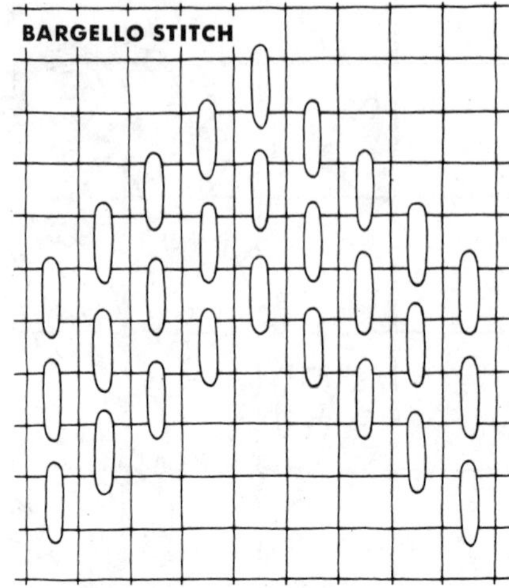

DIRECTIONS: Cut canvas 2 5/8" (6,5 cm) wide and the length of your waist measurement plus 3" (7,5 cm). Fold canvas lengthwise into thirds so that belt is 9 meshes wide. Mark the center back. Starting 1" (2,5 cm) from one end, and using colors in any sequence, work Bargello Stitch (see diagram) through all three layers; stop at center back. Repeat from other end. Overcast both long edges, working through same meshes covered by outermost Bargello Stitches. Block (see page 28). Attach buckle, folding back 1 1/2" (3,8 cm) on ends. Turn ends under diagonally and tack securely in place.

GEOMETRIC PILLOWS AND PINCUSHION (shown on page 4)

Sizes: Large Pillow — 10 x 10" (25,5 x 25,5 cm)

Pincushion—3 1/4 x 3 1/4" (8,1 x 8,1 cm)

Jewelry Pillow—6 x 6" (15 x 15 cm)

Bracelet Pillow—9 1/2 x 3 1/2" (24,2 x 8,9 cm)

MATERIALS: Large Pillow — 14" (35,5 cm) square of #12 mono canvas; DMC tapestry yarn, 8.7 yd. (8,0 m) skeins: 5 Burgundy #7115, 3 Rose #7135, 2 each Blue Green #7861 and Light Violet #7895, 1 Pale Apricot #7917, 5 Fuschia #7155, and 6 Lavender #7255; 11 x 11" (28 x 28 cm) square of velvet; thread; polyester fiberfill.

Pincushion—7 1/4" (18,6 cm) square of #10 mono canvas; 1 skein each same colors as Large Pillow, omitting Rose and Lavender, plus 2 extra skeins Burgundy; 4 1/4 x 4 1/4" (10,6 x 10,6 cm) square of velvet; thread; polyester fiberfill.

Jewelry Pillow—10" (25,5 cm) square #10 mono canvas; DMC tapestry yarns: 2 skeins each Navy #7307, Teal #7860 and Light Teal #7595; 3 each Blue Gray #7593, Bright Blue #7995 and Aqua #7952; 1 skein each Pale Apricot #7917 and Pale Blue #7800; 7" (18 cm) square of velvet; thread; polyester fiberfill.

Bracelet Pillow—13 1/2 x 7 1/2" (34,2 x 19,2 cm) piece of #10 mono canvas; DMC tapestry yarns: 1 skein each Teal #7860, Turquoise #7807 and Pale Apricot #7917; 2 skeins Pale Blue #7800; 3 each Dk. Blue Green #7596 and Aqua #7952; 4 Blue Green #7861; 10 1/2 x 4 1/2" (26,7 x 11,4 cm) piece of velvet; thread; polyester fiberfill.

DIRECTIONS: Fold canvas in half lengthwise, then crosswise; mark center. Design is worked in Scotch and Continental Stitches (pages 13 and 9), plus Cashmere Stitch (page 11) for Large Pillow. Starting at center, follow chart and color key opposite to work center motif in Scotch Stitch. For Bracelet Pillow, work another motif on each side of center, allowing the last row of the center motif to be the first row of the motifs on either side. Work succeeding rows around center motifs as follows.

Large Pillow —1 Burgundy Scotch, 1 Lavender Cashmere, 1 Fuschia Continental, 1 Burgundy Cashmere, 1 Fuschia Continental, 3 Lavender Scotch, 1 Burgundy Continental, 1 Rose Cashmere, 1 each of Burgundy, Fuschia and Burgundy Continental, 1 Lt. Violet Scotch, 1 Rose Cashmere, 1 Blue Green Continental, 3 Lavender Scotch, 1 Rose Cashmere, 1 Blue Green Continental and 2 Burgundy Continental rows.

Pincushion—1 row Burgundy Continental.

Jewelry Pillow—1 row each of Navy, Pale Blue, and Aqua Continental, 1 each Lt. Teal, Teal, and Bright Blue Scotch, 1 Pale Apricot Continental.

Bracelet Pillow—1 row Turquoise Continental.

FINISHING: Block finished needlepoint (see page 28). Trim canvas to within 1/2" (1,2 cm) of the design. With right sides together, pin velvet to canvas and stitch a 1/2" (1,2 cm) seam, leaving an opening for turning. Trim corners, turn right side out and stuff firmly. Slipstitch opening.

Tassels: Make 4 tassels as follows. Large Pillow—1 skein Fuschia per tassel; Pincushion—1/2 skein Burgundy per tassel; Jewelry Pillow—1/2 skein Aqua per tassel; Bracelet Pillow—½ skein Blue Green per tassel. Wind yarn around a 3½" (9 cm) wide strip of cardboard. Thread a needle with a strand of yarn and run it under the yarn along one edge of cardboard; remove needle and tie yarn firmly. Cut yarn along other edge; remove cardboard. To form a "head," wrap another strand around tassel a few times, ½" (1,2 cm) from knot, and use the needle to run the end into the wrapping. Sew tassels to corners.

Color Key

LARGE PILLOW; PINCUSHION		JEWELRY PILLOW	BRACELET PILLOW
⊠	Fuschia	Blue Gray	Turquoise
▲●	Burgundy	Navy	Teal
■	Pale Apricot	Pale Apricot	Pale Apricot
○	Fuschia	Blue Gray	Pale Blue
▲	Lt. Violet	Bright Blue	Blue Green
⬡	Burgundy	Navy	Dk. Blue Green
●	Blue Green	Lt. Teal	Aqua
⊙	Lt. Violet	Bright Blue	Pale Blue
△	Fuschia	Blue Gray	Teal
◩	Pale Apricot	Pale Apricot	Dk.Blue Green
⊗	Burgundy	Navy	Pale Apricot

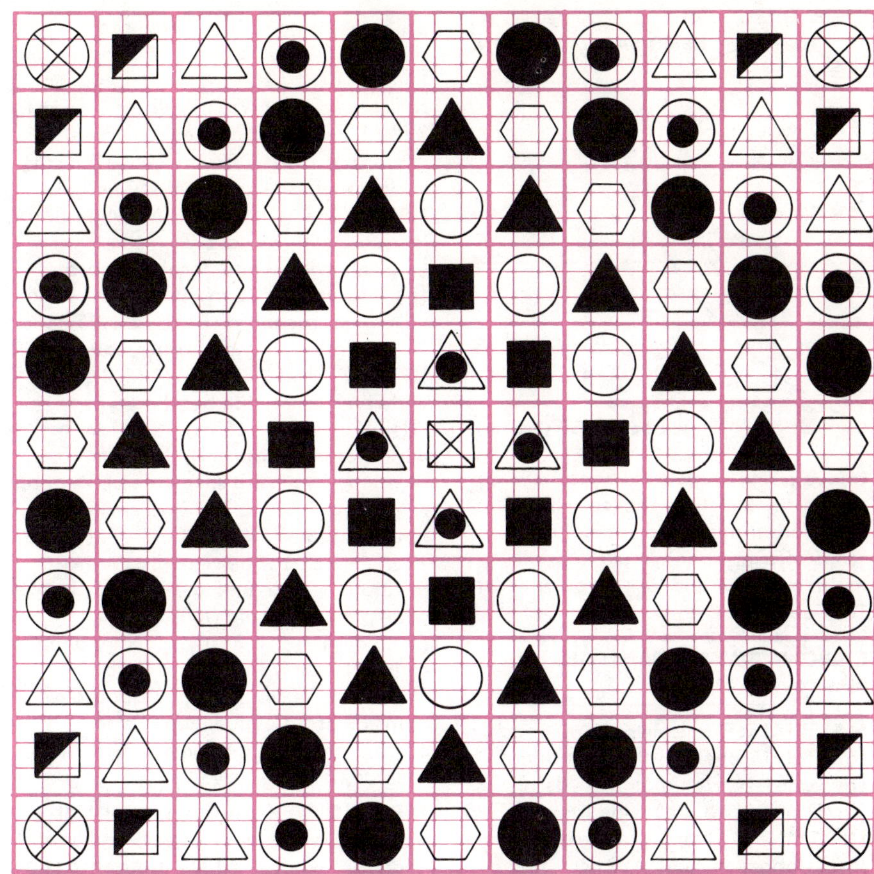

PASTEL PILLOW (shown on page 29)

Size: 14 x 14" (35,5 x 35,5 cm)

MATERIALS: ½ yd. (0,50m) lightweight fusible interfacing, ½ yd. (0,50 m) satin fabric for pillow back; 14" (35,5 cm) square knife-edge pillow form; ⅝" (1,5 cm) wide Offray polyester satin ribbon, as follows: 5 yds. (4,60 m) Wedgewood (A); 4¼ yds. (3,95 m) Iris (B); 3½ yds. (3,25 m) each Aqua (C), Light Orchid (D) and Misty Turquoise (E).

DIRECTIONS: Cut ribbon into 15" (38 cm) lengths as follows: 12 A, 10 B, and 8 each C, D, and E. Cut fusible interfacing 15 x 15" (38 x 38 cm) and place it fusible side up on the ironing board. Following the weaving method described on page 36, weave ribbons over the interfacing in this order: A, B, C, D, E, A, B, C, D, E, A, B, A, E, D, C, B, A, E, D, C, B, A. Fuse in place, following the interfacing manufacturer's directions.

FINISHING: Cut pillow back fabric 15 x 15" (38 x 38 cm). With right sides together, pin top to back. Stitch them together with a ½" (1,2 cm) seam, leaving a 10" (25,5 cm) opening for turning. Trim corners. Turn right side out, insert pillow form and slipstitch the opening.

SQUARE SACHET (shown on page 29)

Size: 6 x 6" (15 x 15 cm)

MATERIALS: 1¼ yds. (1,20 m) ¾" (2 cm) wide floral jacquard ribbon; 1¾ yds. (1,60 m) ⅜" (1 cm) wide picot-edged satin ribbon; 6 x 6" (15 x 15 cm) piece satin to match ribbon and lightweight fusible interfacing, 1½ yds. (1,45 m) 1" (2,5 cm) wide picot-edged taffeta ribbon; polyester fiberfill or potpourri.

DIRECTIONS: Cut floral ribbon into 7 strips and satin ribbon into 10 strips, each 6" (15 cm) long. Place interfacing fusible side up on ironing board. Arrange the floral ribbon vertically, sides touching, over interfacing. Without overlapping the picots, weave the satin ribbon over and under the vertical strips. Anchor with pins as described on page 36; then fuse. Cut taffeta ribbon 50" (127 cm) long. Join ends with a French seam. Gather one edge to form a ruffle that fits around ribbon weaving. With right sides together, pin the gathered edge of the ruffle to the edge of the ribbon weaving; machine baste. With right sides together, stitch front to satin back in ½" (1,2 cm) seam, leaving an opening for turning. Turn and stuff with fiberfill to which you've added a few drops of cologne, or with potpourri.

HEART SACHET (shown on page 29)

Size: about 4 x 5" (10 x 12,5 cm)

MATERIALS: 3½ yds. (3,20 m) ⅛" (3 mm) wide Offray polyester satin ribbon in each of three shades of pink; 5½ x 5½" (14 x 14 cm) piece satin or taffeta fabric to match ribbon and lightweight fusible interfacing; ½ yd. (0,50 m) ½" (1,2 cm) wide pregathered lace trim; small floral appliqué; polyester fiberfill or potpourri.

DIRECTIONS: Cut ribbon into 66 pieces, each 5½" (14 cm) long. Save remainder. Place interfacing fusible side up on ironing board. Over interfacing, arrange 44 strips vertically with sides touching, alternating colors. Anchor as described on page 36. Leaving ⅛" (3 mm) spaces between ribbons, weave remaining strips horizontally over and under vertical strips, alternating colors. Save any leftover strips. Anchor as described on page 36; fuse.

FINISHING: Enlarge heart pattern (see pages 20-21) and place on weaving so ribbons run diagonally; cut out. Using same pattern, cut satin back. With right sides together, pin front to back. Stitch a ½" (1,2 cm) seam, leaving an opening for turning. Trim, clip, and notch seam. Turn right side out and press. Stuff with fiberfill to which you've

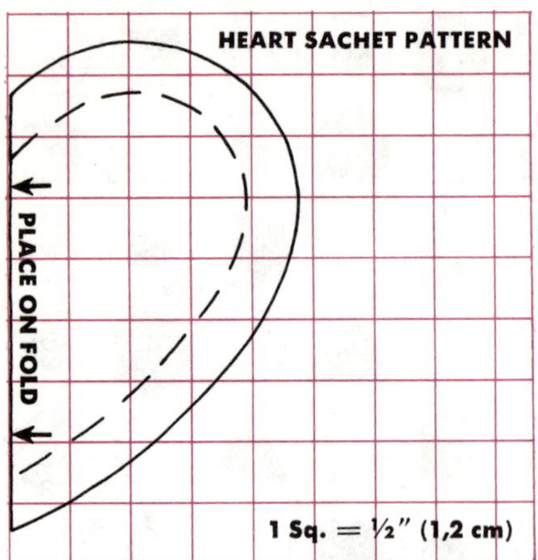

added a few drops of cologne, or with potpourri. Slipstitch the opening. Slipstitch lace trim around edge of heart. From leftover ribbon, make a small multi-loop bow and tack to top of heart. Tack appliqué over bow.

RIBBON-TRIMMED CAMISOLE

(shown on page 29)

MATERIALS: Camisole pattern; peach satin fabric for camisole (see pattern envelope); approximately 3 yds. (2,75 m) ⅜" (1 cm) wide Iris and 1 yd. (0,95 m) ⅜" (1 cm) wide Orchid satin ribbons; thread to match ribbons.

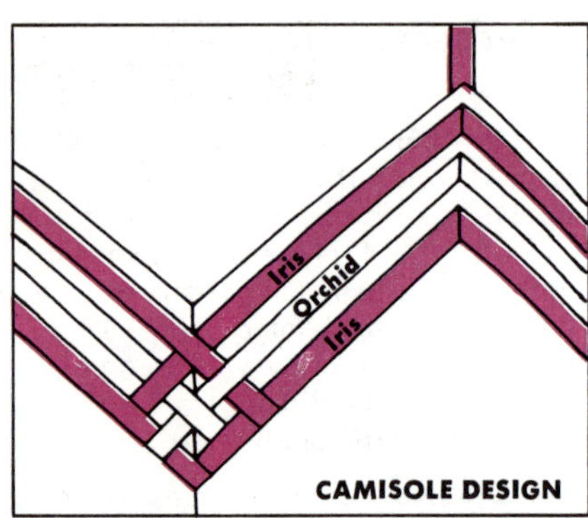

DIRECTIONS: Using the strap pattern piece, cut two lengths of Iris ribbon for straps and set aside. Following diagram, arrange remaining ribbons on camisole front; miter corners and, at center, weave ribbons and turn ends under. Pin, then stitch ribbons in place along both edges, using matching thread. Assemble camisole as your pattern directs, using the ribbon set aside for straps.

WICKER SERVING TRAY

(shown on page 29)

Size: Our tray is 21 x 14½" (53,5 x 36,7 cm) overall with inside dimensions of 18½ x 12½" (47,2 x 31,7 cm).

MATERIALS: (requirements may vary with tray size): Wicker tray; white spray paint; assorted ribbons: We used 14 different Offray ribbons. 1¾ yds. (1,65 m) ⅞" (2,2 cm) wide dotted hot pink grosgrain (A); 1½ yds. (1,45 m) ⅞" (2,2 cm) wide dotted pink grosgrain (B); ¾ yd. (,70 m) 1½" (3,8 cm) wide dotted pink grosgrain (C); 1 yd. (,95 m) 1¼" (3,1 cm) wide white floral jacquard (D); ¾ yd. (,70 m) ⅞" (2,2 cm) wide white floral jacquard (E); 1¼ yds. (1,20 m) ¾" (2 cm) wide mini-floral jacquard (F); 1 yd. (,95 m) ¾" (2 cm) wide pink floral jacquard (G); 1¼ yds. (1,20 m) ½" (1,2 cm) wide pink and white beading-type (H); 1¾ yds. (1,65 m) ½" (1,2 cm) wide hot pink satin (I); 1¾ yds. (1,65 m) 1½" (3,8 cm) wide pink satin (J); ½ yd. (,50 m) ½" (1,2 cm) wide pink gingham taffeta (K); 1 yd. (,95 m) 1½" (3,8 cm) wide pink gingham taffeta (L); 1 yd. (,95 m) 1½" (3,8 cm) wide pink grosgrain (M); 2 yds. (1,85 m) 1½" (3,8 cm) wide hot pink satin (N); ¾ yd. (,70 m) fusible interfacing; fusible web; cardboard to fit inside of tray; glue; heavy clear acetate or 1/16" (1,5 mm) thick acrylic sheet to fit inside tray.

DIRECTIONS: If desired, spray-paint your tray white, applying several light coats. Allow drying time after each coat. Cut interfacing to fit inside of tray. Place interfacing fusible side up, on ironing board. Following diagram, cut and arrange ribbons A-M over interfacing, anchoring with pins as described on page 36. Start by placing ribbons that run in one direction. Then weave those that run in the opposite direction and anchor them with pins. When all ribbons are woven in place, fuse. Trim ends of ribbons even with edge of interfacing. Cut ribbon N to fit around edge of weaving as a border, allowing for mitering at corners. Cut fusible web strips the same width and length. Using web as manufacturer directs, fuse ribbon border in place. Glue ribbon weaving to cardboard; insert in tray. Insert acetate or acrylic over ribbon weaving.

CLUTCH PURSE

(shown on page 30)

Size: about 5 x 8" (12,5 x 20,5 cm)

MATERIALS: J. & P. Coats Deluxe Six Strand Floss: 1 skein each Crimson #120, Lt. Cardinal #143, Beauty Pink #65, Lt. Steel Blue #69, Baby Blue #7-A, Avocado #216, Chartreuse #5-A, Yellow #9, Sun Gold #223, and Gold Brown #51-C; 12 x 20" (30,5 x 51 cm) piece each of even-weave fabric with 21 threads per inch (8 per cm), matching lining and nonwoven interfacing; thread to match fabric; 1 yd. (0,95 m) decorative cord.

DIRECTIONS: Mark the lengthwise center of the fabric with hand basting. Using 3 strands of floss in a tapestry needle throughout, work Cross-stitch embroidery design (see pages 34-35) following the chart. **NOTE:** each square on chart equals 2 threads of fabric. The large arrow shows the center of the design, which should line up with the basting stitches. Begin working at small arrow, 1¼" (3,2 cm) from lower edge of fabric and 5 threads to the right of center. When design is complete, press piece as directed on page 28.

FINISHING: To make a pattern for purse, enlarge the pattern diagram as described on pages 20-21, tracing broken foldlines as well. Using this pattern, cut out purse shape (centering the curved flap section over the embroidery), interfacing and lining. Matching

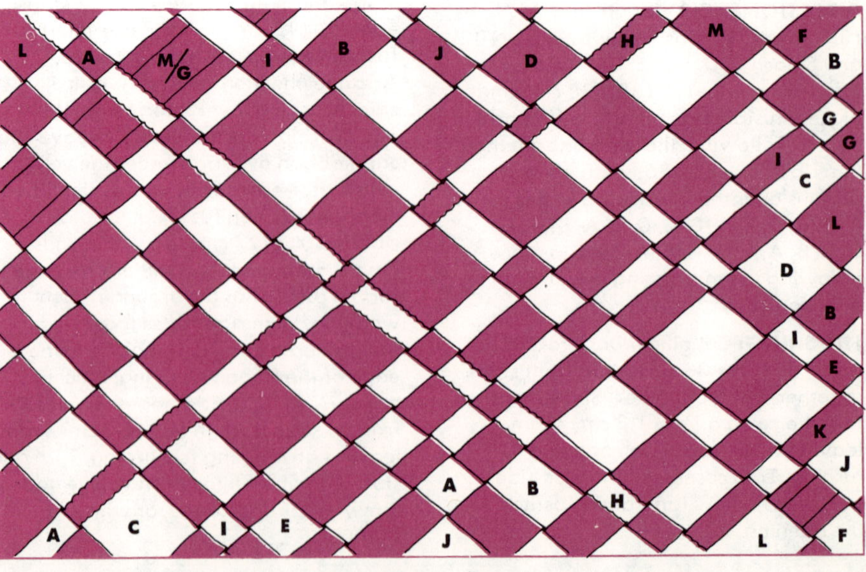

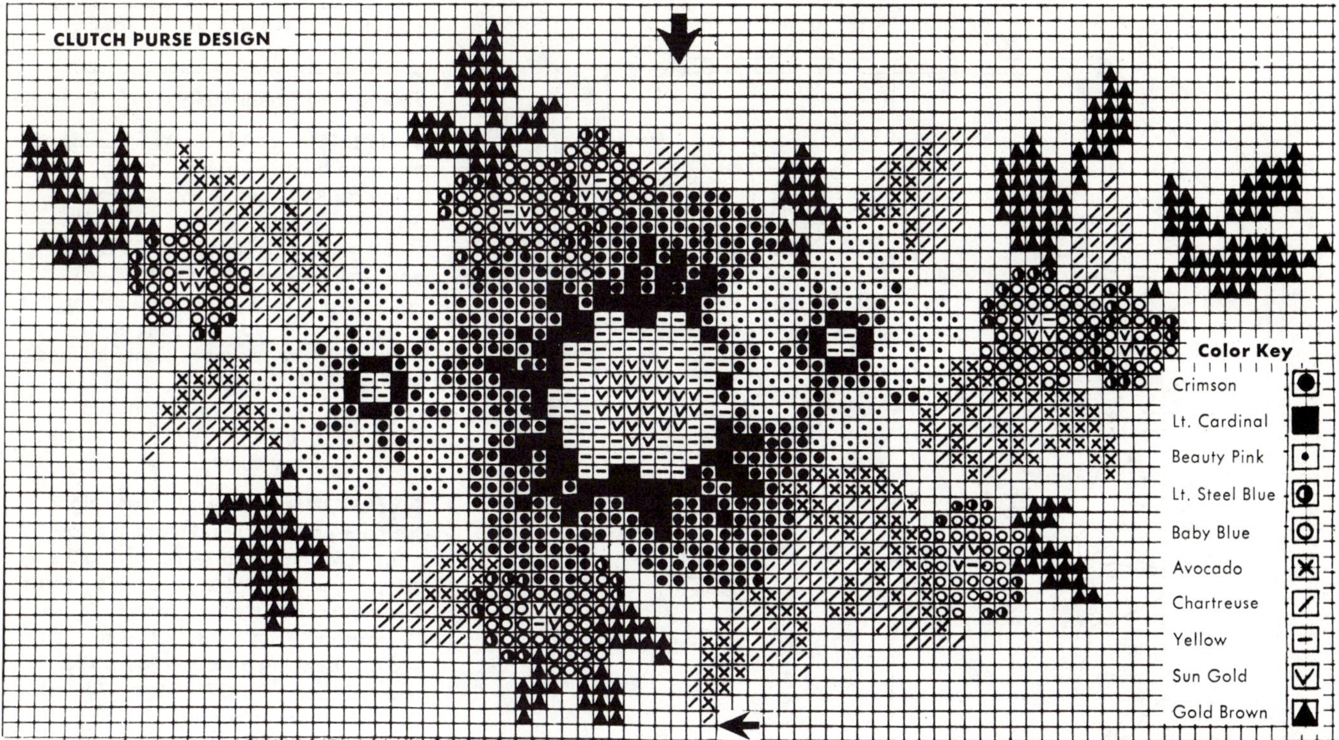

edges, baste interfacing to wrong side of lining. Then, with right sides together, pin lining to purse shape and stitch a 5/8" (1,5 cm) seam, leaving an opening for turning along short straight edge. Trim seams and corners and notch the curve; press seam open. Turn right side out, press, and slipstitch opening closed. Fold straight end up along foldline so it meets other foldline. Whipstitch the side edges together securely. Sew decorative cord to side and flap edges and add a snap for fastening if desired.

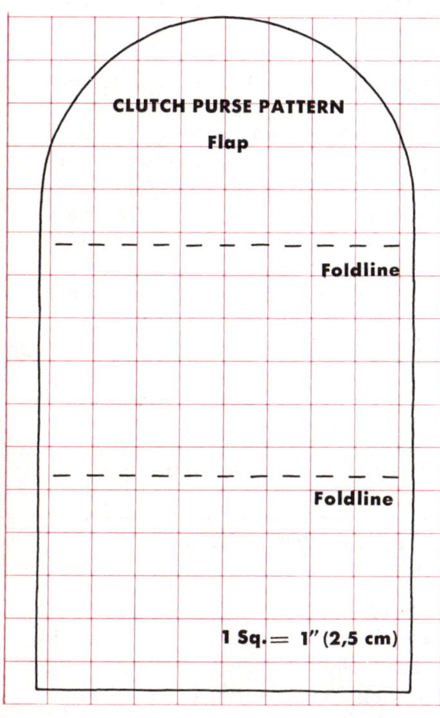

PLACEMAT, NAPKIN AND COASTER

(shown on page 30)

Sizes: Placemat—18½ x 13" (47 x 33 cm); **Napkin**—16 x 16" (40,5 x 40,5 cm); **Coaster**—4½ x 4½" (11,2 x 11,2 cm).

MATERIALS: (for 1 of each): ½ yd. (0,50 m) even-weave fabric, at least 36" (90 cm) wide, with 20 threads to the inch (8 per cm); DMC Six-strand Cotton Embroidery Floss: 1 skein Spring Green #907 and 2 skeins each Red #606 and Golden Yellow #972.

DIRECTIONS: Following fabric grain, cut fabric along a thread to sizes listed above. Staystitch ½" (1,2 cm) from all edges, following the fabric thread. Using 3 strands of Red in needle, and working crosses over two fabric threads, work border in Cross-Stitch (pages 34-35) all around placemat and coaster, and around lower left quarter of napkin, ¾" (2 cm) from edges. Then, following chart, embroider a single flower motif on the napkin and coaster, and three motifs on the placemat. On coaster, center the motif from side to side, and begin bottom of flowerpot 5 threads up from border. On placemat, begin motif 21 threads up and 16 threads in from border, with 6 threads between motifs; on napkin, begin 15 threads up and 14 in from border.

Press embroidery as directed on page 28. Then, to form fringe, carefully pull out threads up to staystitching all around each piece.

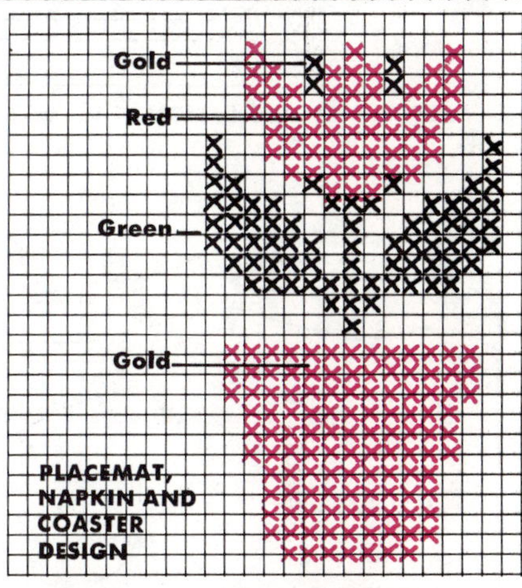

BED AND BATH MONOGRAMS

(shown on page 31) See pages 94-95.

LATCH HOOK RUGS

(shown on page 32)

Sizes: Boston Fern—31 x 34" (78,5 x 86,5 cm)
Galaxy—20 x 27" (51 x 68,5 cm)

MATERIALS: Rug canvas with 3½ meshes per inch (2,5 cm): for Boston Fern, 35 x 38" (89 x 96,5 cm); for Galaxy, 24 x 31" (61 x 78,5 cm); Spinnerin Rug Yarn in colors and amounts specified on page 84; latch hook; materials for finishing specified on page 39.

DIRECTIONS: To make the rugs, use the design diagrams on page 84 and the latch hook technique on page 39. Before finishing, trim excess canvas to 1" (2,5 cm).

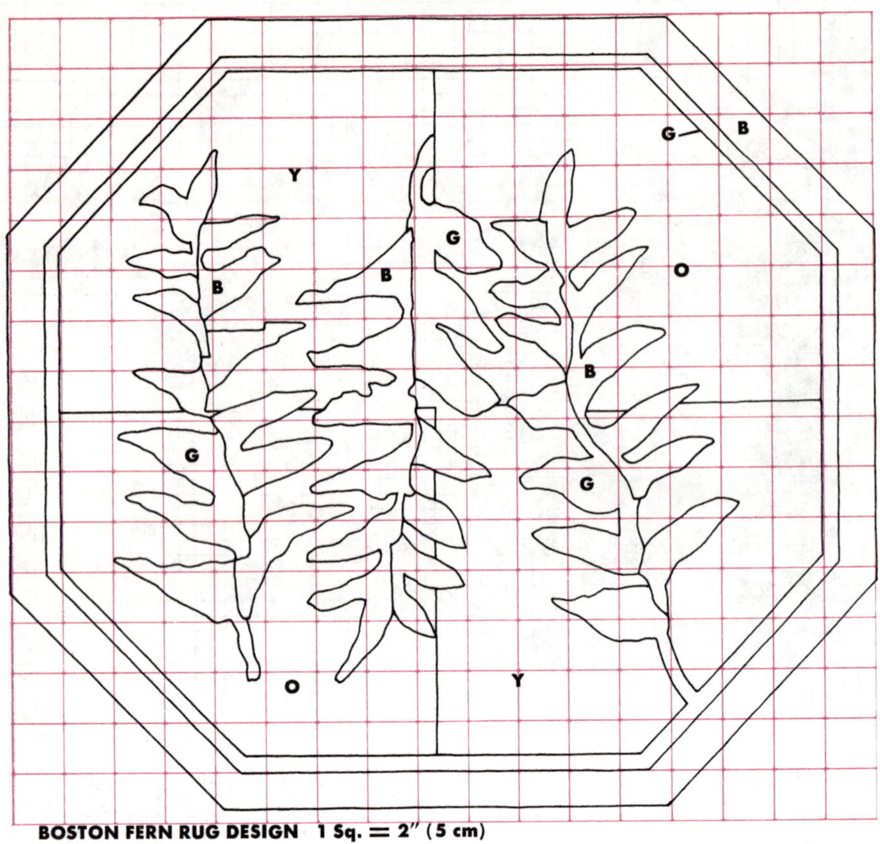

BOSTON FERN RUG DESIGN 1 Sq. = 2" (5 cm)

GALAXY RUG DESIGN 1 Sq. = 1½" (3,8 cm)

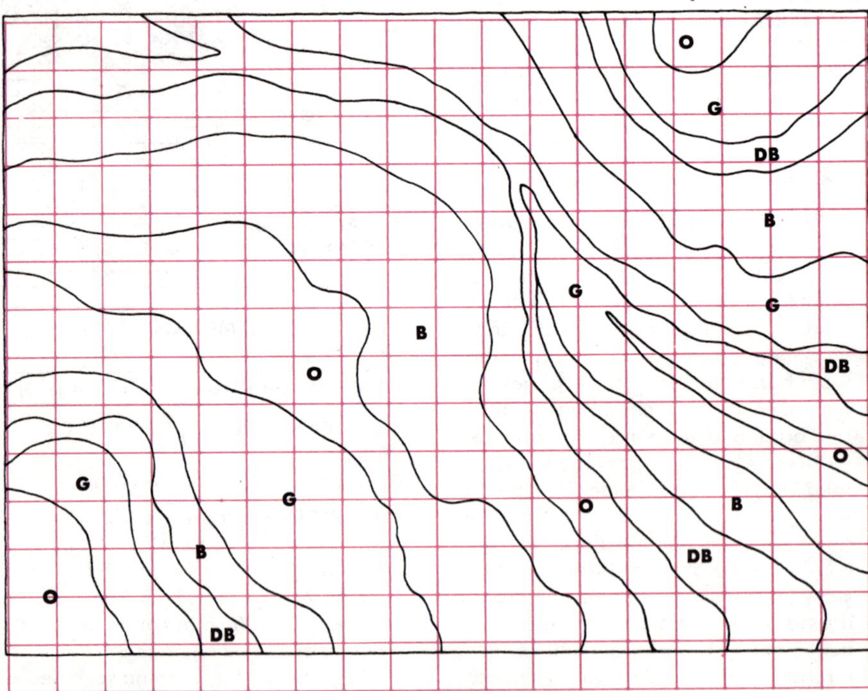

BOSTON FERN RUG
Color Key and Yarn Amounts

Symbol	Color	Packages Needed
B	Black	9
Y	Yellow	12
G	Antique Gold	7
O	Burnt Orange	11

GALAXY RUG
Color Key and Yarn Amounts

Symbol	Color	Packages Needed
DB	Dark Brown	4
G	Gold	7
O	Burnt Orange	6
B	Brick	7

BARN WALL HANGING

(shown on page 41)

Size: 33 x 43" (84 x 109 cm)

MATERIALS: 45" (115 cm) wide cotton or cotton-blend fabrics: 1½ yds. (1,40 m) Red, 1 yd. (0,95 m) each Bright Blue and Pale Yellow, ½ yd. (0,50 m) Canary Yellow, Pale Green and Spring Green, ¼ yd. (0,25 m) each Purple, Dark Green and Bright Yellow, and ⅛ yd. (0,15 m) each Orange, Navy, Maroon, Light Pink and Medium Pink; 1 yd. (0,95 m) 45" (115 cm) wide lightweight muslin; 72 x 90" (183 x 229 cm) pkg. quilt batting; yellow thread.

DIRECTIONS: Enlarge diagram, right (see pages 20-21) and make a paper pattern for each shape. Following the diagram and color key, use the patterns to cut out fabric sections for appliqués. Cut muslin 33 x 43" (84 x 109 cm). From Red, cut backing 35 x 45" (89 x 115 cm) and rod casing 5 x 37" (12,5 x 94 cm). Cut two layers of batting 33 x 43" (84 x 109 cm).

Arrange appliqués on muslin, following diagram. Pin or fuse the pieces in place (see page 50). Zigzag-stitch all raw edges with yellow thread, using a wide, closely-spaced stitch. Stitch a weathervane over the barn in zigzag stitch, as shown on the diagram.

Center batting on backing fabric, allowing a 1" (2,5 cm) border all around. Place the appliquéd top over the batting and backing. Baste as for a quilt, page 51. Turn under ¼" (6 mm) on the short ends of the casing and stitch. Fold casing in half lengthwise, wrong sides together. On the outside, center casing at the top of the backing, matching raw edges. Baste in place. Turn under ½" (1,2 cm) along raw edges of backing, including casing, toward the front. Turn edges toward the front again, overlapping the raw edges of the picture. Pin and stitch edges in place through all layers. Do not miter corners. Machine-quilt around the barn, sun, silo, inner edges of the blue border and along the line that runs across the picture at the base of the barn and silo, through all layers.

RUFFLED PATCHWORK PILLOW

(shown on page 41)

Size: 21 x 21" (53,5 x 53,5 cm), including ruffle

MATERIALS: 45" (115 cm) wide cotton or cotton-blend fabrics: ⅛ yd. (0,15 m) each Yellow, Green, Blue, Purple and Orange, and 1¼ yds. (1,15 m) Red;

thread to match fabrics; 15" (38 cm) square each of muslin and quilt batting; 14" (35,5 cm) square knife-edge pillow form.

DIRECTIONS: NOTE: Use ½" (1,2 cm) seams throughout. Cut 4½" (11,5 cm) squares of fabric as follows: 4 Purple, 3 each Red and Blue, 2 each Green, Orange and Yellow. From remaining Red, cut a 15" (38 cm) square for pillow back and enough 8" (20,5 cm) wide bias strips for ruffle to measure about 3 yds. (2,75 m) when pieced.

Stitch squares together in the order shown in color on the Patchwork Diagram, below, forming four strips; sew strips together to form a 15" (38 cm) block. Press seams open as you go.

To quilt the block, sandwich batting between the patchwork block and the muslin, matching edges. Baste together as described on page 51. Then, using thread to match, machine-quilt the block in the diagonal design shown in the Patchwork Diagram.

Ruffle: Join bias strips, including ends, to make a continuous piece; press seams open. Fold strip in half lengthwise; press fold lightly. To gather opposite edge, make two rows of long machine stitches, ¼" and ⅜" (6 mm and 1 cm) from raw edges. Divide ruffle into four equal parts; mark with pins. Pin ruffle to right side of pillow top, matching raw edges and placing pins at corners. Pull up the bobbin threads until ruffle fits; distribute fullness evenly, allowing a little extra at corners. Baste. Finish pillow same as for Pastel Pillow, described on page 81.

RUFFLED PATCHWORK QUILT

(shown on page 41)

Size: 63 x 63" (160 x 160 cm), including ruffle

MATERIALS: 45" (115 cm) wide cotton or cotton-blend fabrics: ½ yd. (0,50 m) each Yellow, Orange and Green, ⅝ yd. (0,60 m) Blue, ⅞ yd. (0,80 m) Purple and 6⅝ yds. (6,10 m) Red; thread to match fabrics; 72 x 90" (183 x 229 cm) pkg. of quilt batting (or use 2 pkgs. if a thicker quilt is desired).

DIRECTIONS: NOTE: Use ½" (1,2 cm) seams throughout. Cut 4½" (11,5 cm) squares of fabric as follows: 64 Purple, 48 each Red and Blue, and 32 each Green, Orange and Yellow. From Red cut two 57" (145 cm) lengths for quilt back. From remaining Red, cut enough 9" (23 cm) wide bias strips for ruffle to measure 12⅛ yds. (11,50 m). Following instructions for Pillow, above,

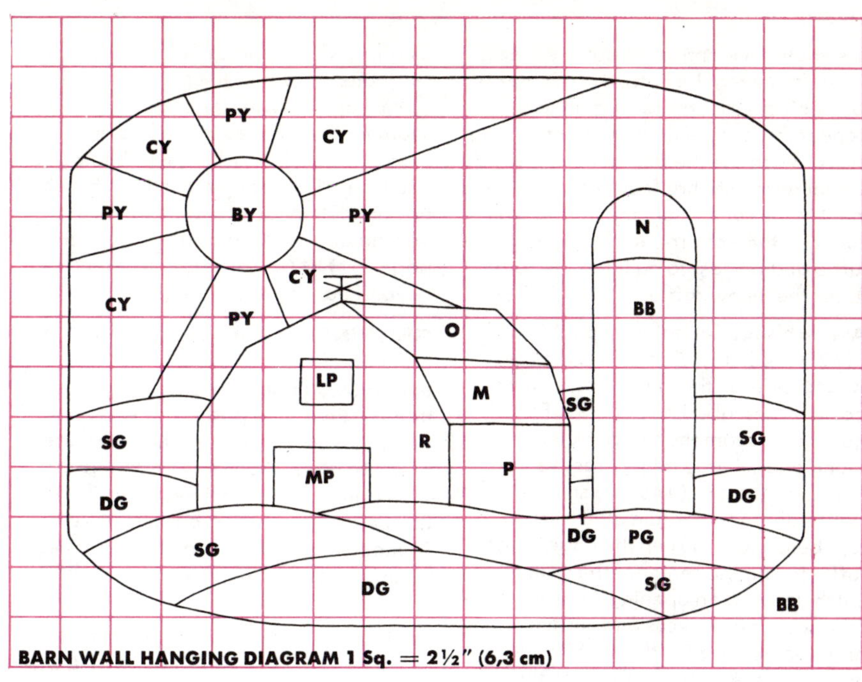

BARN WALL HANGING DIAGRAM 1 Sq. = 2½" (6,3 cm)

Color Key

R—Red
BB—Bright Blue
PY—Pale Yellow
CY—Canary Yellow
PG—Pale Green
SG—Spring Green
P—Purple
DG—Dark Green
BY—Bright Yellow
O—Orange
N—Navy
M—Maroon
LP—Light Pink
MP—Medium Pink

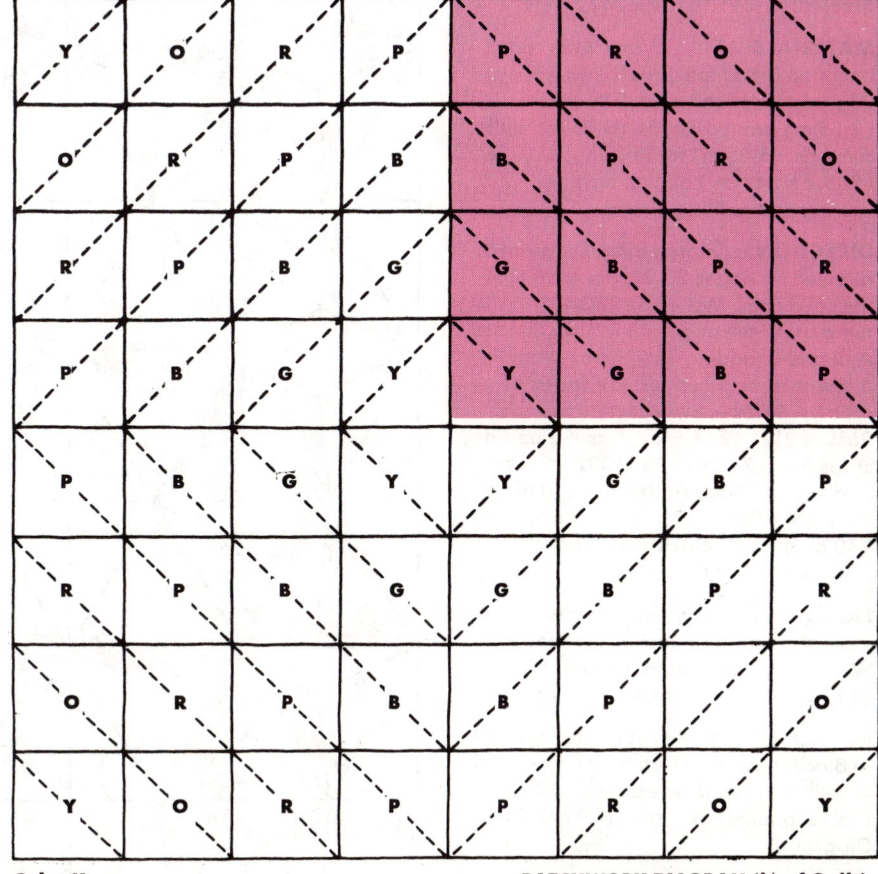

Color Key

P—Purple
R—Red
O—Orange
Y—Yellow
G—Green
B—Blue

PATCHWORK DIAGRAM (¼ of Quilt)

assemble 16 identical 16-square blocks. Then, following the Patchwork Diagram, join 4 blocks to form 1/4 of quilt top. Repeat three more times with remaining blocks. Arrange the four quarters, which are identical, so that four Yellow squares meet in the center; join the quarters as you did the squares and blocks. Make ruffle and baste it to quilt top the same as for the Pillow ruffle.

Assembling: Cut batting 56 x 56" (142 x 142 cm). Center it over the *wrong* side of the quilt top; then hand-baste as described on page 51. For quilt back, seam the two back lengths along one selvage edge; press seam open. Trim to 57" (145 cm) square. With right sides together, pin quilt back to top, being sure to keep the edge of the ruffle facing the center of the quilt. Stitch, leaving an opening for turning. Trim seam allowances and corners and turn quilt right side out. Slipstitch opening closed. Using matching thread, machine-quilt along the diagonal lines shown in the diagram.

TWINKLING STARS QUILT

(shown on pages 42-43)

Size: 80¼ x 95" (204 x 241,5 cm)

MATERIALS: 45" (115 cm) wide cotton or cotton-blend fabric as follows: 2⅞ yds. (2,65 m) solid, 2¾ yds. (2,55 m) print, 5½ yds. (5,05 m) white, 5½ yds. (5,05 m) for backing; 81 x 96" (205,7 x 244 cm) pkg. of batting; sewing and quilting thread.

DIRECTIONS: Enlarge Block Diagram as directed on pages 20-21, drawing only the solid lines. Make patchwork templates (see pages 48-49) for Shapes A, B and C, adding ⅜" (1 cm) seam allowances to all edges. Cut fabric as follows: **Solid** — 2 border strips, each 96¼ x 2¼" (244,5 x 5,7 cm), 2 border strips, each 79½ x 1¼" (202 x 3,2 cm), and 210 of Shape A; **Print** — 210 of Shape B; **White** — 210 of Shape A and 140 of Shape C; **Backing** — two 95" (241,5 cm) lengths.

NOTE: The quilt is 5 blocks wide and 7 blocks long, for a total of 35 blocks. When assembling quilt top, use ⅜" (1 cm) seams and press all seams open.

For each block, piece shapes together as in Block Diagram, starting at center and working outward (see page 50). Sew blocks together as shown in the Quilt Diagram.

With right sides together, sew border strips to quilt top, attaching short strips first. Mark quilting lines on quilt top with chalk or a soft, well-sharpened pencil, using the dashed lines on the Block Diagram as guides; lines are about ⅜" (1 cm) apart. With right sides together, seam the long edges of the backing pieces; then trim backing width to 80¼" (204 cm). Trim batting to same size as backing. Then layer and baste the top, batting and backing as described on page 51. **NOTE:** Borders will extend beyond batting and backing.

FINISHING: Stretch and fasten quilt to a quilting frame, or use a large embroidery hoop. Hand-quilt along the marked lines (see page 51). After quilting is complete, turn the raw edges of the borders under ⅜" (1 cm); press. Turn borders over backing, so that finished width of short borders is ¼" (6 mm) and width of long borders is ¾" (2 cm); slipstitch in place.

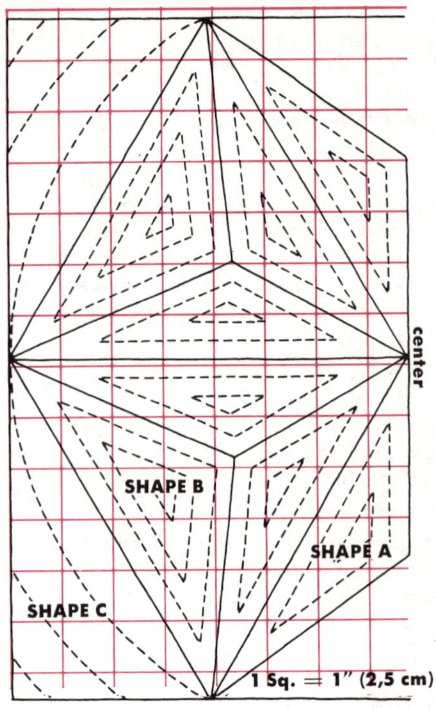

TWINKLING STARS BLOCK DIAGRAM (½ of block)

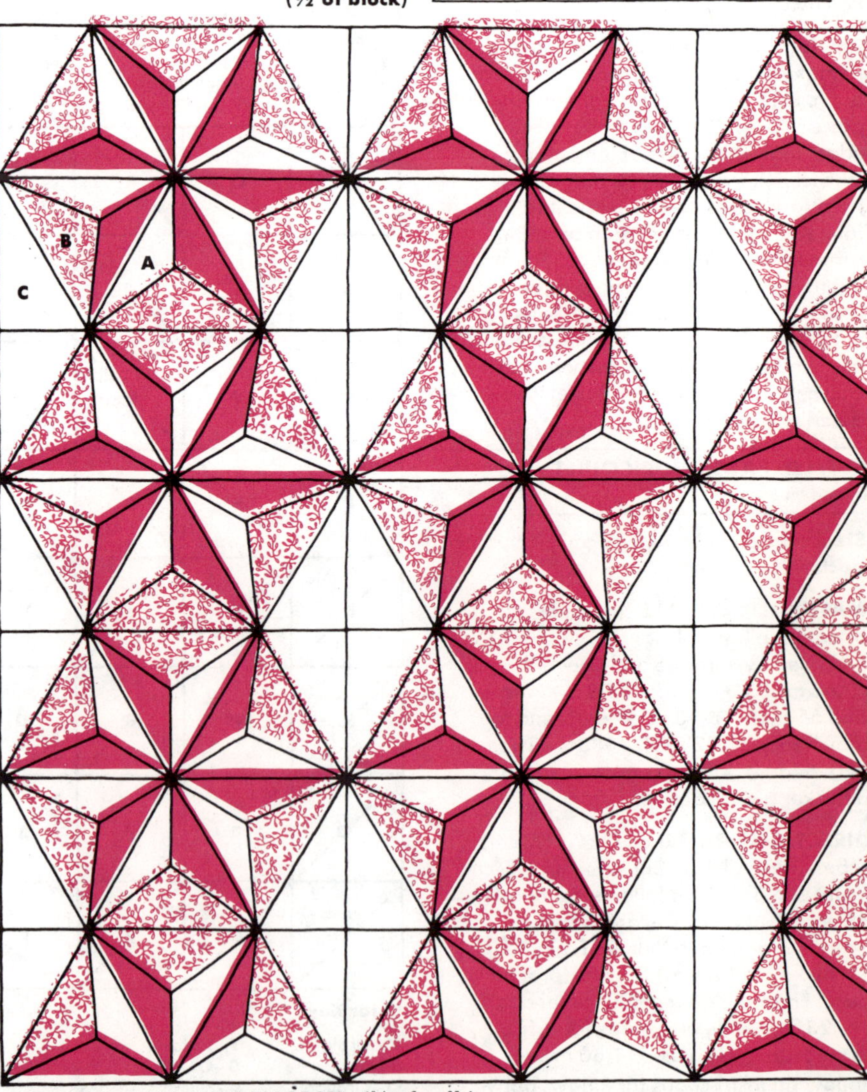

TWINKLING STARS QUILT DIAGRAM (¼ of quilt)

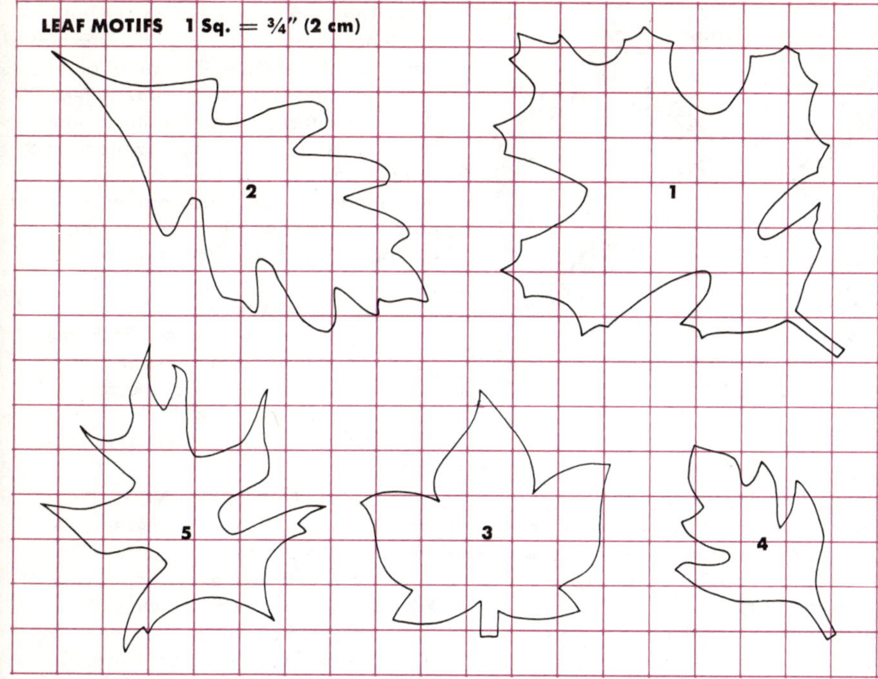

PLACEMAT, CHAIR CUSHION AND POT HOLDER (shown on page 44)

Sizes: Placemat — 19 x 14" (48,5 x 35,5 cm); **Chair Cushion** — about 15 x 15" (38 x 38 cm); **Pot Holder** — 8½" (21,6 cm) diameter.

MATERIALS (for all three items): 45" (115 cm) wide cotton or cotton-blend fabrics: 1 yd. (0,95 m) checked gingham, ½ yd. (0,50 m) each medium solid and print A, ¼ yd. (0,25 m) print B, ⅛ yd. (0,15 m) each print C and dark solid; ½ pkg. (crib size) quilt batting; thread to contrast with fabrics.

DIRECTIONS: From print A, cut placemat top 19 x 14" (48,5 x 35,5 cm). From gingham, cut chair cushion top and back 15 x 15" (38 x 38 cm); taper the sides to make one edge 13" (33 cm) *or to fit your chair*. From medium solid, cut placemat back same size as top, and two 8½" (21,6 cm) circles for pot holder. Enlarge leaf motifs; see pages 20-21. Cut leaves as follows: Leaf #1—2 of print A; #2—1 of print A and 1 of gingham; #3—1 of print B and 1 of print C; #4—2 of print C and 1 of dark solid; #5—1 of dark solid. From remaining gingham, cut enough 1" (2,5 cm) wide bias strips to fit around placemat and pot holder, and two 1½ x 16" (3,8 x 40,5 cm) straight strips for cushion ties. From remaining print A, cut 1" (2,5 cm) wide bias strips to fit around chair cushion. From batting, cut one piece each the same size as placemat and pot holder, and two pieces same size as chair cushion.

For each item, place batting between top and back fabric, aligning all edges. Baste as described on page 51. Using the photograph on page 44 as a guide, pin or fuse leaves to tops (see page 50). Zigzag-stitch around edges of leaves, through all layers, with a wide, closely-spaced stitch. Add zigzagged center vein and stem to leaf on pot holder.

FINISHING: Trim corners of placemat and chair cushion, rounding them off slightly. Bind raw edges of each item with the reserved bias strips, piecing as necessary; zigzag-stitch in place along inner edge of bias, being sure to catch in bias on underside. Turn ends under and lap over the starting ends. For chair cushion ties, press under ¼" (6 mm) on long edges of straight gingham strips, fold in half lengthwise and press again. Stitch along both edges. Fold ties in half crosswise; sew through fold on underside of cushion at rear corners. Using any fabric, cut a 1½ x 5" (3,8 x 12,5 cm) bias strip. Stitch as for chair ties, form into a loop and sew to pot holder.

BLUE BOUCLÉ SWEATER (shown on page 53)

Sizes: Directions are for size 10. Changes for sizes 12, 14 and 16 are in parentheses.

MATERIALS: 8 oz. (224 g) lightweight bouclé or looped nylon yarn; No. 8 knitting needles OR SIZE TO GIVE GAUGE; 1 pair shoulder pads; ¼ yd. (0,25 m) lining fabric to match yarn.

GAUGE: 4 sts = 1" (2,5 cm); 6 rows = 1" (2,5 cm).

DIRECTIONS: NOTE: Work with double strand of yarn throughout. **Back:** Cast on 60 (64-68-72) sts. Work in Garter St (see page 60), inc 1 st each side every 17th row 4 times. Work even on 68 (72-76-80) sts for 15 more rows, or until piece measures 14" (35,5 cm) to underarm. **Armhole Shaping:** Bind off 3 sts at beg of next 2 rows and 1 (1-2-2) st at beg of next 4 rows. Work even on 58 (62-62-66) sts for 39 (41-43-45) rows. Bind off 12 (14-14-16) sts at beg of next 2 rows. Loosely bind off remaining 34 sts for neck.
Front: Work same as Back.
Sleeves: Cast on 44 (46-48-50) sts. Work in Garter St until piece measures 16" (40,5 cm). Bind off 3 sts at beg of next 2 rows and 1 st each side every other row 13 (14-15-16) times. Work even on 12 sts for 2 rows. Bind off.
FINISHING: Using 1 strand of yarn, sew shoulder seams. Sew sleeve cap to armholes. Sew side and sleeve seams. To cover shoulder pads, trace the shoulder pad onto paper and add ⅝" (1,5 cm) all around for seam allowances. Using paper pattern, cut two pieces from lining fabric for each cover. With right sides together, stitch the cover, leaving an opening large enough to insert the pad. Trim the seam, clip or notch curves and turn cover right side out; press. Insert the pad and slipstitch the opening closed. Sew shoulder pads into garment, so that straight edges extend into sleeves ¼" (6 mm) beyond armhole seams.

RED SWEATER WITH CHEVRONS
(shown on page 53)

Sizes: Directions are for Small (6-8). Changes for Medium (10-12) and Large (14-16) are in parentheses.

MATERIALS: J. & P. Coats "Knit-Cro-Sheen", 175 yd. (166 m) ball: 20 balls #126 Spanish Red and 1 ball #10-A Canary Yellow; Nos. 8 and 9 knitting needles OR SIZE TO GIVE GAUGE; Size G crochet hook.

GAUGE: Stockinette St on No. 9 needles: 9 sts = 2" (5 cm); 11 rows = 2" (5 cm).

DIRECTIONS: NOTE: Work with 4 strands held tog throughout. **Back:** With No. 8 needles and Red, cast on 73 (81-91) sts. Work in k 1, p 1 ribbing for 1½ (2-2½)" [3,8 (5-6,3) cm]. Change to No. 9 needles and work in Stockinette St (see page 61) until piece measures 11½ (12½-14)" [29,2 (31,7-35,5) cm]; end with a p row. **Raglan Armholes:** Bind off 4 sts at beg of next 2 rows. **Next row:** K 1, k 2 tog through back of sts, k to last 3 sts, k 2 tog, k 1. **Following row:** P. Repeat last 2 rows 17 (20-23) times more. Bind off remaining 29 (31-35) sts.

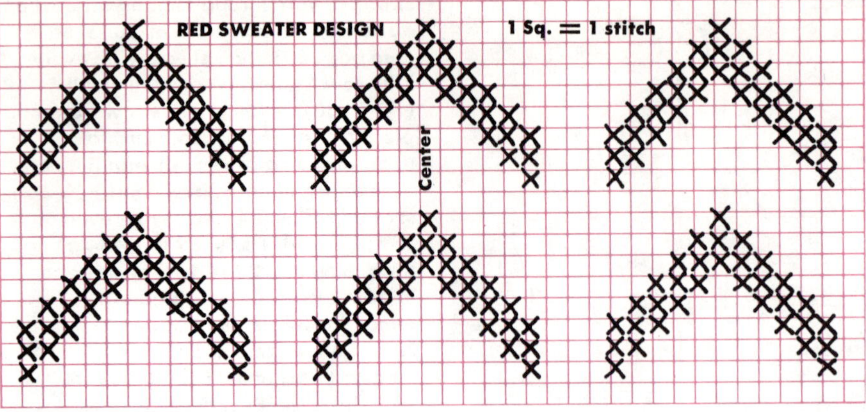

Front: Work same as Back, discontinuing raglan shaping when 35 (37-41) sts remain on needle; end with a p row.
Neck Shaping: Row 1: K 1, k 2 tog through back of sts, k 2, k 2 tog. Turn. **Row 2 and all even rows:** P. **Row 3:** K 1, k 2 tog through back of sts, k 2 tog; turn. **Row 5:** K 1, k 2 tog; turn. **Row 7:** K 2 tog. Cut thread and fasten. Attach thread, bind off center 21 (23-27) sts, and work on remaining 7 sts to correspond to opposite side.
Sleeves: With No. 8 needles and Red, cast on 34 (38-42) sts. Work in ribbing as for Back. Change to No. 9 needles and work in Stockinette St, inc 1 st at both ends of row every 1¼" (3,2 cm) 8 (9-10) times. Continue on 50 (56-62) sts until piece measures 17½ (18-18½)" [44,2 (46-47,2) cm].
Raglan Shaping: Work same as for Back. Bind off remaining 6 sts.
FINISHING: With thread, mark vertical center of Front. With 4 strands of Canary Yellow in tapestry needle, following chart, work embroidery in Duplicate St, (see page 63), beginning at center, 14 rows down from neck edge. Sew raglan seams. Sew side and sleeve seams. With crochet hook and 4 strands of Red, work a row of reverse sc (see page 71) around neck edge, working from left to right. Cut thread and fasten.

DOLL (shown on page 54)

Size: About 15" (38 cm) high
MATERIALS: Sport yarn: 2 oz. (56 g) Beige for doll, 1 oz. (28 g) Light Blue for dress, and small amount of Brown; Nos. 5 and 3 knitting needles OR SIZE TO GIVE GAUGE; stitch holder; tapestry needle; polyester fiberfill for stuffing; small button.
GAUGE: Garter St on No. 5 needles: 6 sts = 1" (2,5 cm); on No. 3 needles: 7 sts = 1" (2,5 cm).
DIRECTIONS FOR DOLL: Arms (make 2): With No. 5 needles and Beige, cast on 14 sts. Work in Garter St (see page 60) until piece measures 5½" (14 cm). Cut yarn, leaving 18" (46 cm) end. Thread this end through tapestry needle and draw through the sts on the knitting needle; remove knitting needle. Draw yarn through sts again, pull up tightly and fasten.
Legs (make 2): With No. 5 needles and Beige, cast on 16 sts. Work as for Arms until piece measures 6½" (16,2 cm).
NOTE: For striped "socks", work last inch (2,5 cm) before foot in Brown and Beige, alternating rows as desired.
Next row (start of foot): Attach Brown. K 8, place remaining 8 sts on a holder, and cast on 4 sts for foot. Continue with Brown on 12 sts for ⅞" (2,2 cm); bind off, leaving 18" (46 cm) end. Slip sts from holder onto needle; with Brown, cast 4 sts onto other needle. K sts from holder, then continue as for other half of foot.
Body: With No. 5 needles and Beige, cast on 34 sts. Work in k 1, p 1 ribbing for 3 rows. Then work in Garter St until piece measures 5⅛" (13 cm). **Next row:** Sl 1, k 2 tog across row, end k 1. **Next row:** K. Repeat last 2 rows once. Cut yarn, leaving end. Finish as for Arm.
Head: With same needles and yarn, cast on 28 sts. Work in k 1, p 1 ribbing for 3 rows. Continue in Stockinette St (see page 61) until piece measures 2½" (6,3 cm), end with a p row. **Next row:** Sl 1, k 2 tog across row, end k 1. **Next row:** P. Repeat last 2 rows once. Finish as for Body.
FINISHING: With matching yarn, sew arms, legs and body into tubes, matching ends of k rows. Set aside. Block head (see page 64), p side up, to 2½ x 4⅝" (6,3 x 11,5 cm) rectangle. Sew head as for other parts. Stuff firmly, then close opening by drawing tapestry needle, threaded with yarn, through loops of cast-on sts and pulling firmly. Fasten securely and cut ends. Stuff body and close opening as for head. Stuff legs, feet first; close opening by overcasting. Cut two 7" (18 cm) lengths of yarn. Thread a large-eyed needle with one length and sew through one stitch at top of foot; tie in bow. Repeat for other foot. Stuff and close arms same as legs. Wind a few turns of yarn tightly around lower arms to form wrists. Sew head and arms to body with running stitches, alternating between body and other part. Place doll in sitting position and sew on legs. For hair, knit several yds. (m) of Brown into a swatch. Steam swatch; when dry, ravel it. Cut the resulting curly yarn into 14" (35,5 cm) lengths and sew the middle of each strand along the midline of the doll's head from front to back. Add ribbon bows if desired. With Brown, embroider eyes.
DIRECTIONS FOR DRESS: NOTE: Dress is worked vertically, from side to side. If you want the dress to have stripes, work 2 or 3 rows in Brown every ½" (1,2 cm).
Front: With No. 3 needles and Light Blue, cast on 5 sts. K 2 rows, then cast on 5 sts at end of row. K 2 more rows, then cast on 5 more sts. Continue in this way until you have 40 sts on the needle to underarm. Work even for ½" (1,2 cm), end at underarm. Cast on 7 sts for armhole. K 1 row. **Next row:** *K 29 sts only, turn and k back to hemline. **Next 2 rows:** K across *all* sts. Repeat from * until piece measures 2½" (6,3 cm) from armhole edge; the partial rows add fullness to the lower part of the dress. AT THE SAME TIME, when first shoulder strap is ⅝" (1,5 cm) wide, shape neck as follows: Bind off 5 sts for side of neck. Work even until lower edge of neck measures 1½" (3,2 cm). Then cast on 5 sts for other side of neck and work even until second shoulder strap is the same width as first one; this should happen 1 row after discontinuing the partial rows. Bind off 7 sts for armhole, then work even for ½" (1,2 cm), end at underarm. *At beg of next row, bind off 5 sts and k to end. **Next row:** K. Repeat from * until no sts remain.
Back: Work same as Front until ⅝" (1,5 cm) from neck side edge, end at neck. For opening, bind off 18 sts at beg of next row. Finish row. **Next row:** K, casting on 18 sts at end of row. Finish as for Front.
FINISHING: Sew side and shoulder seams. Sew button at top of one side of back opening; make a thread or yarn loop on opposite side.

HORSES (shown on page 54)

Sizes: Directions are for 7" (18 cm) horse. Changes for 3½" (9 cm) horse are in parentheses.
MATERIALS: Small amount of sport yarn; No. 5 (3) knitting needles OR SIZE TO GIVE GAUGE; scraps of contrasting

mohair yarn or fur-like fabric for mane and tail; scrap of felt for ears; polyester fiberfill for stuffing.
GAUGE: Garter St on No. 5 needles: 6 sts = 1" (2,5 cm); on No. 3 needles: 7 sts = 1" (2,5 cm).
DIRECTIONS: Beg at hind leg, with No. 5 (3) needles, cast on 40 (25) sts. Work in Garter St (see page 60) for ¾ (½)" [2 (1,2) cm]. **Next row:** Bind off first 32 (20) sts, finish row. **Next row:** K 8 (5) sts, then cast on 3 (2) sts at end of row for stomach. Work even on 11 (7) sts for body until piece measures 1¼ (⅝)" [3,2 (1,5) cm] from bound-off sts, end at stomach edge. **Next row:** Bind off 3 (2) sts, k remaining sts, then cast on 15 (9) sts for neck. K the 23 (14) sts, then cast on 32 (20) sts tightly for front leg. Work on 55 (34) sts until front leg is same width as hind leg, end at lower edge. **Next row:** Bind off 49 (30) sts. Work on remaining 6 (4) sts for head for another ¾ (½)" [2 (1,2) cm]. Bind off. Make another piece in the same way.

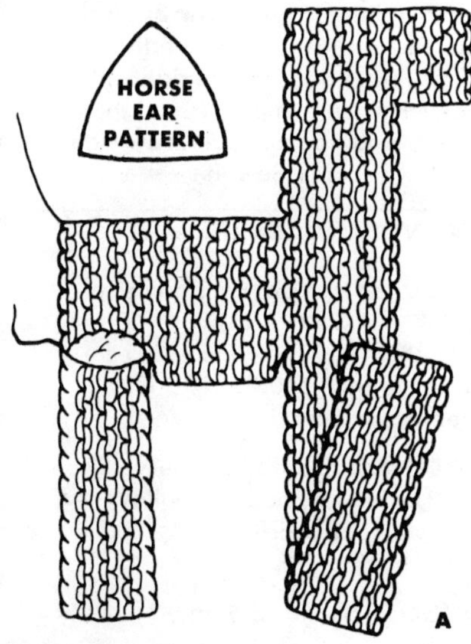

FINISHING: On each piece, fold up bottom of legs to meet body. Sew outer edges of legs tog, stuffing as you sew (A); leave tops of legs open. With open tops of legs tog, sew stomach edges tog, then sew tops of legs tog. Sew remaining edges of horse tog, adding stuffing as you sew. Make a mane and tail from yarn or fur-like fabric and sew in place. Using pattern, cut ears from felt and sew in place, making a tiny tuck at base of ear. Embroider eyes with contrasting yarn.

WOMAN'S PATCHWORK SWEATER

(shown on page 55)

Sizes: Directions are for size 8. Changes for sizes 10, 12 and 14 are in parentheses.
MATERIALS: Unger's Skol, 1.6 oz. (45 g) ball: 7 (8-8-9) Medium Brown (A), 2 each of Beige (B) and Natural (C); Nos. 8 and 10 knitting needles OR SIZE TO GIVE GAUGE.

GAUGE: 7 sts = 2" (5 cm); 5 rows = 1" (2,5 cm).

DIRECTIONS: NOTE: When making squares, twist yarns on wrong side when changing colors to prevent holes.
Back: With No. 8 needles and A, cast on 60 (64-68-72) sts. Work in k 2, p 2 ribbing for 3" (7,5 cm), inc 6 (5-4-3) sts evenly across row—66 (69-72-75) sts. Change to No. 10 needles and Stockinette St (see page 61). **Row 1:** K 22 (23-24-25) B, k 22 (23-24-25) A, k 22 (23-24-25) B. **Row 2:** P 22 (23-24-25) B, p 22 (23-24-25) A, p 22 (23-24-25) B. Repeat Rows 1 and 2, 15 (15-16-16) times more—32 (32-34-34) rows. **Row 3:** K 22 (23-24-25) C, k 22 (23-24-25) B, k 22 (23-24-25) C. **Row 4:** P 22 (23-24-25) C, p 22 (23-24-25) B, p 22 (23-24-25) C. Repeat Rows 3 and 4, 15 (15-16-16) times more—32 (32-34-34) rows. Mark beg and end of next row for start of armholes. **Row 5:** K 22 (23-24-25) A, k 22 (23-24-25) C, k 22 (23-24-25) A. **Row 6:** P 22 (23-24-25) A, p 22 (23-24-25) C, p 22 (23-24-25) A. Repeat Rows 5 and 6, 15 (15-16-16) times more—32 (32-34-34) rows. With A only, continue to work even in Stockinette St for 12 rows. **Shape Shoulders:** Bind off 7 (7-8-8) sts beg next 4 (2-6-4) rows, then 8 (8-0-9) sts beg next 2 (4-0-2) rows—22 (23-24-25) sts. Place remaining sts on a holder.
Front: Work same as for Back to underarm. Mark for underarm as for Back. Work until last Row 6 is completed. **Shape Neck:** K 28(29-30-31) A sts, slip center 10(11-12-13) sts to a holder, attach a 2nd ball A, k 28(29-30-31) sts. Working both sides at the same time, dec 1 st at each neck edge every row 3 times, every other row 3 times — 22(23-24-25) sts each side. Work to shoulder as for Back. **Shape Shoulders:** At each arm edge, bind off 7(7-8-8) sts every other row 2(1-3-2) times, then 8(8-0-9) sts 1(2-0-1) time.
Neckband: Sew left shoulder seam. On right side, starting at right back shoulder, with No. 8 needles and A, pick up 68 (70-72-74) sts around neck (this includes all sts on holders). Work in k 2, p 2 ribbing for 2½" (6,3 cm). Bind off in ribbing. Sew right shoulder and neckband seam. Fold neckband in half to inside and sew in place.
Sleeves: With No. 10 needles and A, on right side, pick up 59(59-63-63) sts along armhole edge, from marker to marker. Beg with a p row and work in Stockinette St. Work even for 1" (2,5 cm). Dec 1 st each end of next row, then every 1½ (1¾-1½-1¾)" [3,8 (4,5-3,8-4,5) cm] 8(7-8-7) times more — 41(43-45-47) sts. Work even until 16" (40,5 cm) from beg, or 3" (7,5 cm) less than desired length, end with a k row; p 1 row, dec 13 sts evenly across — 28 (30-32-34) sts. Change to No. 8 needles. Work in k 2, p 2 ribbing for 3" (7,5 cm). Bind off in ribbing.
FINISHING: Sew sleeve and side seams, using matching color yarn. Press lightly on wrong side.

MAN'S STRIPED SWEATER

(shown on page 55)

Sizes: Directions are for size 38. Changes for sizes 40, 42 and 44 are in parentheses.
MATERIALS: Unger's Skol, 1.6 oz. (45 g) ball: 7 (7-8-8) Brown (A), 4 (5-5-5) Taupe (B), 3 (3-4-4) Off White (C), 3 (3-4-4) Rust (D); Nos. 9 and 10 knitting needles OR SIZE TO GIVE GAUGE.
GAUGE: On No. 10 needles: 7 sts = 2" (5 cm).
NOTE: Carry yarns not in use along side edge. However, if color has to be carried too many rows, break off and reattach when needed. When working with 2 colors, carry yarns loosely across back of work to prevent puckering.
DIRECTIONS: Back: With No. 9 needles and A, cast on 71 (73-77-79) sts. Work in k 1, p 1 ribbing for 4" (10 cm), inc 1 st each end of last row—73 (75-79-81) sts. Change to No. 10 needles and pat. **Row 1:** With B, k on wrong side. **Row 2:** With B, k on right side. **Row 3:** * P 1 A, p 1 B; repeat from *, end p 1 A. **Row 4:** K 1 A, k 1 B; repeat from *, end k 1 A. **Rows 5 and 6:** With A, p. **Rows 7-10:** With B, work in Seed St (see page 64). **Rows 11, 12:** With C, k. **Row 13:** With A, p on wrong side. **Row 14:** With A, p. **Rows 15, 16:** With C, k. **Rows 17, 18:** With D, k. **Rows 19-22:** With A, k. **Rows 23, 24:** With C, k. **Rows 25-28:** With D, k. **Rows 29, 30:** With A, k. **Rows 31, 32:** With D, k. **Rows 33-36:** With C, k. **Rows 37-39:** With B, work in Seed St. **Rows 40 and 42:** * K 1 A, k 1 B, repeat from *, end k 1 A. **Rows 41 and 43:** * P 1 A, p 1 B; repeat from *, end p 1 A. **Row 44:** With A, p. **Row 45:** With A, k. **Row 46:** With B, k. **Row 47:** With B, p. **Row 48:** With B, k. Repeat Rows 3 through 48 for pat. Work even until 18" (46 cm) from beg, or desired length to underarm. Place a marker at each end for armholes. Work even until armhole measures 8¾ (9¼-9½-10)" [22,2 (23,5-24,2-25,5) cm]. **Shape Shoulders:** Bind off

7 (7-7-8) sts beg next 6 (4-4-6) rows, then 0 (8-9-0) sts beg next 0 (2-2-0) rows—31 (31-33-33) sts. Place remaining sts on a holder.

Front: Work same as for Back until armhole measures 6 (6½-6½-7)" [15 (16,2-16,2-18) cm], end on wrong side—73 (75-79-81) sts. **Shape Neck:** Work 29 (30-31-32) sts and place on a holder, work center 15 (15-17-17) sts and place on another holder for neck, work remaining 29 (30-31-32) sts. Keeping continuity of pat, at neck edge, dec 1 st every row 4 times, every other row 4 times—21 (22-23-24) sts. Work to shoulder as for Back. **Shape Shoulder:** At arm edge, bind off 7 (7-7-8) sts every other row 3 (2-2-3) times, then 0 (8-9-0) sts 0 (1-1-0) times. Place the 29 (30-31-32) sts from holder onto No. 10 needles. Attach yarn at neck edge and work to correspond to other side, reversing shaping.

Sleeves: With No. 9 needles and A, cast on 33 (33-35-35) sts. Work in k 1, p 1 ribbing for 4" (10 cm), inc evenly across last row to 39 (39-41-41) sts. Change to No. 10 needles and pat st as for Back. Inc 1 st each end every 1½ (1¼-1¼-1¼)" [3,8 (3,2-3,2-3,2) cm] 8 (9-10-11) times—55 (57-61-63) sts. Work all inc sts into pat. Work even until 20 (20-21-21)" [51 (51-53,5-53,5) cm] from beg, or desired length. Bind off loosely with one color.

Neckband: Sew left shoulder seam. With No. 9 needles and A, on right side, pick up 76 (76-80-84) sts around neck (this includes sts on holders). Work in k 2, p 2 ribbing for 2" (5 cm). Bind off in ribbing. Sew right shoulder and neckband seam.

FINISHING: Sew straight edge of sleeve to armhole, from marker to marker. Sew sleeve and side seams. Press seams lightly on wrong side.

CABLED V-NECK PULLOVERS

(shown on page 56)

Sizes: Directions are for bust or chest size 34" (86,5 cm). Changes for sizes 36, 38, 40, 42 and 44" (91,5; 96,5; 102; 107 and 112 cm) are in parentheses.

MATERIALS: Columbia-Minerva Shannon, 3 oz. (84 g) ball: 8 (8-8-9-9-9) balls; Nos. 6 and 8 knitting needles OR SIZE TO GIVE GAUGE; cable or dp needle.

GAUGE: Stockinette St on No. 8 needles: 9 sts = 2" (5 cm); 6 rows = 1" (2,5 cm).

Back: With No. 6 needles, cast on 78 (82-86-90-94-98) sts. Work in k 1, p 1 ribbing for 2½" (6,3 cm). Change to No. 8 needles. Work even in Stockinette St (see page 61) until piece measures 15" (38 cm) for Women, 17" (43 cm) for Men, or desired length to underarm, end with p row. **Shape Armholes:** Bind off 2 (2-3-3-4-4) sts at beg of next 2 rows. Dec 1 st each side every other row 4 (4-4-5-5-6) times—66 (70-72-74-76-78) sts. Work even until armholes measure 8 (8½-9-9½-10-10½)" [20,5 (21,7-23-24,2-25,5-26,7) cm], end with p row. **Shape Shoulders:** Bind off 6 (6-7-8-7-8) sts at beg of next 2 rows; then 7 (8-8-8-9-9) sts at beg of next 4 rows; slip these 26 sts to a holder to be worked later.

Front: Work same as for Back to end of ribbing. Change to No. 8 needles and pat as follows: **Row 1:** * K 12 (13-14-15-16-17), p 2, k 6, p 2, repeat from * 2 times, end k 12 (13-14-15-16-17). **Row 2:** * P 12 (13-14-15-16-17), k 2, p 6, k 2; repeat from * 2 times, end p 12 (13-14-15-16-17). **Rows 3 and 4:** Repeat Rows 1 and 2. **Row 5—Cable Row:** * K 12 (13-14-15-16-17), p 2, slip next 3 sts to cable needle and hold in back of work, k next 3 sts, k 3 sts from cable needle, p 2; repeat from * 2 times, end k 12 (13-14-15-16-17). **Row 6:** Repeat Row 2. **Rows 7 and 8:** Repeat Rows 1 and 2. Repeat these 8 rows for pat. Work even until Front measures 14" (35,5 cm) for Women, 16" (40,5 cm) for Men, or 1" (2,5 cm) less than Back to underarm, end with p row. **Shape Neck and Armholes:** Work across 39 (41-43-45-47-49) sts; attach another ball of yarn and work to end. Working each side separately, work 1 row even. Dec 1 st at each neck edge; then dec 1 st at same edge every 4th row. AT THE SAME TIME, when same length as Back to underarm, shape armholes as on Back. Keeping arm edges even, continue to dec 1 st at neck edge every 4th row until 20 (22-23-24-25-26) sts remain on each side of neck. Work even until armholes are same length as Back to shoulders. **Shape Shoulders:** At each arm edge, bind off 6 (6-7-8-7-8) sts once; then 7 (8-8-8-9-9) sts every other row twice.

Sleeves: With No. 6 needles, cast on 40 (42-44-46-48-50) sts. Work in k 1, p 1 ribbing for 2½" (6,3 cm), inc 4 sts evenly spaced across last row—44 (46-48-50-52-54) sts. Change to No. 8 needles and Stockinette St. Work even for 4 rows. Inc 1 st each side of next row; then every 8th row 9 (9-10-10-10-10) times more—64 (66-70-72-74-76) sts. Work even until Sleeve measures 18" (46 cm) for Women, 20" (51 cm) for Men, or desired length to underarm. **Shape Cap:** Bind off 2 (2-3-3-4-4) sts at beg of next 2 rows. Dec 1 st each side every other row 14 (15-16-17-16-15) times; then every 4th row 0 (0-0-0-1-3) times. Bind off 3 sts at beg of next 4 rows. Bind off remaining sts.

FINISHING: Sew left shoulder seam. **Neckband:** With No. 6 needle, from right side of work, k across sts on back holder, pick up and k 1 st in each row along left neck edge having an even number of sts, pick up 1 st at center and mark this st for center st, pick up 1 st in each row along right neck edge same as on left neck edge. **Row 1:** P 1, k 1 in ribbing to center st, p center st; beg with a p or a k st the same as st before center st, work in ribbing to end. **Row 2:** Work in ribbing to 1 st before center st, sl next st as to p, sl center st to dp needle and hold in front of work, sl st from right needle back to left needle, insert left needle from left to right in center st and sl this st to left needle, k 3 sts tog through back loops, work in ribbing to end. **Row 3:** Work even. Repeat last 2 rows until 1" (2,5 cm) from beg, end on right side. Bind off all sts loosely in pat. Sew right shoulder and ribbing seam. Sew side and sleeve seams. Sew in sleeves.

PULLOVER AND SCARF (shown on page 65)

Sizes: Directions are for Small size (32-34" [81,5-86,5 cm]) bust. Changes for Medium (36-38" [91,5-96,5 cm]) and Large (40" [102 cm]) are in parentheses. Scarf is one size.

MATERIALS: Columbia-Minerva Shannon, 3 oz. (84 g) ball: for pullover—6 (6-7) balls; for scarf—2 balls; Size I crochet hook.

GAUGE: 3 sc = 1" (2,5 cm); 3 rows = 1" (2,5 cm).

DIRECTIONS: Back: Ch 51 (57-63) to measure approximately 16 (18-20)"[40,5 (46-51) cm]. **Row 1 (right side):** Work 1 sc in 2nd ch from hook and in each ch across; 50 (56-62) sts. Ch 1, turn. **Row 2:** Work 1 sc in each sc. Repeat Row 2 twice more (4 rows sc). Ch 2, turn. **Row 5:** 1 hdc in 2nd ch from hook, ch 1, sk 1, * 1 hdc in next st, ch 1, sk 1; repeat from * across, end 1 hdc. Ch 1, turn. **Row 6:** Work 2 sc in each ch across row. Repeat Rows 5 and 6 for pat. Work even until piece measures 21" (53,5 cm) from beg, end with a sc row.

Shape Neck: Work first 7 (8-9) hdc, turn. Continue to work on these sts only for 2½" (6,3 cm) more. Cut yarn and fasten. Attach yarn to other side of neck and work as for opposite side.

Front: Work same as Back.

Sleeves: Ch 43 (47-49) to measure 14 (15-16)" [35,5 (38-40,5) cm] for lower edge. Work in sc for 4 rows as for back—42 (46-48) sts. Work in pat as for Back until 18" (46 cm) from beg or desired length to underarm, end with sc row. Cut yarn and fasten.

FINISHING: Sew shoulder seams. Mark off 7 (7½-8)" [18 (19,2-20,5) cm] from shoulder seams on back and front for armholes. Sew in top of sleeves between these markers. Sew underarm and sleeve seams.

Neck Edging: From right side, beg at left shoulder, work 2 rows of sc around entire neck edge. Cut yarn and fasten.

Scarf: Ch 21 to measure 7" (18 cm). Work 1 row of sc. Change to pat as for pullover and work even until 58" (147,5 cm) from beg, end with sc row.

Fringe: Cut about 60 strands of yarn 12" (30,5 cm) long. Using 3 strands, knot fringe in every ch-1 sp across each narrow edge.

PEACH SHAWL (shown on page 65)

Size: About 42" (107 cm) long at center.

MATERIALS: Unger's Dolly, 1.4 oz. (40 g) ball—10 balls; Size G aluminum crochet hook OR SIZE TO GIVE GAUGE.

GAUGE: 5 sts = 1" (2,5 cm); 7 dc rows = 3" (7,5 cm).

DIRECTIONS: Shawl starts at the point. **Base Row:** Ch 8, join with a sl st to form a ring. Ch 4, turn. **Row 1:** 7 dc in ring. Ch 4, turn. **Row 2:** Dc in first dc, ch 3, dc back in same dc (forms a V st), ch 1, skip 1, 1 dc in each of next 3 sts, ch 1, skip 1, dc in next dc, ch 3, dc back in last dc worked (V st), dc in top of turning ch. Ch 4, turn. **Row 3:** 7 dc under ch-3 of V st, ch 1, 1 dc in each of next 3 dc, ch 1, 7 dc under ch-3 of V st, dc in top of turning ch. Ch 4, turn. **Row 4:** Dc in first dc, ch 3, dc back in last st worked (V st), ch 1, skip 2 dc, 1 dc in each of next 3 dc, ch 1, skip 1, dc in next st, ch 1, skip ch and dc, dc in next dc (center st of 3 dc), ch 1, skip dc and ch, dc in next st, ch 1, skip next dc, 1 dc in each of next 3 dc, ch 1, skip 1, dc in next dc, ch 3, dc back in last st worked (V st), dc in top of turning ch. Ch 4, turn. **Row 5:** 7 dc under ch-3 of V st, ch 1, dc in next dc, ch 1, skip center dc, dc in next dc, (ch 1, dc in next dc) 4 times, ch 1, skip center dc, dc in next dc, ch 1, 7 dc under ch-3 of V st, dc in top of turning ch. Ch 4, turn. **Row 6:** Dc in first dc, ch 3, dc back in same st (V st), ch 1, skip 2 dc, 1 dc in each of next 3 dc, ch 1, skip 1, dc in next st, (ch 1, skip ch, dc in next dc) 8 times, ch 1, skip 1, 1 dc in each of 3 sts, ch 1, skip 1, dc in next dc, ch 3, dc back in last st worked (V st), dc in top of turning ch. Ch 4, turn. **Row 7:** 7 dc under ch-3 of V st, ch 1, dc in next dc, ch 1, skip center dc, dc in next dc, (ch 1, dc in next dc) 10 times, ch 1, skip center dc, dc in next dc, ch 1, 7 dc under ch-3 of V st, dc in top of turning ch. Ch 4, turn. **Row 8:** Work a V st in first st, ch 1, skip 2 dc, 1 dc in each of 3 sts, ch 1, skip 1, dc in next st, (ch 1, skip ch, dc in next dc) 14 times, ch 1, skip 1, 1 dc in each of 3 sts, ch 1, skip 1, V st in next dc, dc in top of turning ch. Ch 4, turn. **Row 9:** 7 dc under ch-3 of V st, ch 1, dc in next dc, ch 1, skip center dc, dc in next dc, (ch 1, dc in next dc) 16 times, ch 1, skip center dc, dc in next dc, ch 1, 7 dc under ch-3 of V st, dc in top of turning ch. Ch 4, turn. **Row 10:** V st in first dc, ch 1, skip 2, 1 dc in each of next 3 sts, ch 1, skip 1, dc in next st, (ch 1, skip ch, dc in next dc) 20 times, ch 1, skip 1, 1 dc in each of 3 sts, ch 1, skip 1, V st in next st, dc in top of turning ch. Ch 4, turn. **Row 11:** 7 dc under ch-3 of V st, ch 1, dc in next dc, ch 1, skip center st, dc in next dc, (ch 1, dc in next dc) 22 times, ch 1, skip center dc, dc in next dc, ch 1, 7 dc under ch-3 of V st, dc in top of turning ch. Ch 4, turn. **Row 12:** V st in first dc, ch 1, skip 2, 1 dc in each of 3 sts, ch 1, skip 1, dc in next st, (ch 1, skip ch, dc in next dc) 26 times, ch 1, skip 1, 1 dc in each of 3 sts, ch 1, skip 1, V st in next st, dc in top of turning ch. Ch 4, turn. **Row 13:** Same as Row 5, repeating (ch 1, dc in next dc) 28 times. **Row 14:** Same as Row 6, repeating (ch 1, dc in next dc) 32 times. **Row 15:** Same as Row 5, repeating (ch 1, dc in next dc) 34 times. **Row 16:** Same as Row 6, repeating (ch 1, dc in next dc) 38 times. **Row 17:** Same as Row 5, repeating (ch 1, dc in next dc) 40 times. **Row 18:** Same as Row 6, repeating (ch 1, dc in next dc) 44 times. This row has 46 eyelets between 3 dc at each side edge. Ch 4, turn.

Start center design: Row 19: 7 dc under ch-3 of V st, ch 1, dc in next dc, ch 1, skip 1, dc in next dc, (ch 1, dc in next dc) 22 times, ch 3, skip next ch, dc and ch, dc in the next dc, (ch 1, dc in next dc) 22 times, ch 1, skip 1 dc, dc in next dc, ch 1, 7 dc under ch-3 of V st, dc in top of turning ch. Ch 4, turn. **Row 20:** Same as Row 6, repeating ch 1, dc in next dc for eyelets to within ch-3 space (do not work in dc just before ch-3), ch 1, 7 dc under ch-3, ch 1, skip next dc, complete row as for Row 6 (make sure same number of eyelets are on each side of center 7 dc shell). **Row 21:** Same as Row 5 , repeating ch 1, dc in next dc for eyelets to within 2 dc before center 7 dc shell, ch 3, skip next dc, dc in next dc, ch 1, skip 2 dc of shell, 1 dc in each of next 3 dc of shell, ch 1, skip 2 dc of shell, dc in next dc, ch 3, skip next dc, dc in next dc (2 ch-3 spaces made), complete row as for Row 5. Ch 4, turn. **Row 22:** Same as Row 6, repeating ch 1, dc in next dc for eyelets to within dc before the ch-3, ch 1, 7 dc under ch-3 for shell, ch 1, skip next dc, dc in next dc (center of 3 dc), ch 1, skip next dc, 7 dc under ch-3 for shell, complete as for Row 6. Always make sure there are same number of eyelets on either side of shell patterns (2 shells worked). Ch 4, turn. **Row 23:** Same as Row 5 to within 2 dc before first 7 dc shell, ch 3, skip the next dc, dc in next dc, ch 1, skip 2 dc of shell, 1 dc in each of 3 dc of shell, ch 1, skip 1 dc, dc in next dc, ch 3, skip next dc, dc in first dc of shell, ch 1, skip 1 dc, 1 dc in each of 3 dc, ch 1, skip 1, dc in last dc of shell, ch 3, skip next dc, dc in next dc (3 ch-3 spaces), complete as for Row 5. **Row 24:** Same as for Row 6 to within dc before ch-3 space, ch 1, 7 dc for shell under ch-3, ch 1, skip next dc, dc in next dc (center of 3 dc), ch 1, skip next dc, 7 dc under ch-3, ch 1, skip next dc, dc in next dc (center of 3 dc), ch 1, skip next dc, 7 dc under ch-3, ch 1, skip next dc, complete row as for Row 6 (3 shells worked). Work in this manner as for Rows 23 and 24, gaining 1 extra ch-3 space on all odd rows and 1 extra shell on all even rows until there are 25—7 dc shells, ending with Row 68. **Row 69:** Same as Row 5, work to within dc before shell, ch 1, * dc in first dc of shell, ch 1, skip 1 dc, dc in next dc, ch 1, skip 1 dc, dc in next dc, ch 1, skip next dc, dc in next dc, ch 1, dc in next dc, ch 1; repeat from * across shells, complete row as for Row 5. Alternating beg and end of Rows 6 and 5 and ch 1, dc eyelets in between, continue in pattern for 12 rows more, or desired size. Fasten off.

Scalloped edge along slanted sides: Join with a sl st at top edge. On right side, 7 dc in first ch-3 space, sl st through ch-4 of row below, * 7 dc in next ch-3 space, sl st in ch-4 of row below; repeat from * to point; at point work 8 dc in space for shell; continue along other side of shawl to correspond to other side. Fasten off. Do not block.

LACY COLLAR (shown on page 65)

MATERIALS: 1 ball J. & P. Coats "Knit-Cro-Sheen"; No. 1 steel crochet hook.

DIRECTIONS: Starting at neck edge of collar, ch 105, having 7 sts per inch (2,5 cm). **Row 1 (right side):** Dc in 4th ch from hook and in next 11 ch; * 2 dc in next ch, dc in next 14 ch. Repeat from * across — 109 dc, counting first ch-3 as 1 dc. Ch 1, turn. **Row 2:** Sc in first dc, * ch 3, sk next dc, sc in next dc. Repeat from * across, end with sc in top of ch-3 — 54 ch-3 lps. Ch 5, turn. **Row 3:** Sc in first lp; * 5 dc in next lp (forms a shell); sc in next lp, ch 3, sc in next lp. Repeat from * to last 2 lps, shell in next lp; end (sc, ch 2, dc) in last lp — 18 shells. Ch 1, turn. **Row 4:** Sc in first lp, *ch 3, sc in 2nd dc of next shell, ch 3, sk next dc of same shell, sc in next dc, ch 3, sc in next lp. Repeat from * across, working last sc of final repeat in last lp formed by turning ch — 54 lps. Ch 5, turn. **Rows 5-9:** RepeatRows 3 and 4 twice, then Row 3 once. Cut thread and fasten. Press collar lightly, stretching outer edge very slightly.

FLORAL AFGHAN (shown on page 66)

Size: 36 x 54" (91,5 x 137 cm)

MATERIALS: Knitting worsted type yarn: 18 oz. (504 g) Off-white, 4 oz. (112 g) each Yellow, Orange and Dark Green, and 2 oz. (56 g) Light Green; Size E or F crochet hook.

GAUGE: 1 square = 17¾ x 17¾" (45 x 45 cm)

DIRECTIONS: Follow the diagram for colors, picking up and dropping them as needed. Carry colors not in use loosely behind work. **NOTE:** Diagram shows odd-numbered rnds only; each square represents one 3-dc group. Work each even-numbered rnd in same colors as previous odd-numbered rnd.

Square: Starting in center, with Off-white, ch 8 and join with sl st to form a ring. Begin using chart. **Rnd 1:** Ch 3 (counts as first dc), 2 dc in ring, ch 3, * 3 dc in ring, ch 3, repeat from * twice, sl st in first dc. **Rnd 2:** Sl st in top of 2nd and 3rd dc, * (sc, ch 3, sc) in next ch-3 sp, ch 3, repeat from * around, sl st in first sc. **Rnd 3:** Ch 3 (counts as first dc), (2 dc, ch 3, 3 dc) in corner, 3 dc in next ch-3 sp, * (3 dc, ch 3, 3 dc) in corner, 3 dc in next ch-3 sp, repeat from * around, sl st in first dc. **Rnd 4:** Sl st in 2nd and 3rd dc, * (sc, ch 3, sc) in corner, ch 3, (sc between next two 3-dc groups, ch 3) twice, repeat from * around, sl st in first sc. **Rnd 5:** Ch 3, (2 dc, ch 3, 3 dc) in corner, (3 dc in next ch-3 sp) three times, * 3 dc, ch 3, 3 dc) in corner, (3 dc in next ch-3 sp) three times, repeat from * around, sl st in top of first dc. Repeat Rnds 4 and 5, adding two ch-3 or 3-dc groups to each side of square each rnd. Work until there are 15 dc rnds. Work 5 more squares in same way.

FINISHING: Crochet squares together as follows: With wrong sides together, using Off-white, work 1 sc through corner of both squares, * (ch 3, sc) between next two 3-dc groups, repeat from * to end. Add squares until you have 3 rows of 2 squares each. With Dark Green, work 1 row of dc all around, working 1 dc in each dc and 5 dc in corners. Cut yarn and fasten.

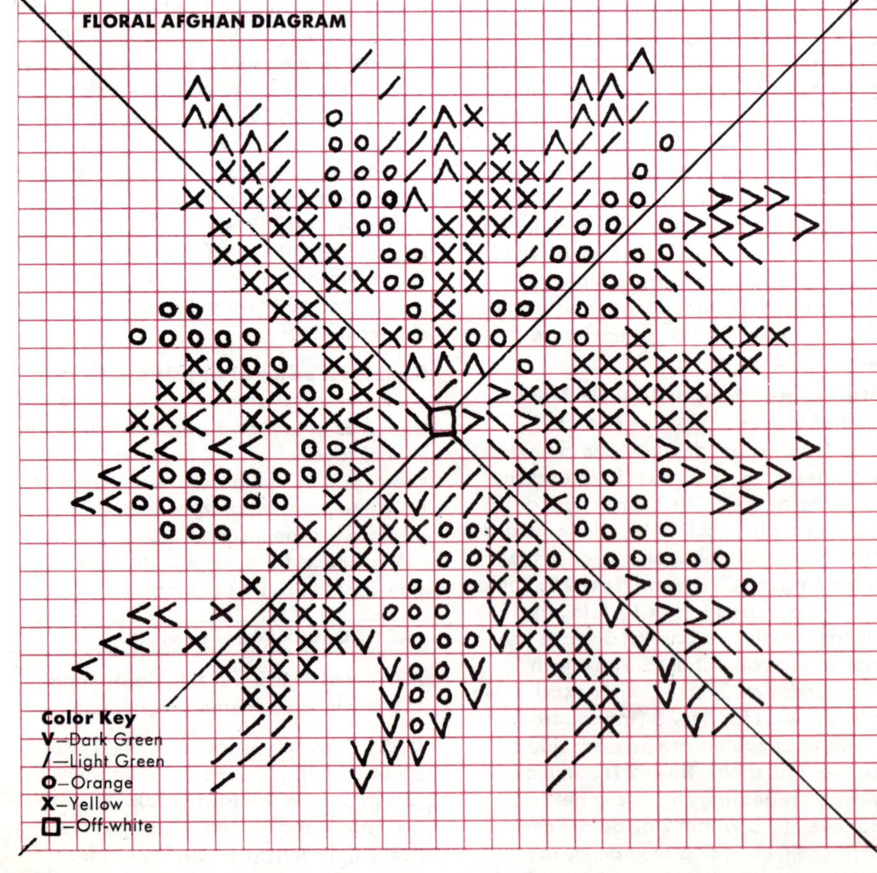

CRIB COVERLET (shown on page 66)

Size: 32 x 57" (81,5 x 145 cm)

MATERIALS: 4-ply knitting worsted type yarn: 12 oz. (336 g) Off-white and 3 oz. (84 g) each of five other colors; Size G crochet hook OR SIZE TO GIVE GAUGE.

GAUGE: 1 square = 3½" (9 cm).

DIRECTIONS: Each square is made with 3 different colors. Use one color for Rnds 1 and 2 and a different color for Rnd 3, varying them at random; use Off-white for Rnd 4 of every square.

Square: With first color, ch 4, join with sl st to form a ring. **Rnd 1:** 8 sc in ring. **Rnd 2:** Sl st in first sc, ch 3; keeping last lp on hook, 2 dc in same sc, yo, draw through all 3 lps, ch 2; (keeping last lp of each dc on hook, 3 dc in next sc, yo, draw through all 4 lps on hook, ch 2) 7 times, sl st in top of first tr group. Cut yarn and fasten; join second color. **Rnd 3:** Ch 3, 2 dc in same sp, (3 dc, ch 1, 3 dc) in next ch-2 sp for corner, * 3 dc in next ch-2 sp, (3 dc, ch 1, 3 dc) in next ch-2 sp; repeat from * twice; sl st to top of corner ch-1 sp. Cut yarn and fasten; join Off-white. **Rnd 4:** Ch 3, (2 dc, ch 1, 3 dc) in corner sp, 3 dc in each of next 2 sps between 3-dc groups, * (3 dc, ch 1, 3 dc) in corner ch-1 sp, 3 dc in each of next 2 sps between 3-dc groups; repeat from * twice, sl st in top of ch-3. Cut yarn and fasten.

Make 144 squares. With Off-white, sc or sew squares tog, having 9 squares across and 16 down. If desired, work a row of reverse sc (work from left to right) loosely all around. Press lightly on wrong side.

GEOMETRIC THROW (shown on page 67)

Size: 46 x 60" (117 x 152,5 cm)

MATERIALS: Coats & Clark Red Heart® "Preference" 4-Ply Handknitting Yarn: 14 oz. (392 g) each #353 Taupe and #322 Fawn Beige, and 10½ oz. (294 g) #109 Ecru; Size K or No. 10½ afghan hook 14" (35,5 cm) long OR SIZE TO GIVE GAUGE.

GAUGE: 3 sts = 1" (2,5 cm); 2 rows = 1" (2,5 cm).

DIRECTIONS: First Section: Starting at lower edge, with Taupe, ch 132, having 3 ch per inch (2,5 cm). Following the directions on pages 75-76, work Rows 1 and 2 of Afghan St. **Row 3, first half:** *Insert hook under next 2 vertical bars and draw up a lp, insert hook in top lp of next ch st following last 2 vertical bars used, yo and draw up a lp. Repeat from * to last vertical bar, insert hook through last vertical bar and the st directly behind and draw up a lp — 132 sts. **Second half:** Work off lps as for Row 2. Repeat Row 3 for pat until you have worked 12 rows. Now work **Narrow Strip: Next row, first half:** Work in pat until there are 17 lps on hook, draw up a lp in next vertical bar — 18 sts. Do not work over remaining sts. **Second half:** Work off lps as for Row 2. **Following row:** Repeat Row 3 over 18 sts. Work even in pat until piece measures 58" (147,5 cm). **Last row:** Sk first vertical bar, sl st in next bar and in each bar across. Fasten yarn. **Second Section: Next row, first half:** On right side, insert hook under next free vertical bar following last st used for previous narrow strip. With Beige, yo and draw up a lp, insert hook under next 2 vertical bars and draw up a lp, insert hook in top lp of next ch st following last 2 vertical bars used, yo and draw up a lp; then complete row in pat — 114 sts.

Second half: Work as for Row 2. Work in pat until you have worked 12 rows with Beige. **Second Strip:** With Beige, work over 18 sts as for previous strip until piece reaches top edge of previous strip; work last row as before. **Third Section and Strip:** With Ecru, work as for previous section over 96 sts for 12 rows, then over 18 sts as for previous strip. **Fourth Section and Strip:** With Taupe, work over 78 sts for 10 rows, then over 14 sts as before. **Fifth Section and Strip:** With Beige, work over 64 sts for 10 rows, then over 14 sts as before. **Sixth Section and Strip:** With Ecru, work over 50 sts and 10 rows, then over 14 sts. **Seventh:** With Taupe, work over 36 sts for 8 rows, then over 8 sts. **Eighth:** With Beige, work over 28 sts for 8 rows, then over 8 sts. **Ninth:** With Ecru, work over 20 sts for 8 rows, then over 8 sts. **Tenth:** With Taupe, work over 12 sts for 6 rows, then over 4 sts. **Eleventh:** With Beige, work over 8 sts for 6 rows, then over 4 sts. **Last Strip:** With Ecru, work over 4 sts until strip is same length as previous strip. Complete as before.

FINISHING: Join long edges of strips as follows: Using one of the colors of adjacent strips, with right side up and matching ends of rows, sc strips tog. **Border: Rnd 1:** On right side, attach Ecru to corner, ch 2; working from *left to right*, keeping work flat, (*hdc in edge, ch 1. Repeat from * to next corner; in corner, work hdc, ch 1 and hdc; ch 1) 4 times. Join with sl st to first hdc. Fasten yarn. **Rnd 2:** With Beige, ch 2; working from *left to right*, (*hdc in next ch-1 sp, ch 1. Repeat from * to next corner ch-1 sp; in corner sp, work hdc, ch 1 and hdc; ch 1) 4 times. Join and fasten. **Rnd 3:** With Taupe, work as for Rnd 2. To block, see page 74.

V-NECK PULLOVER (shown on page 68)

Sizes: Directions are for Small size. Changes for Medium and Large are in parentheses.

MATERIALS: Spinnerin Cashmere Plus, 20 g (.7 oz.) ball: 12(13-14) #705 Light Beige MC and 3(3-4) #700 White CC, OR Baby and Fingering, 1 oz. (28 g) ball: 8(9-10) #6105 Dk. Beige MC and 4(5-5) #6100 White CC; Size 0 steel crochet hook OR SIZE TO GIVE GAUGE.

GAUGE: Pat 1 — 11 Post Sts = 2" (5 cm); 7 rows = 2" (5 cm).

Pat 2 — 5 Picot Mesh Pat (10 sts) = 2" (5 cm); 5 rows = 2" (5 cm).

STITCHES AND ABBREVIATIONS:
Front Post dc (FP): Yo, insert hook from front to back and again to front at left of st (st lies on top of hook in front of work), draw lp thru and complete st as a dc. After first row, work post sts around post sts of previous row.

Back Post dc (BP): Work same as FP but insert hook from back to front and again to back (st lies on top of hook in back of work).

Pat 1 — Post St Ribbing (worked over a multiple of 2 sts + 1): **Row 1 (right side):** FP around stem of 2nd dc from hook, dc in next dc, *FP around stem of next dc, dc in next dc; repeat from * to end. Ch 3, turn. **Row 2:** BP around post of 2nd dc from hook, dc in next dc,* BP around post of next dc, dc in next dc; repeat from * to end. Ch 3, turn. Repeat these 2 rows for Rib Pat.

Pat 2 — Picot Mesh (worked over a multiple of 2 sts + 1): **Row 1:** Ch 5, sc in 4th ch from hook (first picot), ch 1, sk 1 st, sc in next st, * ch 4, sc in 4th ch from hook (picot), ch 1, sk 1 st, repeat from * to end, turn. **Row 2:** Ch 5, picot, ch 1, sc in center of next picot,* picot, ch 1, sc in center of next picot; rep from * to end, turn. Repeat Row 2 for Picot Mesh Pat.

DIRECTIONS: Back: With CC, ch 87 (99-111). **Foundation Row:** Dc in 4th ch from hook and in each ch to end. Ch 3, turn — 85(97-109) sts. Beg with Row 1, work Pat 1 for 3" (7,5 cm), end with Row 2. Fasten CC, join MC, turn. Beg with Row 1, work Pat 2 to 15" (38 cm) from beg, end with Row 2. **Armhole — Row 1:** Working 3 sl sts, sl st along side of picot, sc in center of picot (1 picot dec at beg of row), complete row in pat, turn. Repeat this row 7(9-11) times more — 4(5-6) picots dec at each armhole edge and 69(77-85) sts counting picots as 1 st. Work even in pat until armholes measure 7(7½-8)" [18(19,2-20,5) cm]. Fasten yarn.

Front: Work same as Back to 13" (33 cm) from beg, end with Row 2. Mark picot at center front. **(NOTE:** When counting picots, count sc at end of row as a picot.) **V-Neck and Armhole:** Work in pat to marked picot, sc in marked picot, turn. Dec 1 picot at neck edge every other row (working decs as for armhole) 7(8-9) times AND AT THE SAME TIME, when piece measures same as Back to underarm, at armhole edge dec 1 picot every other row 4(5-6) times. Work even until armholes measure same as Back to shoulder. Fasten yarn. Join MC to marked picot at center of last full row, sc in marked picot, sc thru center of next picot, complete row in pat. Work other side to correspond, reversing all shaping.

Sleeves: With CC, ch 45(49-53). Beg with Foundation Row, work in Rib Pat as on Back on 43(47-51) sts to 4" (10 cm) from beg, end with Row 2 of pat. Fasten CC, join MC, turn. **Inc Picot Mesh Row:** Ch 5, sc in 4th ch from hook (picot), ch 1, sc in first st, picot, ch 1, † sk 1 st, (sc in next st, picot, ch 1) twice †; repeat between †'s 3(4-5) times more — 10 (12-14) picots; sk 1 st, (sc in next st, picot, ch 1, sk 1 st) 7(6-5) times, *(sc in next st, picot, ch 1) twice, sk 1 st; repeat from * to last 2 chs, sc in next ch, picot, ch 1, sc in last ch, turn—53(61-67) sts; 27(30-33) picots counting last sc as a picot. Beg with Row 2, work Pat 2 to 19" (48,5 cm) from beg, or 2" (5 cm) more than usual length to cap, end with Row 2. **Cap: Row 1:** Work same as Row 1 of Back Armhole to 1 picot before last sc, end sc in center of next picot, turn — 1 picot dec each end of row, leaving 25(28-31) picots. Repeat this row 9(10-11) times more, leaving 7(8-9) picots. Fasten yarn.

FINISHING: Sew shoulder, side and sleeve seams. Set in sleeves. **Neckband — Row 1:** From right side join CC to point of V at center front. Being sure to work an uneven number of sts, work in dc evenly spaced around entire neck edge, end at point of V. Ch 3, turn. **Row 2:** Dec 1 dc each end of row, work Row 2 of Pat 1. **Row 3:** Dec 1 dc each end of row, work Row 1 of Pat 1 to end. Ch 1, turn. **Rows 4 thru 6:** Dec 1 sc each end of row, work in sc, end Row 6 with ch 1, turn. Beg with Row 1 and dec 1 st each end of row, work in Pat 1, working around sc post for 2 more rows. Fasten yarn. Sew edges tog at center front.

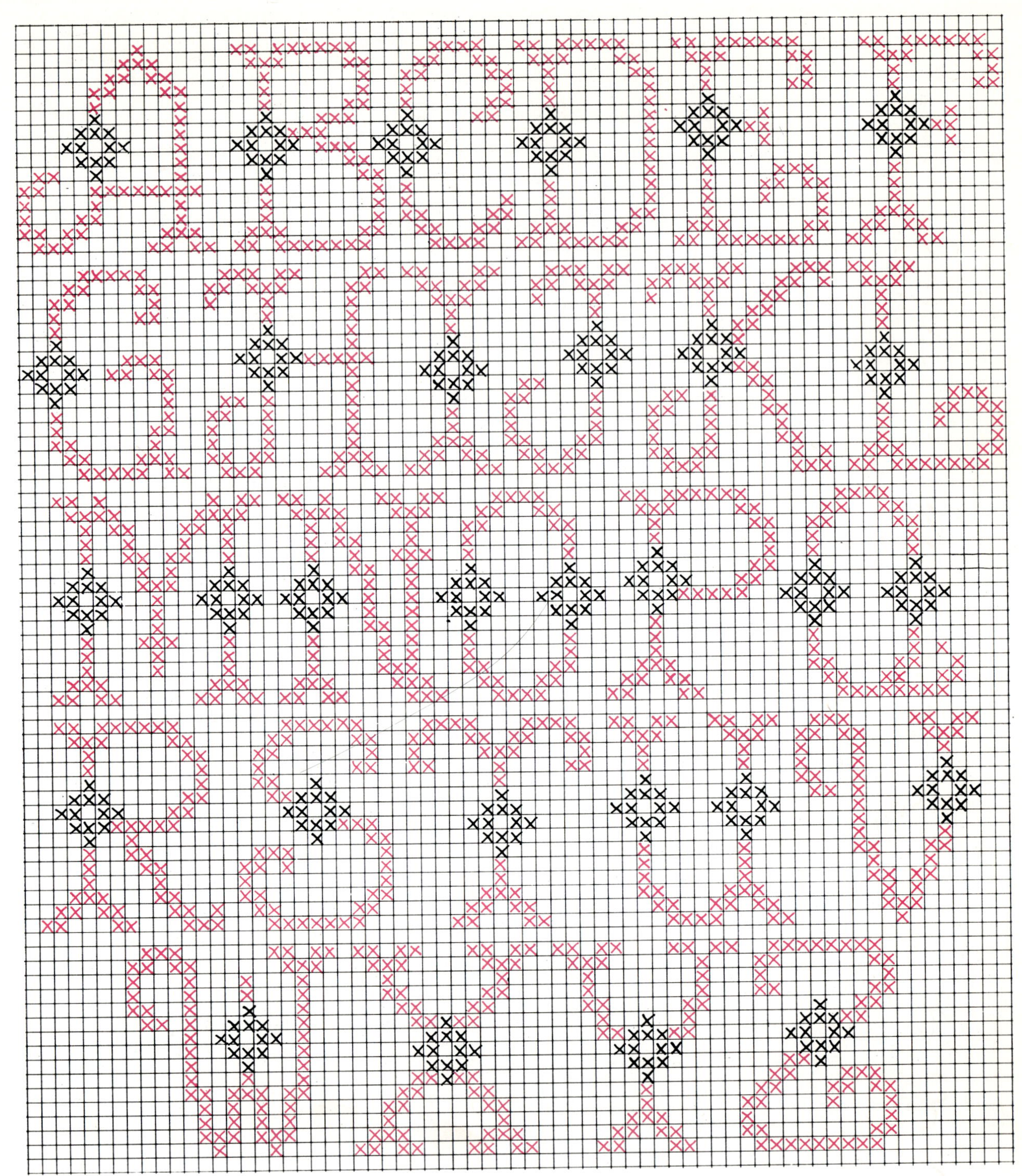

BED AND BATH MONOGRAMS

(shown on page 31)

DIRECTIONS: If desired, enlarge or reduce monograms (see pages 20-21). Transfer the motifs to sheets, pillowcases, towels or other items such as table linens, handkerchiefs, scarfs and garments, following the directions on pages 33 and 34. Following the stitch diagrams on pages 22-27 and 34-35, work embroidery, using the key on this page for stitches and number of strands of cotton embroidery floss. Choose colors to coordinate with your decorating scheme or with the colors of your garment or fashion accessories.

Stitch Key and Thread Amounts

Symbol	Stitch	No. of Strands
X	Cross-stitch	3
A	Satin Stitch	2 (pillowcase) 3 (towel)
B	Stem Stitch	2 (pillowcase) 3 (towel)
C	French Knot	3 (pillowcase) 6 (towel)
D	Lazy-daisy Stitch	6

B
A
D
D
A
D
B
C
A
C
C
B
A
B

INDEX

RESOURCES

Shirley Botsford Design Associates, Inc., 682 Avenue of the Americas, New York, NY 10010

Coats & Clark, Inc., 72 Cummings Point Road, Stamford, CT 06902

Columbia-Minerva, 295 Fifth Avenue, New York, NY 10016

The DMC Corporation, 107 Trumbull Street, Elizabeth, NJ 07206

Liz Dominick of Domino Patchworks, 100 Avenue of the Americas, New York, NY 10013

Sara Gutiérrez

Ruth J. Katz

C. M. Offray & Son Inc., 261 Madison Avenue, New York, NY 10016

Paternayan Brothers, Paterna Persian Yarn, 312 E. 95th Street, New York, NY 10028

Spinnerin Yarns, 230 Fifth Avenue, New York, NY 10001

The Stearns & Foster Company, Cincinnati, OH 45215

William Unger & Co., 230 Fifth Avenue, New York, NY 10001

Ursula von Wartburg

Marcia Whalen

Erica Wilson Needle Works, 232 East 59th Street, New York, NY 10022